Sustainable English Language Teacher Development at Scale

Also available from Bloomsbury

Achievement for All in International Classrooms, Sonia Blandford
Initial English Language Teacher Education, edited by Darío Luis Banegas

Sustainable English Language Teacher Development at Scale

Lessons from Bangladesh

Edited by Ian Eyres, Robert McCormick and Tom Power

BLOOMSBURY ACADEMIC

LONDON · NEW YORK · OXFORD · NEW DELHI · SYDNEY

BLOOMSBURY ACADEMIC
Bloomsbury Publishing Plc
50 Bedford Square, London, WC1B 3DP, UK
1385 Broadway, New York, NY 10018, USA

BLOOMSBURY, BLOOMSBURY ACADEMIC and the Diana logo are
trademarks of Bloomsbury Publishing Plc

First published in Great Britain 2019

A catalogue record for this book is available from the British Library.

A catalog record for this book is available from the Library of Congress.

ISBN: HB: 978-1-3500-4347-3
       ePDF: 978-1-3500-4348-0
       eBook: 978-1-3500-4349-7

Typeset by RefineCatch Ltd, Bungay, Suffolk
Printed and bound in Great Britain

To find out more about our authors and books, visit www.bloomsbury.com
and sign up for our newsletters.

This book is dedicated to the memory of our great friend and colleague Jenny Leach (1949–2007), whose pioneering work in the application of new communication technologies, in particular the use of mobile phones to support teaching and learning in Sub-Saharan Africa, provided English in Action with both an inspiration and a foundation.

'EIA has been able to add to the global knowledge and debate around teacher professional development, by proposing a specific model based on five elements and by putting teachers at the centre of the classroom, and evidencing what works in the classroom and to build teachers' capacities.'

DFID Project Closure Review

Contents

Illustrations

Figures

Tables

Contributors

Shamim Ahmed, Education Consultant, Splenor Services Limited, Bangladesh.

Rehnuma Akhter, Education Specialist, Cambridge Education, a member of the Mott MacDonald Group, UK.

Sonia Burton, Research Analyst, Rady Children's Hospital San Diego, USA.

Sharmistha Das, Senior Consultant Education/Education Adviser, EIA, Cambridge Education, a member of the Mott MacDonald Group, UK.

Elizabeth J. Erling, Professor of ELT Methodology, University of Graz, Austria.

Ian Eyres, Senior Lecturer, Education, The Open University, UK.

Malcolm Griffiths, Lecturer, International Teacher Education, The Open University, UK.

Claire Hedges, Senior Programmes Manager, The Open University, UK.

Masuda Khatoon, Head of Schools Programme, British Council, Bangladesh.

Rama Mathew, Professor of Education, University of Delhi, India.

Robert McCormick, Emeritus Professor of Education, The Open University, UK.

Amol Padwad, Associate Professor and Head, Dept. of English, J.M. Patel College, India.

David Pedder, Professor of Education, The University of Brighton, UK.

Tom Power, Director, International Teacher Education Development, The Open University, UK.

Bikash Chandra Sarkar, Head of materials development, English in Action, Cambridge Education, a member of the Mott MacDonald Group, UK.

Fauzia Shamim, Professor and ELC Coordinator, Taibah University, Saudi Arabia.

John Shotton, Director, Mott MacDonald.

Mike Solly, Senior Advisor, English for Education systems, The British Council, UK.

Marc van der Stouwe, Manager in International Development/Project Director EIA, Cambridge Education, a member of the Mott MacDonald Group.

Christopher Walsh, Academic Professor in Education, Victoria University, Melbourne, Australia.

Clare Woodward, Lecturer, International Teacher Education, The Open University, UK.

Kirsten Zindel, Deputy Team Leader, EIA, Cambridge Education, a member of the Mott MacDonald Group, UK.

Acknowledgements

Like English in Action (EIA) itself, the production of this book has very much been a collaboration, involving not only the named authors and editors, but many other past and present members of the EIA family. We should like therefore to thank individually a number of colleagues from The Open University and Cambridge Education who gave invaluable advice and feedback concerning various chapters and the book as a whole. By name, they are: Mostan Zida Alnoor, Sudeb Kumar Biswas, M. Obaidul Hamid, S. M. Azmul Karim, Mourie Nishad, Mir Md Arafat Rahaman, Rubayet Mollika Rahman, Zakera Rahman, Ruma Rebecca Rodrigues, Md Ashraf Siddique, and Sue Williamson (Cambridge Education); and Lina Adinolfi, Frank Banks and Alison Buckler (Open University). Thanks are also due to Hannah Wilkinson (Cambridge Education) for her work to bring the book to a wide audience. We are especially grateful to Julie Herbert (Open University), not just for her expert attention to the typescript but also for the countless times she has saved the day and helped bring this complex endeavour to a surprisingly smooth conclusion.

Though they are far too many to list individually, we should also like to acknowledge all those past and present members of the EIA team and others who took part in the many discussions and conversations, formal and informal (many of them on the balconies of the Aristocrat Inn, Dhaka) which shaped the thinking behind both the Programme itself and the present volume. Of great value among these indirect contributors we would include many of the Programme's teachers and teacher facilitators, and other local staff whose skills and enthusiasm enabled the Programme to work in the places that really matter.

We are grateful to The Open University's Centre for Research in Education and Educational Technology (CREET) for its support for the book's development.

Foreword

John Shotton, Director, Mott MacDonald

When in 2007 it became clear that the British government's Department for International Development (DFID) wanted to respond positively to a request from the Government of Bangladesh (GoB) for financial and technical support in order to deliver a national sustainable English-language teacher-development programme that would contribute to the economic development of the country, I well remember the voices of cynicism that emerged. The whole prospect was viewed with suspicion. In the eyes of many, this could only be yet another post-colonial initiative that would look to elevate the English language above and over local languages.

Nothing could have been further from the truth. For those of us who were involved in the design of the EIA Programme, this was an opportunity to work closely with the GoB to look to effect change within and across a national educational system, with the interests of the mass of the population, and within that the poor, at its heart.

As the content of this book reveals, the success has been enormous. Over a nine-year period, the opportunity to generate change inside classrooms in both government and civil society-supported schools has been grasped and delivered. Of course, this is mostly in English classes at both the primary and secondary level, but such has been the impact of pedagogical transformation in those classes that the GoB, through its education-delivery system, is now looking to effect similar change across the curriculum, and the role that English in Action (EIA) has played has been significant.

There are lessons to be learned here about key elements of the development agenda and the use of aid which supports the same. Nothing has been imposed, and the Programme has been delivered with the full participation and agreement of the GoB. The Programme has also been supported by a team of outstanding Bangladeshi professionals who have been critical to its success, and who will be a great resource for the country as it looks to develop its educational offer. Further, EIA invested in 'getting a pilot right' where content was first tried and tested.

As the person who was honoured to lead the EIA Design Team, I am humbled to see the strapline 'Changing Learning, Changing Lives' having really come to fruition, as I am eager to learn about the full positive effect and impact from the content of this book.

Abbreviations

ABL	activity-based learning
AL	Awami League
AV	audio-visual
AUEOs	Assistant Upazila Education Officers
BNP	Bangladesh Nationalist Party
BRC	Block Resource Centres (India)
CEFR	Common European Framework of Reference for Languages
CfE	centre for excellence
CLT	communicative language teaching
CM	cluster meeting
CoE	centre of excellence
CP	classroom practice
CPD	continuous professional development
CT	core trainer
CTG	caretaker government
DEEP	Digital Education Enhancement Project
DFID	Department for International Development
DIET	District Institutes of Education and Training (India)
DPE	Directorate of Primary Education (Bangladesh)
DPEd	Diploma in Primary Education
DRC	District Resource Centres (India)
DU	Dhaka University
EFA	Education for All
EfT	*English for Today*
EIA	English in Action
EIL	English as an international language
ELC	English language competency
ELF	English as a lingua franca
EL4T	English language for teachers
ELT	English language teaching
ELT	English language teacher alt. teaching
ELTIP	English language teaching improvement project

EMI	English medium of instruction
EO	education officer
ERS	English reading scheme
ESD	Education for Sustainable Development
ESP	English for specific purposes
ESP	Education for specific purposes
FIVDB	Friends In Village Development in Bangladesh
GEMR	Global Education Monitoring Report
GESE	Graded Examinations in Spoken English
GMR	Global Monitoring Report
GoB	Government of Bangladesh
HEI	higher education institute
HTs	head teachers
IELTS	International English Language Testing System
IER	Institute for Education and Research
ILO	International Labour Organization
INSET	in-service training
I&S	institutionalization and sustainability
ITE	initial teacher education
JICA	Japan International Cooperation Agency
LMIC	low-to-middle income countries
MAV	mediated authentic video(s)
MDGs	Millennium Development Goal(s)
MFL	modern foreign language
NALAP	National Literacy Acceleration Program
NAPE	National Academy for Primary Education
NCTB	National Curriculum and Textbook Board
NGO	non-governmental organization
NSA	National Student Assessments (Bangladesh)
ODL	open-distance learning
OU	The Open University
OU-PGCE	Open University's Post-Graduate Certificate in Education
PEDP	Primary Education Development Programme
PK	pedagogical knowledge
PMO	Prime Minister's Office (Bangladesh)
PSQL	primary school quality level
PTI	primary teacher training institute
PTR	pupil–teacher ratio

QA	quality assurance
RCT	randomized control trial
RME	research, monitoring and evaluation
RNGPS	registered non-government primary school
SBT	subject-based training
SBTD	school-based teacher development
SC	Save the Children
SDG	sustainable development goal(s)
SESIP	Secondary Education Sector Investment Programme
SIEF	Strategic Impact Evaluation Fund
SK	subject knowledge
SMC	school management committee
TA	technical assistance
TD	teacher development
TDC	teacher development co-ordinator
TDPs	teacher development programmes
TEL	technology-enhanced learning
TESSA	Teacher Education in Sub-Saharan Africa
TESS-India	Teacher Education through School-based Support in India
TF	teacher facilitator
TG	Teachers' Guides
TPD	teacher professional development
TQI	Teaching Quality Improvement Project (Bangladesh)
TQI-SEP	Teaching Quality Improvement Secondary Education Project
TTC	teacher training college
UCEP	Underprivileged Children's Educational Programmes
UEO	Upazila Education Officer
VfM	Value for Money
ZEST	Zambian Education School-based Training

Introduction

Effecting Change Within and Across a National Education System

Tom Power, Ian Eyres and Robert McCormick

Purpose and approach

English in Action (EIA) consisted of two components: BBC Janala, a non-formal learning service for adults; and the EIA Teacher Development Programme for primary and secondary schools. Both components received multiple international awards for the innovative use of new pedagogies and technologies to improve the teaching and learning of English language in Bangladesh and the Programme as a whole was considered by the UK's Department for International Development (DFID) to be one of its 'flagship projects',[1] and one that had made a 'positive impact' on the quality of English language learning in government schools.[2] This book is about the EIA schools component,[3] which was widely judged to be one of the most successful large-scale teacher development projects in low-to-middle income countries (LMICs), reaching 43,000 primary teachers (21 per cent of the workforce), 11,000 secondary teachers and over 7 million schoolchildren across Bangladesh.

The purpose of this book is to provide a detailed, analytical and critical account of the EIA teacher development programme, setting out lessons learned during the ten years of implementation from 2008–18.

EIA was initiated at the request of the Government of Bangladesh (GoB), to significantly improve the number of people able to communicate in the English language, at levels that would enable them to participate fully in economic and social activities. The project was funded by UK aid through DFID and was managed by Cambridge Education.[4] The Open University was technical lead on the EIA Programme, which sought to improve students' English language proficiency by enabling teachers to implement communicative language teaching (CLT) practices in their classrooms. EIA developed from initial design, Phase 1 (2008), followed by three main three-year phases: Phase 2 – Pilot (2008–11), which included baseline research, developmental testing (2008–09) and a pilot cohort (2010–11) reaching 750 teachers; Phase 3 – Upscaling (2011–14), reaching a further 12,000 teachers (in two cohorts, 2011–12 and 2013–14); and Phase 4 – Institutionalization (2014–17, subsequently extended to 2018), reaching over 40,000 more teachers within and through government systems (Table 0.1 summarizes this development).

The Programme related to global educational challenges as encapsulated in the United Nations' Millennium Development Goals at Programme inception and later the Sustainable Development Goals (SDGs) at Programme completion, 'to ensure inclusive and equitable quality education for all'. EIA reflects the partners' commitment to international development and openness.

> The Open University's mission is to be open to people, places, methods and ideas. We promote educational opportunity and social justice by providing high-quality university education … We deliver flexible, adaptable and scalable programmes in partnership with governments, NGOs, funding institutions and local partners.[5]

EIA drew upon prior Open University (OU) research and development programmes for teachers in LMICs, particularly the Digital Education Enhancement Project (DEEP)[6] but also Teacher Education in Sub-Saharan Africa (TESSA).[7] This informed an approach to teacher development underpinned by clear principles, namely that: (i) educational change had to start with teachers and build upon their existing or potential strengths; (ii) new teaching practices were best developed in the context of classroom and school realities; (iii) teachers would learn best from each other and should not be expected to introduce change alone; (iv) teachers were likely to need new tools and resources to support the development of new practices; (v) for teachers and

Table 0.1 The four phases of EIA's development

Phase 1 (2008)	Phase 2: Pilot (2008–11)		Phase 3: Upscaling (2011–14)	Phase 4: Institutionalization (2014–17/18)
	2008–10	2010–11		
Initial design	Baseline and developmental testing	Pilot cohort 700+ teachers	Cohort 2 (2011–12) Cohort 3 (2013–14) 12,000 teacher total	40,000 teachers

students alike, new practices should be enjoyable, effective and confidence inspiring – respect and affirmation were essential; (vi) teachers would develop a sense of agency and professional identity through shared action and reflection; (vii) simplistic 'deficit' analyses of teachers' knowledge and practice were rejected, whilst the multifaceted complexity of introducing, owning and sustaining change in low-resource classrooms, schools, communities and education systems was acknowledged and embraced.

Similarly, the Programme's promoted classroom pedagogy was also based on already established principles of CLT (see, e.g. Howatt 1984). These were articulated as follows:

- **communicative purpose:** learners take part in activities that involve reading, writing, speaking and listening in order to communicate. The teacher's (English) language is used purposefully, for example in setting up activities, managing the classroom, asking questions and giving feedback.
- **student-centredness:** the focus is shifted from the teacher to the learners' active involvement.
- **interaction:** the traditional emphasis on copying, repetition and translation gives way to interaction between teacher and learner(s) and between learners working in groups and pairs.
- **participation:** all learners take an active part in each lesson.
- **integrated skills:** reading, writing, speaking and listening are learnt together and support each other.
- **grammar in context:** grammar is taught in the context of communicative language use, rather than through decontextualized rules.

The ways in which the Programme attempted to embody both principles of teacher development and CLT resulted in an innovative and adaptable approach to school-based professional development for English language teachers.

Teachers' exploration of new classroom practices in the setting of their schools was conceived as the core driver of teacher professional development. Teachers were filmed carrying out CLT activities in their classrooms with their students, with narration added to help others approach these examples of practice critically (see Chapter 6). Such 'mediated-authentic videos' provided offline through mobile technology became the external stimulus for developing teachers' understanding of subject pedagogy. Replacing the traditional role of the 'teacher trainer', the mobile phone and AV resources became known locally as 'the trainer in the pocket'. To help teachers adapt and apply these activities to their own teaching, various levels of support were provided, including classroom resources and Teachers' Guides, peer and head teacher support in school, and regular peer-support meetings in an out-of-school setting for twelve to eighteen months. Two teachers from each group of local schools were given extra support, so that they could facilitate other teachers' engagement with the Programme. The four defining features of this approach to teacher development were that it was focused on classroom practice, was peer-supported, school-based and enhanced by mobile technology.

These principles and practices, along with supporting evidence, are laid out and analysed in subsequent chapters. Most chapters are written by members of the EIA Programme team (from the OU and Cambridge Education), and these chapters conclude with a summary of the lessons learnt. The book is structured as four parts, each concluding with a chapter written by a critical author, to provide an external perspective and analysis.

Framing questions

Each of the book's four parts is set around a framing question, and these questions and a brief synopsis of all the chapters are outlined below.

Part 1: Context (Chapters 1–3)

This part of the book sets out the context in which the EIA Programme was developed, and aims to give the reader an understanding of the challenges and opportunities faced by those who designed and implemented the strategies presented and critiqued in subsequent chapters. Together, the first two chapters address the question: why did the government of Bangladesh seek support to improve English language, as a skill for development?

In the final critical chapter of Part 1, Fauzia Shamim echoes and amplifies the questions posed in Chapter 2, about the impact of English on national economies, and examines EIA's determination to work with the existing context.

Part 2: Teacher professional development in low-to-middle-income countries (Chapters 4–7)

The first three chapters in this part are concerned with teacher professional development (TPD), covering the literature for this area, and the implementation of TDP within EIA, both in terms of the overall model of TPD and the use of technology to provide video support to teachers. Together, the chapters examine the question: what kinds of professional development approach enable teachers in low-to-middle income countries to improve their professional knowledge and practice?

The fourth 'critical comments' chapter, written by David Pedder, considers the approach to TPD advocated in the earlier chapters and examines its foundation.

Part 3: English language teaching (Chapters 8–10)

All chapters of Part 3 address matters of English language teaching, including the core features of the model adopted by EIA, and the implications for the Programme of the low level of English proficiency among many teachers. At the heart of the chapters is the question: how were improved English language teaching (ELT) practices envisaged, developed and supported through EIA?

In the concluding critical chapter of Part 3, Amol Padwad considers EIA's approach to ELT, commenting on the benefits of a practice-based intervention and the place of improving teachers' proficiency through classroom English.

Part 4: Strategic issues (Chapters 11–14)

Addressing the strategic issues of the EIA Programme, the first three chapters cover quite different, though related, topics that brought EIA from a pilot project to an institutionalized 'programme', including the research, monitoring and evaluation programme of EIA, sustainability, through embedding and institutionalizing, and how the idea of scale was achieved within a value for money (VfM) framework. The question the three chapters address in their different ways is: which issues were critical for any programme that wants to institutionalize and sustain its approach?

The critical comment chapter by Ahmed Shamim examines these strategic issues in the light of his experience in Bangladesh.

An invitation to readers

This introduction merely touches upon the rich and sometimes contentious or challenging accounts presented in subsequent chapters. Readers are invited to reflect upon a number of dilemmas/tensions that run through the book, including:

1. possible tensions between responding to what was practical and possible in local contexts across Bangladesh, and agendas set by internationally accepted approaches and norms;
2. the effect of scale on the activities and how that was affected by the length of the project and the consequent iterative nature of its development;
3. the contribution that 'distance learning' and 'mobile learning' may make to significant improvements in the quality of education (in keeping with the requirements of the SDGs), when these are ultimately manifested as improvements in face-to-face pedagogies.
4. the need to think creatively and radically to develop principled and pragmatic approaches, even when there is a shortage of evidence on which to base action, whilst, where possible drawing on, and contributing to, the international evidence base of 'what works'.

How the Programme responded to these challenges is the subject of three of the book's four sections, but the first part sets out the institutional and national context in which these challenges were presented.

Notes

1   Letter on the Programme's closure, Jim McAlpine, DfID Bangladesh, Acting Head of Office, 19 December 2017.
2   Throughout the book the Department for International Development will be referred to as DFID.
3   Subsequent use of 'EIA' throughout this book is intended to refer only to the EIA schools component, not BBC Janala.
4   Cambridge Education is a member of the Mott MacDonald Group.
5   http://www.open.ac.uk/about/main/mission (accessed 30 October 2017).
6   See www.open.ac.uk/deep (accessed 29 October 2017).
7   See www.tessafrica.net (accessed 29 October 2017).

Part One

Context

The first part of the book sets out the context in which the EIA Programme was developed, with a major goal of giving the reader an understanding of the challenges and opportunities faced by those designing and implementing the strategies presented and critiqued in subsequent chapters. Chapter 1 explores the wider physical, political, social and educational environment of Bangladesh at the time of the Programme's inception. It indicates how Bangladesh has progressed economically to become a LMIC, but nevertheless faces formidable issues in relation to improving the quality of its education, including in English language. Chapter 2 focuses more narrowly on the country's linguistic history, and on the sometimes contentious place of English within this. It also examines critically the rationale for promoting the learning of English in a country like Bangladesh, examining the focus on promoting English-language competency in the population to improve the economy; such improvement was the overall goal of EIA. Together, the two chapters address the question: why did the Government of Bangladesh seek to support the improvement of its citizens' proficiency in the English language, as a skill for development?

In the concluding critical chapter of Part 1, Fauzia Shamim echoes and amplifies the questions posed in the preceding chapter, about the impact of English on national economies, arguing that English skills can only be of value in the context of a 'strong educational base' which supports improvements in literacy, numeracy and employability skills. Shamim also recognizes EIA's early baseline research and determination to work with the existing context as significant factors in the Programme's success at classroom level.

Part One

Context

1

The Educational Context of Bangladesh

An Overview

Sonia Burton, Ian Eyres and Robert McCormick

Introduction

Bangladesh has developed from being one of the poorest and least-developed countries in the world to being classified as a Lower-Middle-Income Country (LMIC) with a Gross National Income (GNI) per capita of $1,190 in 2014.[1] Its Gross Domestic Product (GDP), growing at 6.6 per cent, currently stands at $195 billion, and the growth rate of the population (at the time of writing, around 161 million) continues to fall.[2] Nevertheless, it experiences considerable and growing income inequality: over the past forty years, there has been perennial transfer of income from the lower four quintiles of households to the highest quintile and the bottom 20 per cent experiencing the greatest fall in income share (Matin 2014). A number of factors exacerbate this situation: Bangladesh's large and growing population; political instability; poor infrastructure; and geography and weather conditions (vulnerability to climate change and natural disasters), to name but a few. The World Bank summarized the challenges:

> To sustain growth, Bangladesh needs urgently to implement structural reforms, expand investments in human capital, increase female labor force participation, and raise productivity through increased global value chain integration. Reducing infrastructure gaps and improving the business climate would allow new productive sectors to develop and generate jobs.[3]

In particular, the World Bank identified job creation as Bangladesh's top priority.

The English in Action (EIA) Programme was initiated to improve the lives of 25 million Bangladeshis by giving them access to English language learning opportunities, through which they can enhance their English language skills. Improving their English increases their access to jobs requiring such skills and thus to higher levels of income; at a national level, income is improved and poverty is reduced. The Programme aimed to improve English language skills across all demographic groups, including poor and more socially excluded people, such as ethnic minorities.

This chapter provides a contextual backdrop to EIA's schools component at the time of its inception in order to paint a picture of the conditions and circumstances within which the Programme was designed and initially implemented. It begins by outlining key factors relating to the country's geographical, social, cultural, economic, political and technological context, and moves on to describe the educational context and key issues pertaining to it. Through this, it presents evidence from EIA's baseline studies and elsewhere – in relation to teachers, students and schools – in order to illustrate life in schools in Bangladesh. It moves on to consider the typical pedagogy and teacher motivation in Bangladeshi schools and provides an account of a typical Bangladeshi teacher's work and home life. Finally, it reflects on the lessons for any project on English language teaching in how to meet the challenges a developing country, such as Bangladesh, poses.

Geographical, social, technological and political context

Bangladesh, located in the north-eastern part of South Asia, is a semi-tropical country with lush green vegetation, monsoon rains and one of the largest deltas in the world. At the foot of the Himalayas, its low-lying land is interlaced by three great rivers: the Ganges (in Bangladesh, the Padma), the Brahmaputra (in Bangladesh, the Jamuna), and the Meghna, which all flow south into the Bay of Bengal. The many tributaries of these rivers are often interlinked, making parts of the country difficult to reach. It is the deposits of these rivers that provide Bangladesh with a rich, productive agricultural soil, with rice as the main cereal crop and staple food.

Despite the rich agricultural land, less favourable aspects of Bangladesh's meteorological and geographical conditions mean it experiences substantial rainfall and much of the land is under water for considerable periods of the year. This makes it difficult to establish and maintain infrastructure, such as roads, electricity and internet, and leaves communities cut off and isolated.

Although Bangladesh is a relatively small South Asian country, with an area of around 148,000 square kilometres,[4] its population is large and while growth was for many years falling, since 2007 it has 'stabilized' at around 1.2 per cent.[5] At the time of EIA's inception (2007), Bangladesh's total population stood at just under 147 million people (161 million at the time of writing)[6] and population density was at around 1,126 people per square kilometre (1,237 in 2015).[7] The population density of the Netherlands – a similarly low-lying country – is, in contrast, about half that of Bangladesh. The considerable population size and continuing growth place much pressure on the education system, which must provide for this increasing demand. This, at a time when spending on education is inadequate: although Bangladesh had aspirations to become not just a LMIC, but a MIC (Middle Income Country), its educational spending is well below what is required (less than 2 per cent of GDP averaged over 2010–2014; *The Daily Star* 2016) compared to other MICs (e.g. China at 4 per cent).

In terms of technology, internet and mobile phone use were low at the time of EIA's conception: in 2007, just 1.85 per cent of people used the internet[8] and 23.5 per cent had a mobile phone subscription;[9] in 2015, these figures had increased to 12.1 per cent[10] and 81.9 per cent[11] respectively. The EIA infrastructure studies found the following (EIA 2009h & j):

- the growth rate for fixed telephone lines (ownership of which is low) had been very modest in comparison with the growth in mobile phone subscriptions;
- mobile phone subscriptions reached 46.69 million by mid-2009, with high rates of access in rural areas;
- computer ownership and access to the internet remained at very low levels. The figure for internet users in 2007 was 0.32 per cent, much lower than the already low figure cited above;
- the overall national figure for internet usage was 3 per cent, but there was considerable variation by location. While 8 per cent of metropolitan dwellers had used the internet, only 1 per cent of those in rural areas had done so. Variation by gender was also high: 4 per cent of males had used the internet compared with 1 per cent of females.

Other technologies, such as television and radio, were available to around a quarter of the population, and electricity available to a third of rural households, but in all parts of the country the supply was found to be unstable. Note that the Bangladeshi government has bold plans to build on this in its effort to reach MIC status by 2021, and established the Vision 2021 policy incorporated as part of its Digital Bangladesh policy (GoB 2012).

Politically, the country was administered locally through six divisions[12] (Barisal, Chittagong, Dhaka, Khulna, Rajshahi, Sylhet), and within these, 64 districts. The districts are divided into upazilas, under an Upazila Nirbahi Officer. There are around 500 upazilas, and within each one, villages are grouped to form a union, each having an approximate population of 25,000.

At the national level, Bangladesh has faced ongoing political instability since its establishment in 1971 (Chapter 2 will consider the political social and cultural issues that influenced the country's sociolinguistic development). Since parliamentary democracy was restored in 1991, two parties, the Awami League (AL) and the Bangladesh Nationalist Party (BNP), each under what has been described as 'dynastic political leadership' (Hossain 2000: 509),[13] have competed for power. The result, Hossain argues, is a 'winner takes all' system which gives all formal power to the successful party and leaves the opposition to engage 'in mobilization, protest or other negative politics' (Osman 2010: 330). This was evident during the caretaker government (CTG) in 2006, which took over from the BNP to organize the election process. The withdrawal of the AL from the pending election in early 2007 (because the two parties could not agree on the election) led to a state of emergency backed by the military and the CTG continued until the election at the end of December 2008 (which the AL won with a two-thirds majority).

All this instability was during the initial period of EIA's inception, including the period when the Programme was conducting baseline studies in October and November 2008. When the EIA memorandum to help start the Programme went for 'rubber-stamping' by the new AL Education Minister following the election, he declined to sign it as he knew nothing about it. It took a year to come around again, as EIA declined to take action to 'smooth the process'. This resulted in a delay in initial implementation of the Programme, and the instability continued throughout the Programme's life, delaying subsequent cohort starts and periodically causing disruption to its operations.[14] During the Programme, various opposition parties called for a 'Hartal', a nation-wide and often violent strike that affected public transport, which sometimes made attending work and EIA training events difficult. There is also a more sinister backdrop to the party struggles in the actions of radical and violent Islamist groups that have been manifest over the life of the Programme (Vaughan 2007; Wolf 2013) including, in 2016, a devastating attack on a restaurant not far from the EIA office (Manik et al. 2016).

This is the broad context within which education is provided, and EIA had to work.

Educational context

The Bangladeshi education system is organized into three levels: primary, secondary and higher education. Primary level education covers Grades[15] 1–5 (ages six to ten) and secondary Grades 6–12 (ages eleven to seventeen). Whilst the government runs or fully supports a substantial proportion of primary schools (47 per cent in 2005, GoB 2008; almost 60 per cent in 2013, WB 2013a), almost all secondary schools are non-government (i.e. private), a figure unchanged in almost a decade, although they are also supported by government funding (GoB 2008; WB 2013b). At the time of EIA's conception, there were approximately 80,000 primary schools and 18,500 secondary schools operating in Bangladesh, with 16 million and 7 million children attending, respectively (GoB 2008). The greater number of students in primary education reflects the fact that education at this level is compulsory and free.[16] Indeed, it was claimed that universal primary enrolment was achieved in 2012 (GED 2015), although the 'net enrolment rate' quoted by the GoB over the years is usually higher than that given by other bodies (cf. WB 2013a); in 2008 it was 90.8 per cent (UNICEF 2009). More to the point, the proportion of pupils completing up to Grade 5 (the end of primary schooling) was around 70 per cent when EIA started, and by 2010 was 76 per cent (WB 2013a).[17] The estimated number of out-of-school children was 3.3 million (UNICEF 2009), the poor being more likely to be in this group.[18] Some 2 million students are in madrasahs, which largely provide only a Quranic education.

Gender parity had been reached in Bangladesh in primary and secondary schools by 2005, and girls' completion rates are higher than boys' up to junior secondary (Grade 8), though further up the education system this is reversed (WB 2013a). Inequalities are, however, more strongly correlated to location (rural vs urban), district and income, in terms of enrolment (WB 2008), completion and learning outcomes. Thus, as is common in developing countries, students in rural areas do less well in tests and have lower rates of completion, as do those who are poorer (WB 2013a, b). It is also the case that the divisions of Rajshahi and Sylhet lag significantly behind the national average in tests on Bangla and Mathematics (WB 2013b).

The huge numbers of students within the Bangladeshi education system are catered for by a large number of schools and teachers: in the 80,000 primary schools there are 345,000 teachers (GoB 2008). The bulk of primary schools are either government schools or registered non-government primary schools (RNGPS), serving 70 per cent of enrolled primary school children. Though teachers in the RNGPS are, in theory, paid at the same level as in government schools, they do not have the same conditions of employment, including importantly tenure of employment and pensions (GoB 2008). Government primary school teachers are educated at least to secondary-school level (some have degrees, including some with master's degrees). In principle, they receive initial training, though in practice for most teachers this comes some years into their career. At the time of EIA's inception, for primary school teachers this was the one-year Certificate of Education (undertaken at fifty-seven Primary Teachers Training Institutes (PTIs) across the country) and 74 per cent of government primary school (GPS) teachers and 77 per cent of RNGPS had undergone this training (UNICEF 2009). The lateness of this training in a teacher's career means that traditional pedagogies, beliefs and values have years to become entrenched and are unlikely to be changed even by a relatively long residential course. In any event, the National Assessment Survey suggested that the training curriculum may be failing to equip teachers with the competencies required to deliver basic literacy and numeracy provision (UN 2013).[19] In terms of English, EIA studies found that few had the English language ability to teach the level of English they were intended to teach their students (EIA 2009a). Basic in-service training on subjects and pedagogy have been experienced by 25 per cent of GPS teachers and 28 per cent of RNGPS teachers.

The secondary sector is smaller with 18,500 secondary schools (GoB 2008) and 224,000 teachers (WB 2013a). Among the 98 per cent of private schools are an estimated 2000 English-medium schools (Banu 2005). Government secondary school teachers require a first degree and a B.Ed. from a Teacher Training College (TTC), which is usually undertaken in-service. Those in private schools (the large majority) require a first degree but not a B.Ed. and in 2006, more than half of all lower secondary teachers were unqualified to teach. In-service education is provided to secondary teachers only through specific project initiatives, such as Teaching Quality Improvement Secondary Education Project (TQI-SEP).

Teachers often need to supplement their income and 30 per cent of GPS teachers and 63 per cent of RNGPS primary teachers do so, mainly through coaching students outside of school time (GoB 2008). This is often seen as a disincentive for these teachers to improve their practice, since if pupils are successful in school, they do not need to pay for extra lessons. This practice leaves a lot to be desired, as a report for the Special Envoy for Global Education captures when looking at the performance of students in the examination system prior to 2009:

...only 42 percent of students were selected by their teachers to take the Grade 5 exam (Government of Bangladesh 2011c). One quarter of these students failed. This implies that only around one-third of students were able to meet the competency standards set by the exam after five years of schooling. Given that half of the children dropped out prior to Grade 5, the results served to underline the difficult learning environment experienced by Bangladesh's children.

UN 2013: 8[20]

In secondary, according to the same report, 30 per cent of students sitting for the Higher Secondary School Certificate fail, and 50 per cent of students will have dropped out before this stage (UN 2013). When Grade 5 students were tested using National Assessments in 2011, only a quarter acquired relevant competency of Grade 5 Bangla, and only one-third of these students were able to demonstrate competency of Grade 5 Mathematics (WB 2013b). Secondary students do worse: in 2012 a national assessment revealed that the proportion of Grade 9 students who have mastered Grade 8-level competencies in Bangla, English and mathematics are 44 per cent, 44 per cent, and 35 per cent respectively (WB 2013b).

A baseline study conducted by EIA in February 2009 revealed many of the challenges facing teachers: large classes, scarce resources, poor classroom and school conditions (EIA 2009b). In terms of classroom conditions the report observed:

Classrooms are generally clean and tidy, have good natural light and basic teaching equipment like a blackboard and chalk are present there. Often there is sufficient furniture for the students present in class. However, there is little evidence of students' work on display and learning and teaching materials are usually not visible.

EIA 2009c: 9

The classroom environment was better in urban than in rural schools and government schools had less student work on display and less evidence of learning and teaching materials. In only 40 per cent of schools did all the students have a textbook, and in 18 per cent, only 25 per cent or fewer students had one. In most classrooms students had an exercise book.

The official teacher–student ratio was lower (1:49; UNICEF 2009) than the observed class sizes, with sixty to 100 students being found in government schools and thirty to thirty-five in non-government organization schools, though the latter had much less space (EIA 2009c). Such large class sizes always pose a challenge for an innovation like EIA that seeks to change classroom practice, and it alerted the Programme team to take this into consideration when designing the programme.[21] Moreover, discussions with teachers in the pilot phase showed that the belief that large classes prevented the adoption of innovative practices was widely held. Adding to this challenge is the fact that 90 per cent of schools were on a double-shift system: typically Grades 1–2 attend in the morning and Grades 3–5 in the afternoon (UNICEF 2009). When combined with 19 per cent student absenteeism, this means that contact hours are much less than would be expected for primary education. The official contact hours, which exclude shifts and absenteeism, are themselves half the international average of 900–1,000 per year (UNICEF 2009).

This situation does nothing to help teachers improve student learning; although there is no overall relationship between teacher experience and student outcomes, those with experience of twenty years or more are associated with lower student learning outcomes (WB 2013b). Many of these teachers are still relatively young and have at least two decades in the profession ahead of them, and hence an innovation such as EIA has great potential even for them. Motivation, however, appears to be the issue, with few incentives to improve and a poor career ladder (WB 2013b). Many teachers are happy with their job, but the lack of professional development opportunities, feedback or accountability affects their morale (Sandhu and Rahman 2012). EIA could deal with the lack of professional development opportunities, but changes at a local and national level are needed for the other two issues. As will be shown in Chapters 5 and 11, EIA had to work with local education officials – Assistant Upazila Education Officers (AUEOs) – to enable them to observe teachers' classroom practice and to overcome some of the negative attitudes they carried into schools, which do not encourage teachers to innovate in their teaching methods (Baba 2008).

Clearly, given the desire for EIA to make use of reliable technology, relevant aspects of infrastructure and provision constituted important factors. Over the Programme's lifetime there has been evidence of progress in technology use. Given the findings from the baseline studies into technology, internet use and electricity (EIA 2009h, j), it was obvious from this that mobile technology was a good way forward, reinforced by the individual access and usage where almost all teachers and a large proportion of adults owned or had access to a mobile phone, and nearly 40 per cent of students had used one. Only 11 per cent of teachers had access to the internet, fewer than 20 per cent of teachers used audio-visual material for their learning (students hardly at all), and around 10 per cent of both groups used computers for learning. The importance accorded to computer-based learning by the education policies of many developing countries, including Bangladesh, did not seem to be reflected in the reality of communities and schools. The 2010 Education Policy focused on 'conventional' ICT, understandably looking forward to the economic needs of exports related to information technology (Ministry of Education 2010).

Teaching context and pedagogy

The picture of the Bangladeshi classroom has remained static, and observations made at the time when EIA was starting captured the typical pedagogy: 'teachers tend to spend most of their classroom time lecturing or reading textbooks in secondary schools'. This finding was supported by evidence from a Japanese study conducted in 2008 (WB 2013b: 22–3). This sector review by the World Bank also cited an EIA baseline study that painted the same picture for primary schools. Other studies have talked of traditional methods with most of lesson time spent on material taken directly from the textbook (FMRP 2005), or a transmission mode of teaching with a focus on book-based knowledge, and rote learning for memorization (Thorton 2006).

As noted earlier, EIA conducted a baseline study to reveal the nature of classroom practice, specifically in English lessons. A key finding gave a similar picture of the nature of the Bangladeshi classroom to that in the studies cited above:

> Throughout the lessons, teaching from the blackboard or front of the class was the predominant pedagogic approach. As the lesson progressed, teachers tended to read from the textbook, ask closed questions or move around the classroom monitoring and facilitating students as they worked individually. All other pedagogic activities were observed in less than 10 per cent of classes at each of the times sampled.
>
> EIA 2009c: (i)

Other elements of pedagogy seen to be poor were the lack of small group work (used by just over a third of teachers), an over-reliance on ineffective whole-class teaching (used by 60 per cent of teachers) and poor subject knowledge on the part of the teacher (21 per cent of teachers scored less than 50 per cent on a test for their students) (WB 2013b). In particular, this source confirms the centrality of the textbook. The World Bank also pointed out that examinations were confined to testing recall, to the extent that students who used their own words rather than those in the textbook were penalized (WB 2013b)! The EIA study also revealed little use of teaching aids (found in only 2–6 per cent of classes), few stimulating task-based activities and little student participation or interaction (EIA 2009c). On the positive side, teachers had positive interactions with their students and maintained good discipline, and even paid attention to students throughout the classroom, not just those in the front row.

At about the same time, a study of teacher education made the same complaint about pedagogy in that sector (Kraft et al. 2009); newly trained teachers were reproducing what they experienced in school and in their training. EIA was thus set to tackle a lot of these well-established pedagogic positions through its approach to classroom practice, as later chapters will show. What it did not specifically set out to do – it was in no position to – was to revise the examination system, which, given the communicative approach that the Programme advocated, was a challenge: not only did examinations, based as they were on recall, have no place for students to show any interactive abilities, they assessed only reading and writing, and not listening or speaking.

Over a period which extended into the first two years of EIA, Primary Education Development Programme (PEDP) II was funded by a consortium of donors (2004–09). One of the major objectives of PEDP II was to improve the quality of teaching and learning and raise student achievement. Achievement is assessed in the areas of: (i) Primary School Quality Level (PSQL) standards (including provision of adequate/good physical and health and hygiene facilities at schools which helped create a welcoming school environment); (ii) teacher training and deployment; (iii) provision of teaching-learning materials, including textbooks; and (iv) the National Student Assessment and Primary Scholarship Examination. Overall, this project was seen by the World Bank as only 'moderately satisfactory', it having only really started to produce results in the final years of implementation (WB 2011). Although there were improvements in the environment in schools (PSQL standards), there was no fall in teacher–student ratios, but the target numbers for teachers trained were exceeded. Provision of teaching and learning materials resulted in a massive injection of 78 million new textbooks into schools, but the National Student Assessment, although conducted twice, led to tests whose results could not be compared with each other, though in the latter year a revised assessment was on the way to being technically sound. The new primary school examination led to more students taking the examination and high pass rates, though other work by the World Bank cast doubt on their reliability (WB 2013b). As EIA moved into its scale-up and institutionalization phases, the next iteration, PEDP III, was already under way, incorporating the EIA professional development approach and materials, and indeed was part of its institutionalization in the government system, as Chapter 12 will show.

The account in Box 1.1, based on a teacher case study from the EIA Teachers' Lives series (EIA 2013), puts these statistics and general descriptions into the context of the everyday realities for teachers.

Box 1.1: A teacher's life

Osman

Osman works in a government primary school in the upazila of Burichong in the district of Comilla, with his wife, mother, two daughters and one son. All three children attend his school. He sees his main goals in terms of 'maintaining' his family in a 'good manner and at the same time doing a noble job by teaching'.

He gained his BA degree before becoming a teacher, but followed the then standard teacher education course (Certificate in Education) only after he had been a teacher for some time. As well as being a qualified teacher, he trained in library management, as a 'master trainer' for the second Primary Education Development Programme (PEDP II) and as a teacher facilitator for EIA.

According to Osman, as a teacher he is respected by members of his local community and is invited to take part in community meetings as well as social events, such as weddings. People take advice from him because he is seen as 'educated'. While this means that he is, in his own words, 'satisfied' and 'encouraged', one aspect of his work he reports in a less positive way:

> There is nothing that frustrates me as a teacher except the salary scale. The people of other professions think that they are superior and the teachers are inferior, so their attitude sometimes frustrates us.

As well as impacting on his status and his material standard of living, the low salary has consequences for the time Osman has for out-of-school tasks related to teaching. As well as fulfilling family and social responsibilities, Osman works for a life insurance company at weekends and gives private tuition to a group of seven or eight students (some from his own school) early each morning.

Osman's school

In a building he considers 'well built', Osman's school operates a double-shift system, with Classes (Grades) 1 and 2 in the morning and Classes 3 and 4 in the afternoon. Students in Class 5, who are preparing for the national examinations, attend all day. The school is open from 9:30am to 4:15pm (2.15p.m. on Thursday, the end of the week), with a forty-minute lunch break. Because of the shift system, which Osman says is due to a lack of space in the school and not to a shortage of teachers, each lesson lasts only thirty-five minutes, which Osman considers to be 'limited time'.

The number of students on roll for Osman's classes range from the high thirties to more than fifty, but the numbers actually attending ranged from twenty-eight to thirty-five, averaging thirty-three. In each class there were more boys (usually five or six more) than girls, both registered and attending.

Assembly takes place on most days, in between the two shifts, 12:00p.m. to 12:25p.m. Activities include students' reading from the Quran, physical exercise, hoisting the national flag, taking an oath to the country and singing the national anthem. Assembly is also a time for teachers to give students any important information. This leaves little time for Osman to eat lunch, let alone socialize with colleagues, undertake administrative tasks or prepare for the afternoon's lessons.

Osman speaks warmly of his relations with colleagues. The examples of mutual support he gives all relate to personal support that include both prayer and practical financial help, for example to sort out a retiring colleague's problems with his pension. His positive feelings extend to the head teacher, for whom he has high regard. However, although Osman sees him as encouraging and supportive, the head's responsibilities often take him away from the school, absences which Osman can find frustrating.

He describes relations with the wider community, including parents and the School Management Committee (SMC) as 'very collaborative'. In Osman's school, they regularly visit classrooms and make suggestions as to how teaching might be made more effective.

Parents, similarly, are seen by Osman as playing an active role in the life of the school, and are generally satisfied with it. They visit regularly to discuss their child's performance. He talks of a recent meeting, involving all the teachers, the head teacher and the Upazila Education Officer, in which examination results were discussed and parents were urged to encourage their children to come to school. Parents asked for Class 5 children to be given a 'special coaching programme' and this was agreed. The parent–teacher association raises funds for additional materials to support the final exams, as well as religious, cultural, social and sporting activities.

Lessons for EIA

As EIA was planning its approach and materials, the situation it was faced with was one in which it had scope to improve the experience of learners. This chapter has revealed the significant challenges faced by teachers, among them: poor material resources; a lack of appropriate training and preparation; a lack of professional development opportunities; other demands on teachers' time and energy; large classes; poor levels of achievement of students (and in some cases teachers); and disadvantaged groups who were difficult to reach and whose performance was therefore difficult to improve. Equally, there were challenges posed by the wider context, relating to the general physical conditions in schools, teacher salary and progression, the examination system and the expectations of local education officials (e.g. AUEOs) and members of the School Management Committees. More problematic to anticipate or work with, despite long familiar histories, were the effects of geography, poverty and politics. But there were factors in EIA's favour: the buoyant economic growth, the burgeoning global development of mobile technology (in which Bangladesh shared) and a government keen to embrace technology and to meet the challenge of improving its educational quality (as witnessed in its Education Policy 2010 document). EIA had the potential to support effective teaching and learning by supplying improved learning materials, by involving teachers in their own professional development with their colleagues and by doing these things in ways which were manageable (for example, by not taking up too much of teachers' time) and even attractive to teachers, and which placed the latest technology in their hands. The question of why it was considered necessary to focus on the teaching of English is addressed in Chapter 2.

Notes

1 https://datahelpdesk.worldbank.org/knowledgebase/articles/906519; http://www.worldbank.org/en/news/press-release/2015/07/01/new-world-bank-update-shows-bangladesh-kenya-myanmar-and-tajikistan-as-middle-income-while-south-sudan-falls-back-to-low-income (all web addresses in this chapter have been accessed 30 October 2017).

2 http://data.worldbank.org/country/bangladesh?view=chart; http://databank.worldbank.org/data/Views/Reports/ReportWidgetCustom.aspx?Report_Name=CountryProfile&Id=b450fd57&tbar=y&dd=y&inf=n&zm=n&country=BGD.

3 http://www.worldbank.org/en/country/bangladesh/overview#1.

4 http://databank.worldbank.org/data/Views/Reports/ReportWidgetCustom.aspx?Report_Name=CountryProfile&Id=b450fd57&tbar=y&dd=y&inf=n&zm=n&country=BGD; another World Bank source puts it at 130,000 m^2(http://data.worldbank.org/indicator/AG.LND.TOTL.K2?locations=BD).

5   http://data.worldbank.org/indicator/SP.POP.GROW?locations=BD&view=chart.

6   http://data.worldbank.org/indicator/SP.POP.TOTL?locations=BD&name_desc=true.

7   http://data.worldbank.org/indicator/EN.POP.DNST?locations=BD.

8   http://www.internetlivestats.com/internet-users/bangladesh/.

9   http://databank.worldbank.org/data/reports.aspx?source=2&series=IT.CEL.SETS.
    P2&country=.

10 http://wdi.worldbank.org/table/5.12.

11 http://wdi.worldbank.org/table/5.11.

12 The addition of Mymensingh and Rangpur divisions brings this number to eight at
    the time of writing.

13 For analysis of the two dynasties, see Amundsen (2013).

14 Ironically, the later disruptions were caused by the BNP, who among other things
    were objecting to AL not handing over to a CTG prior to an election as required
    by the Constitution.

15 Within Bangladesh, the term universally used for 'grade' or 'year group' is 'class'.
    Thus, the first textbook is for Class 1, and so on.

16 But there are other costs associated with schooling (UNICEF 2009).

17 The World Bank gave reasons for this in its report *Education for All* (WB 2008).

18 The World Bank put the figure at 5 million in 2013 (WB 2013a).

19 Development of a more rigorous and more practice-focused eighteen-month
    training programme – the Diploma in Primary Education (DPEd) – began in 2010
    and by 2015 had been implemented in half of the country's PTIs.

20 Figures given by the World Bank for 2012; the Directorate of Primary Education in
    Bangladesh figures are quite different, with a pass rate of 97 per cent (WB 2013b).

21 However, it is important to note that a study by the World Bank in Bangladesh could
    find an association between Bangla scores and class size only at Grade 5, and not at
    Grade 3, nor in Mathematics at either grade (WB 2013b).

2

The Status and Economic Significance of English in Bangladesh

Perceptions and Consequences

Elizabeth J. Erling and Masuda Khatoon

Introduction

This chapter will provide an overview of the role and status of English in Bangladesh, and specifically its place in various domains in the country, including in education. It will present evidence of the very limited success of implementing communicative language teaching (CLT) in the past and will describe previous attempts to improve English language education in the country. The chapter then explores the premise that the English in Action Programme was built on: that improving English language competence in Bangladesh will improve the economic opportunities of people in the country. This exploration will examine the ways in which the Programme attempted to realize this aspiration, and will also discuss the research undertaken within the Programme that attempted to evidence this relationship.

The political, social and cultural context of English in Action

Bangladesh has, during the last 150 years, been through three political phases that have influenced its sociolinguistic development (and its sociolinguistic development has influenced political change). Several authors have discussed the establishment of English in Bangladesh from its colonial origin, including Hamid (2009; 2011), Hamid and Erling (2016), Hossain and Tollefson (2007), Imam (2005), and Rahman (2007). In the first period, during British rule, there was a push by some social reformers to introduce both English and Western education for Indians (Hamid and Erling 2016). Christian missionaries played a lead role, inevitably for proselytizing purposes. There was some local resistance but, by the early twentieth century, English had become the medium of education in many schools, leading to concerns about the threat to vernacular languages in education (Spear 1938). The demand for English, with its associations with the ruling class, was extensive but access was generally limited to the urban elite (Kachru 1983).

After British Colonial rule ended in 1947 and the territory became a part of Pakistan, the role of English was still contested in relation to Urdu, the official language of Pakistan, and Bangla, which was to become the official language of Bangladesh (cf. Imam 2005). A much greater concern for the population of East Pakistan, however, was the push by the dominant West Pakistan to impose Urdu as the national language. Bangla was the native language of the overwhelming majority of East Pakistan, and the majority native language, in fact, of the whole of Pakistan (57 per cent). Urdu was spoken as a native language by just 3.5 per cent of Pakistan's total population (Thompson 2007). The Pakistani state's decision to adopt Urdu as the national language resulted in student-led civil discontent and a push for the joint establishment of Bangla. During a student procession on 21 February 1952, armed police killed a number of student demonstrators and the deaths provoked wide-spread civil unrest. This 'language martyrdom' was the catalyst for a strong nationalist Bangla language movement which laid the foundation for the establishment of independent Bangladesh in 1971 (see Hossain and Tollefson 2007).

Given this history, it is perhaps not surprising that, on entering this third period, 'Bangla-centric sentimentalities overshadowed any discussions about the role of English within the new nation' (Hamid and Erling 2016: 30). Bangla was firmly established as the medium of instruction in state educational institutions and the nationalistic fervour supporting Bangla led to a long period in which the teaching of English was not seen as a priority and given little or no attention at state level (Rahman 2007). The unintended consequence was that English education was available only in the private sector and therefore only to an elite who were able to afford it.

The role played by English did not divide the political parties. The leaders of successive governments stressed the shedding of the so-called dominance of 'imperial English', and assigned new roles to Bangla in public life to gain popularity. This view of English was understandable, and arguably even advantageous for developing a sense of nationhood during this period. It was not only English that was de-prioritized: regional dialects of Bangla and thirteen languages spoken by ethnic minorities in the hill regions of the country have been neglected, or even ignored in official language policy (Hossain and Tollefson 2007).

During the 1970s and 1980s it became increasingly apparent that standards in English amongst the population were falling (Banu and Sussex 2001), while only a wealthy elite had access to the language, which was already seen as providing social and economic advantage. The Ministry of Education commissioned a special task force to look into falling standards, resulting in the introduction of English as a compulsory subject from Grade One (age six) in 1991, with students having to pass in both English and Bangla in the board examinations.

Despite the promotion of English at policy level and the privileged position of the language in the educational curriculum, the number of English speakers in the country was relatively low at the start of the EIA Programme. In 1996, English was estimated to be used by 3 per cent of the population (Baumgardner 1996: 243). Euromonitor (2010) estimated the number of English-speakers to be much higher than this – around 18 per cent of the population – but little is known about the level of English spoken by this percentage of the population, nor the regularity of use. Given the fact that the standards of English language teaching (ELT) in government schools (and the quality of education in general) have been dramatically low (see Hamid 2011), it might be expected that levels of English amongst the population in general would be rather low.

The place of English in the Bangladeshi national curriculum

With over 40 million students learning English as a compulsory subject throughout the years of primary and secondary education, Bangladesh has one of the largest English-learning populations in the world (Hamid and Erling 2016). It has the same curricular status as Bangla and occupies almost 19 per cent of curricular time. Like Bangla, English is taught every day in class, between one and two class periods of thirty-five to forty-five minutes.

Some pockets of success can be seen in a rise in pass rates in public examinations at the end of Years 10 and 12: that increase has been 70 per cent or higher in the past few years, meaning that larger numbers of students have graduated and progressed to the next level (Hamid 2009). Nevertheless, those who fail in public examinations usually do so in English and/or in mathematics (EIA 2009a; Hamid 2009). However, students' grades are not reliable indices of their levels of English proficiency. (See Chapter 8 for a discussion of the exam system.) In fact, poor levels of English proficiency are common among students and teachers alike in Bangladesh; for example in 2009, there was little evidence of English language progression through primary and secondary school and the majority of students remain at, or even below, the most basic ability levels year after year (EIA 2009a: 2). As noted in Chapter 1, many teachers are assigned to teaching students at higher levels than their own ability in the language. Low levels of English were particularly common in rural areas, where Hamid and Baldauf (2008) found not a single Grade 10 student in a cohort of fourteen students interviewed able to introduce themselves properly after ten years' study of English.

Previous attempts to improve English language education in the country

The need to provide further access to English and improve standards for teaching was identified as far back as 1997, when the English Language Teaching Improvement Project (ELTIP), funded by UK aid and the Government of Bangladesh, ran from 1997 to 2008. ELTIP aimed to introduce a communicative language teaching (CLT) approach in schools within the national curriculum. During its lifetime, ELTIP succeeded in introducing a new textbook series, *English for Today*, which was adopted in schools throughout the country, and provided training to several thousand teachers throughout the country. ELTIP also had some success in making the English curriculum more accessible to students, and in familiarizing teachers with the principles of CLT (Rahman 2007). However, as Chapter 1 indicated, EIA's baseline studies found little evidence of changed classroom practice. In these lessons, students were given little opportunity to interact, and 'none or hardly any' students spoke any English at all. For example, teachers read from the textbook and translated it into Bangla, with them talking most of the time, and students giving one-word responses. Often the communicative methods embedded in the textbook were missed by teachers, who preferred to use the traditional strategies they were familiar with. While some teachers may have been able to talk in general terms 'about' CLT, and were aware that the revised textbook encourages and demands a more participatory approach to learning, for the most part they did not put this into practice.

Thus, for all the investment in educational reform, there was very little visible change in English language teaching and learning. Hamid and Baldauf (2008: 17) argue that it is no wonder that programmes like ELTIP have brought about few significant changes in ELT practices, as teachers continue teaching in the 'same classrooms, surrounded by the same external socioeconomic and political realities, with the same learners, and the same generally inadequate facilities'. Other reasons mentioned as contributing to the failure of previous ELT projects are a lack of resources, limited institutional capacity for English teacher education, and the absence of a co-ordinated monitoring system (Hamid 2011; Hassan 2013; Rahman 2007).

This situation is similar to many other contexts (see de Segovia and Hardison 2009; Hu 2005; Li 1998; Waters and Vilches 2008). Moreover, a survey of the English language education programmes in several countries in the Asia-Pacific region indicated that the significant resources invested in these programmes are not achieving their goals, due to inadequate teacher training and a lack of support for teachers (Nunan 2003).

As will be shown in later chapters, all of the previous challenges of implementing teacher education programmes in Bangladesh and beyond were kept in mind in the design of EIA. The Programme sought to:

- work at scale through innovative but low-cost technologies;
- work within the existing national curriculum;
- include possibilities for teachers to improve their English language competence along with improving their teaching skills;
- recognize the local linguistic landscape (in terms of offering materials in Bangla and English and showing how teachers might mix codes to strengthen learning and communication amongst themselves);
- embed teacher education in schools;
- develop the capacity for peer support and professional networks.

The final section of this chapter looks at how EIA attempted to respond to the additional goal of strengthening economic development in Bangladesh, and at the research undertaken within EIA to evidence this.

Exploring the relationship between English and economic development in Bangladesh

EIA was set up on the premise that improving English language competence in Bangladesh will improve the economic opportunities of people in the country. This was indicated in the inaugural statement about the Programme by the then UK Secretary for International Development, Douglas Alexander: EIA would 'make a valuable and lasting contribution to economic and social development in that country' (Alexander 2008). The focus was on learning English as a technical skill that should contribute to individual and social development, with the implication that the benefit will be felt at the national level. This focus on language as a skill – and not as a medium of cultural expression – could help to downplay the colonial history of English and fears that the promotion of another language might interfere with the national importance of Bangla. Given the language history of Bangladesh, there may be a fear that English language learning functions as 'a displacer of national tradition, an instrument of continuing imperialist intervention, [and] a fierce colonizer of every kind of identity' (Imam 2005: 474). Imam (2005: 482) further noted that '[in] the minds of most people, national identity and learning English are positioned as antagonistic, not complementary'. Thus a focus on English as a language of economic development might have served to de-emphasize suspicions of English as a usurper of local and national cultures (cf. Seargeant and Erling 2011).

Alexander continues that the 'Programme will also address a major skills gap in the Bangladeshi workforce and will help the country become more competitive in both internal and international labour markets' (Alexander 2008). As the Programme website stated:

> English in Action is about equipping the poorest people with language skills that will help them find jobs, engage in entrepreneurial activities and improve their standard of living.[1]

Such Programme statements make assumptions about the relationship between English language learning and economic gain at both the national and individual level without providing an explanation of why or how this will take place (Seargeant and Erling 2011). Alexander points to the Programme's capacity to contribute to conquering unemployment and income inequality:

> A recent Bangladesh Government report identified unemployment and growing income inequality as two major constraints which may prevent the country from achieving the UN's Millennium Development Goals. 'English in Action' will be an important contribution in assisting Bangladesh to overcome such constraints and to improve the livelihoods of its people.
>
> Alexander 2008

However, at the time this statement was made, little was known about the actual relationship between English language proficiency, employability and earnings. There have long been associations with English as a language of opportunity:

> Knowing English is like possessing the fabled Aladdin's lamp, which permits one to open, as it were, the linguistic gates of international business, technology, science and travel.
>
> Kachru 1986: 1

Such perceptions are also present in Bangladesh, with research conducted in rural areas of the country showing a strong belief in the power of English and a desire to be one of those who speak the language for reasons of practicality and prestige (Erling et al. 2014). Thus demands for the language are likely to be quite high, and programmes to enhance or expand ELT are unlikely to meet opposition. More recent research indicates a more complex relationship than is indicated in such policy statements.

Review of research on the relationship between English and economic gain undertaken as part of EIA

Before the launch of EIA in 2008, there was little published research which investigated the relationship between English language skills and economic development in Bangladesh. Studies are, however, increasingly being undertaken in this area in response to a demand for evidence in planning and funding education and development initiatives (see, for example, Erling 2014). EIA also undertook several research projects (see Erling and Power 2014), which serve in some way to justify the project and to show its impact.

The first of these studies (based on an earlier study commissioned by the British Council, which explored the advantages of English for individuals and societies in five countries, including Bangladesh; Euromonitor 2010), found strong relationships between English and economic advantage. Two primary methods were used: interviews conducted with recruitment agencies, corporate businesses, educational institutions and other semi-official sources; a review of salaries in job advertisements. The study concluded that English is seen as offering a key competitive advantage in a difficult employment environment, for getting both a job and a higher salary. In the formal sector employment market, English was found to be the main business language for most of the companies interviewed. Around 86 per cent of representatives of the organizations interviewed felt that English language skills were an important factor in recruiting new employees. In the analysis of job vacancies, 68 per cent required at least an intermediate level of English. The salary gap between someone who can speak English and someone who cannot was found to be 5–15 per cent. In addition, 77 per cent of the respondents from companies stated that employees who speak better English advance faster in their careers than those without a good grasp of the language (Euromonitor 2010).

In 2013, EIA commissioned a follow-up study focusing on Bangladesh with similarly enthusiastic results (Euromonitor 2013). Euromonitor conducted interviews with ten out of the largest twelve recruitment agencies in Bangladesh, mainly located in the capital city of Dhaka. Findings suggested that skills in English help people secure jobs with well-established companies. Employers value language skills for their potential to open up new markets and the ability to communicate with customers and clients in their own language, particularly in jobs that require international travel. Around 40 per cent of jobs advertised on job portals and 20 per cent of jobs advertised in newspapers require English. Some companies also require International English Language Testing System (IELTS) scores.[2] Euromonitor reported that companies required at least an intermediate level of English and were willing to pay more for candidates with excellent command of the language. There was reported to be a 25–30 per cent salary advantage for jobs where the candidate has good English skills.

While the findings of these two Euromonitor studies sound impressive in terms of values of English for individuals, a few caveats must be kept in mind. First of all, the method of interview used in these studies relies almost entirely on participants' perceptions of values of English. That these participants perceive English as being valuable is not surprising given the focus on large, international companies and recruiting firms. Secondly, these studies were wholly concerned with individuals in waged employment in Bangladesh's formal economy, and primarily in Dhaka. While the number of people working in these sectors is large in real terms, it represents only a small percentage of Bangladesh's population (11 per cent, according to ADB 2012). This means that the values for English reported may not be representative of the wider population around the country, who are more likely to work in micro-, small- or medium-enterprises, where language use is likely to be different from large companies. While the review of job advertisements may appear to be a more objective measure, it must be kept in mind that in Bangladesh English language competence may be interpreted by employers as a proxy for being well educated and of elite status (cf. Barsoum 2004; Lockwood 2012). Therefore, such jobs, and the English competence and certification required for them, are likely to be available only to a privileged few, and the value of English reported in these studies is likely to reflect other social and educational advantages.

The role of English in formal sector employment in Bangladesh was further explored in a survey which investigated the demand for, and use of, English by employers and in post-school education (Mott MacDonald 2013). Data collection was limited to the Dhaka area, and the sample of respondents was predominantly male (89 per cent of the 125 respondents), reflecting the current working environment in the formal sector. The respondents included representatives from IT companies, banks, colleges and universities (both public and private), travel and tourism agencies, hotels and restaurants, ready-made garment factories, non-government organizations (NGOs), export agencies and other industries (including newspapers, magazines, advertising agencies and others), again a strong over-representation of the formal sector. The majority were senior managers and/or human resource managers. Findings confirmed the need for, and regular use of, English. However, the extent to which business involves non-Bangla speakers varied from industry to industry, with the hotel and restaurant industry attaching huge importance to English and ready-made garment factories finding it only important for high-level staff. Furthermore, needs for English differ across the industries according to location within Dhaka, type of client, level of position, and type of job. Regarding the hiring of new employees, 64 per cent of respondents said that they are very likely or quite likely to employ candidates having intermediate level English language skills. This research, while limited to the formal sector in the country's capital, shows some indication of the varying demand for English across industries. It suggests, as did Aslam et al. (2010), that values for English depend on the local labour market and sector of employment. However, individuals working outside of the capital or in the informal sector were excluded.

Research conducted by BBC Media Action as part of EIA provides more detail into the value of English for people across socioeconomic groups, among skilled/unskilled workers and in areas outside the capital. This study (Damiani and Gowland 2013) used two existing datasets to explore statistical associations between self-reported levels of English proficiency and two variables related to economic status ('household expenditure' and 'household income after rent'). A self-reported level of English was able to predict a small percentage of the distribution of household income and family expenditure. In other words, a clear difference in the level of self-reported English proficiency translates into a difference in an individual's level of monthly household income or family expenditure. The benefit is greater for those in skilled occupations. The findings do not show a causal relationship but there are positive associations.

Using different methodologies, the studies undertaken in Bangladesh all find evidence of a relationship between English language skills and economic value. However, as the studies are primarily limited to the formal sector, it is difficult to separate values of English language skills from other indicators of social and economic privilege. Even in the BBC Media Action study, which, with participants from across the country, has the most diverse sample the relationship between English and economic value is weak and no causality was determined.

Moreover, while these studies provide some indication of uses for English in the formal sector and values of the language for individuals, they shed little light on how these English language skills were acquired, how language skills might contribute to developing the capabilities of individuals and communities, and whether and how the learning of English can help to counter inequality. It is important, therefore, to look more widely at the evidence available.

Review of international research on the relationship between English and economic gain

The above results from EIA should therefore be seen in the light of other international evidence on the relationship between English language skills and economic value.[3] These studies include data from several international contexts, with at least one of them being in South Asia (Arcand and Grin 2013; Ku and Zussman 2010; Lee 2012). They provide international comparisons about the nature of the relationship between skills in English in a population and economic development at the national level. Three further quantitative studies focus on the value of English at the individual level in the region of South Asia (Aslam et al. 2010; Aslam et al. 2012; Azam et al. 2010).

Taken together, these studies point to the difficulty of singling out the value of English language skills. Thus, it cannot be concluded with absolute confidence that it is English language skills that relate to economic value, but it may in fact be a person's access to higher education and high-quality education (which, in turn, is what makes a person more likely to have had the opportunity to develop English language skills). Moreover, the studies undertaken in South Asia reveal how values of English vary for individuals along with other socioeconomic variables. The obligatory teaching of English in the national curriculum was implemented to provide universal access to the language and to move away from English being available only to the elite. However, these studies suggest that English language skills may not help to level the playing field for people facing disadvantage because of gender, age, ethnicity and class, or because of the types of jobs available to them in their local environment. Such findings suggest that a person from a disadvantaged background is less likely to have experienced high levels of education, or good-quality education, which also means that they are less likely to have gained access to English language skills. They also have fewer opportunities to develop their English language skills in their environment or to come into situations – whether through education or employment – where they use English meaningfully. This trend was not only observed at the individual level but also at the national level. Lee (2012) found that English language skills amongst a population turn into a national advantage only if other factors relating to governance and security are in place.

The message then for language planning and development aid is that (English language) education on its own will not allow a person to overstep other socioeconomic obstacles (cf. Fasih et al. 2012). There is a clear need for larger, systematic change in terms of decreasing the obstacles faced by the most disadvantaged. It is also important to bear in mind that there are larger structural, social and economic issues that contribute to unemployment and inequality, issues that go far beyond an enhancement of ELT. As the International Labour Organization (ILO) argues:

> The low-skill, low-productivity, low-wage economies will not be transformed into high-skill, high-productivity, high-wage economies simply by increasing and improving schools, vocational centres and universities.
>
> ILO 2012: 20

Similarly, English language skills will not necessarily be transformed into employability and access to opportunity. However, the focus on skills in development programmes like EIA places the responsibility for employability on individuals and education systems, and de-emphasizes the need for economic policy to focus on a well-functioning labour market, which leads to a strong demand for adequately trained workers and maximizes the returns from investment in education (cf. Erling 2015).

Conclusion

This chapter shows the historical and linguistic context in which the Programme evolved, in which the Programme attempted to find contextually appropriate solutions for enhancing the quality of ELT nationally. This entailed working at scale with teachers in schools in order to enact sustainable change and recognizing the linguistic landscape in which there are low levels of English, as well as some scepticism towards the language's place in Bangladeshi society. All this needs to be considered in the light of colonial history and the importance attributed to Bangla in the development of the nation.

For EIA, the goal of 'economic development' was always considered at the impact level, i.e. beyond the control of the Programme. It was therefore never set up to be a strong Programme focus (see Chapter 11). That said, the Programme did seek to improve equality of access to quality ELT. Considering previous projects which focused on urban areas and relied on teachers being able to attend training outside of their area, EIA attempted to be highly accessible to individuals, teachers and schools nationally. The schools element worked in six out of the country's eight divisions – at both the primary and secondary level in government – in making use of technologies that supported its use in rural and hard-to-reach areas. Moreover, the Programme did contribute significantly to the available research about the relationship between English and economic gain in the regions. The 2014 Annual Review comments:

> The theory of change sets out a good rationale for the impact of English language skills on economic development. EIA has made a significant contribution to this emerging field of research.
>
> DFID 2014: 16

While there is significant evidence of the Programme contributing to the improving of ELT in the contexts it worked in (explored in detail in Chapters 6, 8 and 9), it is difficult to determine whether any economic development that Bangladesh has experienced can be related in any way to improvements in English language teaching or to EIA. It may simply be that this Programme goal was based on assumptions about English and economic development that were unrealistic. Moreover, more insight could be gained into the potential of English language skills to level out the playing field, to offer opportunities for those who have been traditionally disadvantaged.

Lessons learnt

In reflecting on the principles and the context, several lessons can be drawn out: the complexity of the socioeconomic, linguistic and educational context which has hindered development in Bangladesh despite significant development aid in the past cannot be ignored in the conception of projects such as EIA. It was extremely important to situate EIA within the country's linguistic landscape and within a thorough understanding of previous language-in-education policies and interventions.

In view of the evidence available at the time of EIA's conception about the relationship between English language skills and economic gain, the focus on economic impact was perhaps a distraction (see further Chapter 11). As argued earlier, dealing with English language learning in isolation is unlikely to result in economic improvement. Such projects also ideally need to contribute to larger systemic changes, in which they can contribute more effectively to economic development for the many and not the privileged few. This could involve engagement with other national and development initiatives that focus on economic development and education, as EIA attempted to do by collaborating with Under Privileged Children's Education Programme. Other examples could include developing the private sector, fostering entrepreneurship, supporting opportunities to transform informal employment to small enterprises, and looking at the potential for English language skills (and literacy in general) to support such initiatives.

In view of evidence around the relationship between English language skills and economic development, programme discourses should avoid simplistic assumptions that English language skills necessarily lead to employment opportunities and improved earning potential for individuals. Such discourses are likely to contribute to the unrealistic promotion of English language learning, which results in funding focusing on this, without considering how the wider context of inequality needs to change. While English language projects on their own might serve short-term aims of funders in terms of generating soft power and fostering economic and diplomatic relations, they will not necessarily contribute to wider national development and the promotion of equality – both of which contribute to long-term cohesion and stability.

Notes

1   'About EIA', located at: https://www.eiabd.com/ (accessed May 2017).
2   IELTS is a multi-level examination for English language proficiency.
3   For an extensive overview of these, see Erling, 2017.

The Bangladesh Context

Critical Comments

Fauzia Shamim

Introduction

Teaching English in difficult circumstances has recently received considerable attention (see Shamim and Kuchah 2016; Kuchah and Shamim 2018). While Shamim and Kuchah (2016) focus mainly on the difficulties at the level of the classroom in 'regular' schools, Kuchah and Shamim (2018) extend the definition of difficult circumstances to include the teaching of English in contexts of confinement, refugee camp schools and special education. At the same time, the role of policy in creating difficult circumstances is also highlighted. However, little attention has been paid to sharing the difficulties faced in large-scale, development-aid project planning and implementation (see Holliday 1992 for an exception). Often, these difficulties or contextual-level challenges get masked as 'risks' in project log frames and reports intended for the government and funding agencies; consequently, this information is not easily accessible to policy-makers, teacher educators and, more important, the general English language teaching (ELT) practitioners who are expected to translate this policy into classroom practice. Hence the focus on delineating the context of EIA in terms of the social, political and linguistic landscape in Part 1 of the book is both refreshing and thought provoking.

Westbrook et al. (2013: 4), identifying gaps in current research, call for 'Examples of how a particular piece of research directly impacted on teachers' practices or on policy'. In EIA, research findings from the available literature and extensive baseline studies informed the planning and implementation of various Programme interventions (see Chapters 4 and 5 for details). Equally important is the contribution of research undertaken on language and development, as part of the project. Erling and Khatoon's very candid analysis and critique of the EIA research, as well as international evidence on the relationship between English and economic development (Chapter 2), needs further careful deliberation, particularly in terms of development-aid projects' short- and long-term aims and policies.

Perceptions about the need for English and their impact on policy and practice

A simplistic relationship between English language skills and economic development and increased employability of graduates is often posited as the reason for large-scale interventions in a country's school system, particularly in the developing world.[1] However, Erling (2014: 4) cautions that, 'skills in English are only likely to be of value if a strong educational base is in place'. Similarly, Coleman (2010: 7) concludes, after a review of studies on English and development that: 'a broad-brush approach to the English-development relationship is probably not very useful. Instead, a more fine-grained approach is required, looking at particular types of economy and particular sectors of activity' (see also Mohanty 2017). This is because, as Erling and Khatoon remind us in Chapter 2, a host of factors is involved in providing access to, and gaining proficiency in, the English language – many of them being associated with a higher quality of education and normally available only to the elite section of society. Hence, the benefits of English skills for economic gains are conditional on first levelling out disparities in, for example, gender, urban–rural divide and resource provision in education in general, and English language education in particular (Erling 2015). Despite this, the teaching and learning of English is often promoted as a way of providing equal opportunities to the citizens (Shamim 2011; Williams 2011). Consequently, English is introduced from earlier grades without changing anything else in the system, such as resource provision and teachers' competence in the English language. This leads to a number of challenges and confusions due to a mismatch between rhetoric and classroom realities (Copland et al. 2014).

English is often touted as the language *of* and *for* development around the world (British Council n.d.[2]), even in contexts where there is a common majority language such as Arabic in the MENA region (e.g. Powell-Davies 2015), or for that matter Bangla in Bangladesh. However, as Williams (2011: 47) notes, it often becomes a reason for national division and maintaining the status quo or social inequalities (also see Hamid et al. 2013). Williams (2011: 47) further argues, based on several development indicators in selected African countries such as life expectancy in years, that 'there is no evidence that the use of exoglossic languages such as French and English have contributed to development in proportion to their excessive dominance in educational and other official domains'. Moreover, research indicates that instruction in the mother tongue or local language(s) is an important determinant of educational achievement (e.g. Babaci-Wilhite 2015; Brock-Utne and Alidou 2011). This evidence needs to be considered both by policy-makers in deliberations on language policy, and by education and social development consultants for international aid projects alike.

The professed desire for English in different parts of the world is also linked to neoliberalism and internationalization of education (Doiz et al. 2011; Phan and Barnawi 2015). Hence, English is increasingly being used as the medium of instruction (EMI), particularly in higher education settings in non-native English speaking countries (Dearden 2015). At the same time, the impact of EMI on the quality of teaching and learning, and learners' competence in English and other subjects taught through English is being questioned (see for example, Lei and Hu 2014; Lo and Lo 2014; Shamim et al. 2016; Shohamy 2013). Similarly, concerns have been expressed about the impact of the global spread of English on local languages and culture by a number of researchers in the Arab world, Africa and South Asia (see Belhiah and Elhami 2015; Brock-Utne and Holmarsdotti 2001; Hopkyns 2017; Kirkpatrick and Bui 2016). As Coleman (2011) points out, government pronouncements in favour of English are often made. However, little attention is paid to developing the local languages for improving the impact of healthcare, education and other development activities.

EIA's very realistic appraisal of the impact of simplistic assumptions about the relationship between language and development on the Programme's planning and implementation as a 'distraction' should be an eye-opener for many claiming a causal relationship between English and national/economic development without adequate evidence or, more important, in-depth understanding of the complexity of the variables involved. Also, the discussion above raises an important question: For social and economic development in a multilingual society, what might be more useful: an unequivocal focus on developing English language skills or developing literacy, numeracy, and other employability skills using mother-tongue-based multilingual education?

Theory of change and conditions that make reforms last

In recent years much has been written in the field of English language teaching (ELT) about issues in the transfer of methodology and importance of contextual variables for any reforms to take root in the host culture. As has been pointed out by Coleman (2018) (and the EIA reports quoted in Chapter 1), the country-level statistics such as teacher-to-pupil ratio often do not reflect the reality of class size at the classroom level. Also, they fail to highlight how classes can be crowded even with a smaller number of students due to limited classroom space; in some situations, these 'smaller' classes may take place in shared rooms. The challenges posed by large class sizes for any innovation to take place at the classroom level were realized by the EIA team at the outset, thus alerting them early on to the need for dealing with these challenges. Similarly, it was realized that in Bangladesh, as in several other parts of the world, communicative language teaching had been introduced without much success, mainly due to a mismatch of the methodology with the cultural and social context, and lack of resource planning for its successful use in the classrooms. Accordingly, the EIA project started by undertaking a number of baseline studies to gain a detailed understanding of the context where the innovations were going to take place (see EIA 2009a, b, c). This may be one of the major reasons for its success at the classroom level.

It is now widely acknowledged that contextual features need to be woven into a theory of change for the reform efforts to last in any educational setting. In the context of ELT reforms in particular, it has been pointed out how each context is unique and therefore, needs to be studied thoroughly to develop context-appropriate methodology (Kuchah 2013; Holliday 1992; 1994a). Several studies indicate that there are also contexts within contexts (see for example, Coleman 2018; Holliday 1994b). What this means essentially is that when planning a large-scale intervention, the implementers need to be sensitive to the contextual differences within contexts, such as levels of education, and different sectors in education, including state schools and different types of private schools including NGO and community-based schools.

Classroom-level innovations are influenced by a number of factors, as classrooms are nested within schools, which are influenced by the beliefs and behavioural practices in the immediate community; these, in turn, are governed by language and educational policies as well as the perceptions of the participants in the wider community, and shaped by social, cultural, economic and political factors (Coleman 1996). EIA's focus on identifying the specific features of the context, it seems, allowed the Programme team to identify both challenges and affordances, thus accounting for subsequent successes. However, it is not clear if any major changes in the aims and directions of the Programme were made, during its lifetime, through an ongoing study of changing social and political circumstances or emerging needs of the people, if any, in Bangladesh.[3]

Lessons learnt

Lessons learnt from the EIA Programme provide a number of useful directions for conceptualizing the place of English language education in future development-aid projects. In this section, I will discuss, and expand on, some of the lessons learnt in the EIA Programme for consideration by policy-makers and project planners of international development aid education projects.

Mother-tongue based multilingualism/plurilingualism

Recently, Coleman (2017a) has demonstrated, through a comprehensive review of the changing relationship between language planning and development aid over the last seventy years, that there is evidence of a more questioning attitude towards the role of English in development due to a growing awareness of multilingualism (also see, Coleman 2017b). Hence, there is a need to stand back and look at alternative pathways to language-in-education for development. In this regard, Chumbow (2013) and Glanz (2013) offer a number of strategies for planning and implementation of mother-tongue-based multilingualism policies in Africa. More specifically, Rosekrans and Chatry-Komarek (2012) report on a recent comprehensive and innovative multilingual programme, the National Literacy Acceleration Program (NALAP), in Ghana to promote mother-tongue-based multilingual education in all Ghanian schools. The successes and challenges faced in implementing this programme could be instructive for planning future development-aid education projects.

Another trend that takes account of the reality of the linguistic diversity of a country's population is plurilingualism, or the ability to switch between different languages according to the communicative purpose and demands of the situation. Plurilingualism does not conceptualize languages individually. In contrast, it emphasizes 'the repertoire – the way the different languages constitute an integrated competence' (Canagarajah 2009: 6). As such, Canagarajah (2009) proposes plurilingualism as a way of communication rooted in the ecology of multilingual societies (also see TIRF 2009). In education, this translates into tapping all available linguistic resources in a classroom or 'translanguaging' in order to enhance learning outcomes (see for example Pyhak 2018).

Partnerships in development aid projects

EIA tried to work with local partners such as Underprivileged Children's Educational Programmes (UCEP) and BRAC.[4] However, it is noteworthy that during the lifespan of EIA, at least three other large-scale educational projects were conducted in Bangladesh with the goal of improving education at the primary and secondary levels. Though EIA worked with all these projects *as far as it could* (Chapter 12), as Erling and Khatoon note, multiple inputs working in tandem may be able to build upon and consolidate the gains already made. (Ironically, development-aid projects, by their very nature, need to work 'independently' to achieve their specific goals.)

The specific role of local partners, in development-aid projects needs to be studied and shared more widely. In this regard, Language Teacher Associations (see Smith and Kuchah 2016) could be an important resource for meeting the development and research aims of education projects.[5]

Research on good practice in varying contexts

O'Sullivan (2006) demonstrates how an awareness of some good practices in Ugandan primary-level classrooms may help deal with the issue of introducing quality teaching in large classes. Similarly, Kuchah and Smith (2011) discuss how developing a 'pedagogy of autonomy' may help address challenges in extremely difficult circumstances. (Also see Wedell and Lamb's (2013) portraits of inspiring teachers' practices in Asia, and Westbrook et al. (2013) for teachers' pedagogical practices in formal and informal contexts in developing countries.) In the same vein, Gladys (in press) shares how she facilitated the continuing professional development of two teachers in Cameroon. More important, she identifies how school inspectors could take on a mentoring role, similar to her, to support teachers' continuing professional development. This, and the research conducted by EIA, indicate that research evidence about what works in a specific context is an essential resource in planning future development-aid projects.

Impact assessment of projects

A question that arises even after a cursory look at large-scale educational projects around the world, and in developing countries in particular, is: why is there a limited impact of the reforms introduced on participants' beliefs and practices? It is acknowledged, as pointed out in Chapter 1, that many factors such as the political instability in a country, and rapid change of policy-makers such as ministers, which are outside the control of a project, can impact on its outcomes (see Chapter 12). However, project evaluation needs to go beyond evaluation of outcomes to assess impact to identify any significant improvement in the quality of education and students' life chances more generally.

EIA evaluated the impact of the Programme in terms of learning outcomes of students (see Chapter 11). However, it did not look more generally at, for example, the improvement in student life chances. More to the point, it looked only at impact after a year and ignored any long-term impact. It has been observed that, normally, the project participants, i.e. educational managers, teachers and students, receive some benefits from participation such as study trips abroad, free textbooks, and classroom resources; these 'gains' from the project often lead to positive evaluation of project outcomes. Hence, what is important to gauge is the long-term impact of projects to find out if the introduced practices are institutionalized or have died their natural death soon after the project ends (Shamim 2009).

Dissemination of processes and strategies in development aid projects

Schweisfurth (2011: 1) asks two basic questions based on a comprehensive analysis of seventy-two articles published in the *International Journal of Educational Development* over a period of years on reforms focused on introducing learner-centred education in developing countries: why do the same problems recur repeatedly?; and how do we move beyond the normative 'shoulds' and the practical 'can'ts'?

Normally, challenges in implementing change are shared in reports to funders. Hence, they are not easily accessible when planning further projects, even in the same country.[6] 'Moreover, despite a few outstanding studies there is no tradition of sustained analysis of why some reforms succeed when others fail or what types of reforms have succeeded and what have not, for whom, and under what circumstances' (Cohen and Mehta 2017: 645). Seen in this context, this book-length sharing of EIA successes and challenges is not only a welcome change but may also prove to be a milestone in the history of compiling evidence on international, development-aid, education projects!

Conclusion

Lessons learnt from implementing successfully such a large-scale Programme with an unusually long lifespan of nine years (2008–17) in extremely difficult circumstances must be studied by all students of education and development, in general, and English language education in particular. It is hoped that EIA's work in this regard would motivate similar projects elsewhere to analyse and share what made their system-wide reforms work despite challenging circumstances, and more importantly, indicate where other reform efforts had failed earlier.

Notes

1   See for example, the excerpt quoted in Chapter 2 from the words of the then UK Secretary for International Development at the launch of the project.
2   Mark Robson in the Foreword to *The English Effect* states, 'English makes a significant contribution to sustainable global development.... It is the UK's greatest gift to the world and the world's common language' (British Council n.d.).
3   In fact, it also needs to be considered whether such ongoing work is possible within the framework and limited time span of a project.
4   BRAC is an international development organization based in Bangladesh (http://www.brac.net/ [accessed 30 October 2017]).
5   A conference was held jointly by EIA with BELTA (Bangladesh English Language Teachers' Association) in 2011.
6   The author was denied access to similar project reports in Pakistan by the responsible government officials saying they were marked 'confidential'.

Part Two

Teacher Professional Development in Low-to-Middle-Income Countries

The first three chapters (4–6) of Part 2 are concerned with teacher professional development (TPD), covering the international literature and the approach to implementation within EIA, both in terms of the overall model of TPD and the use of mobile technology to provide video support to teachers. Chapter 4 starts the discussion by examining the imperatives of the Sustainable Development Goals (SDGs) and the need for improved quality and equity of teacher education at scale. It then explores these three elements in relation to common approaches to TPD. This leads to the derivation of characteristics of effective TPD, drawing on the literature from both LMICs and the developed world. In Chapter 5 these imperatives and characteristics are used to examine the approach taken by EIA both initially in the pilot and in later years as scale and institutionalization increased. The third of the chapters (6) picks out the use of technology (ultimately mobile phones) to provide teachers with authentic video of how the various pedagogical techniques could be carried out in Bangladeshi classrooms. These three chapters examine the question: what kinds of professional development approach enable teachers in low-to-middle-income countries to improve their professional knowledge and practice?

In the concluding critical chapter of Part 2, David Pedder considers the approach to TPD advocated in the earlier chapters and examines its foundation. While these comments support the approach taken by EIA, they advocate a more fundamental view of what it means for a whole school to undertake TPD, with a focus on leadership, organizational learning and on teachers confronting their practice-value differences that inevitably exist. This is a radical view, particularly in LMICs.

Approaches to Teacher Professional Development in Low-to-Middle-Income Countries

Tom Power

Introduction

This chapter begins by situating discussion of approaches to teacher development (TD) in the context of the grand societal challenge of *Education for All* (UNESCO 2014), as written into the earlier Millennium Development Goals (MDGs) and now Sustainable Development Goal (SDG) 4: 'to ensure inclusive and equitable quality education for all.' This goal cannot be met without addressing the stark and urgent need for greater numbers of teachers who are adequately equipped with the knowledge and skills to enable effective student learning. Drawing upon personal experiences of work with teachers in LMICs over nearly two decades, the chapter argues against 'blaming teachers' for poor student learning outcomes, and advocates instead the development of better understandings of the often challenging contexts in which teachers practise. The chapter then critically examines common approaches to TD that have often failed adequately to equip teachers for classroom practice, outlining a broadly supported agenda for reform. Recent literature has begun to identify certain characteristics of TD programmes that are increasingly associated with effective student outcomes, in what may be an emerging consensus. These characteristics are briefly outlined, before the chapter closes with lessons learned from English in Action. EIA has both contributed to and benefitted from this emerging evidence base and Chapter 5 illustrates how the implementation of EIA exemplifies such characteristics through a cohesive programme design.

The global challenge

In the early years of the MDGs there were reductions in the number of children out-of-school, but these stalled; by 2015 the number of out-of-school primary-aged children worldwide was rising towards 50 million (Rose 2015). There are currently estimated to be 61 million such children and a further 200 million secondary-aged children, totalling over a quarter of a billion children out of school (UNESCO 2016). Such global challenges are reflected in the national figures for Bangladesh, as Chapter 1 made clear.

Many more children are now 'in-school', but have teachers who are poorly prepared to teach. Whilst teachers' knowledge and practice have been found to account for the majority of variation in student learning outcomes, many teachers in LMICs struggle with rudimentary teaching tasks and student-level subject knowledge (Bold et al. 2016). In Bangladesh, national assessments show the majority of students fail to achieve the required competencies in literacy or numeracy by the end of primary school, or literacy, numeracy and English by the end of junior-secondary school (see Chapter 1). As it is now well established that teachers are *the* single most important determinant of educational quality (Boissiere 2004; Verspoor 2005; Glewwe and Kremer 2006; Rivkin et al. 2005; Bold et al. 2016), such poor performance raises critical concerns about the quality of teaching and, in turn, the processes of teacher preparation and development. As Chapter 1 notes, few Bangladeshi teachers in 2008/9 could communicate in the English language at the level at which they were required to teach, even though the policy intent was for communicative language teaching (CLT), and more recent research has shown only 9 per cent of primary teachers to have a level of English as high as that of the textbooks (Rahman and Jahan 2011).

Implications for teacher development

This chapter argues that inadequate TD, rather than inadequate teachers, is a key contributor to this situation. A global crisis in teacher supply has been identified for some time, signalling the need for new solutions (Moon 2000; UNESCO 2004, 2015a and 2016). It is estimated that Sub-Saharan Africa alone will require six million more teachers by 2030 (UNESCO 2015b). When teacher supply is insufficient to meet demand, this can result in large class sizes and double-shift teaching that reduces the number of hours of tuition for each student (Glewwe and Kremer 2006), as well as lowering recruiting standards to allow further unqualified entrants (UNESCO 2016). All of these effects are seen in Bangladesh (see Chapter 1).

The MDG for education could not be met without addressing both quality and quantity of teacher supply (Lewin and Stuart 2003; Lewin 2011); the same argument is true, perhaps more so, of the SDGs. The large numbers of students out of school, lack of teachers, and particularly of qualified teachers, all indicate insufficient *quantity* of teacher supply. At the same time, students' literacy and numeracy outcomes are poor, even with qualified teachers (Pryor et al. 2012; Hanushek and Rivkin 2010), indicating insufficient *quality* of teacher preparation.

In many LMICs qualified teachers are a relative rarity with thousands of untrained adults present in schools and millions of children still out of school. Classrooms are often highly over-crowded and well above government policy targets for pupil–teacher ratio (PTR). For example, at the time of South Sudan's independence in 2010, fewer than half of the nation's teachers had themselves completed primary education and fewer than one in twenty held a teaching qualification. Yet even so, there were on average 500 children for each classroom or teacher (Power 2013). South Sudan is undoubtedly an extreme illustration, but even in Bangladesh, teacher shortages manifest themselves through out-of-school children (especially in secondary education), large class sizes (often between double and triple the national PTR policy target) and schools working multiple 'shifts' (see Chapter 1). It has been estimated that at present rates the current system of teacher supply would not enable the government to reach the target PTR for at least forty years, even excluding any growth in the school-aged population.[1]

Bangladeshi national statistics on average availability or PTRs also hide substantial inequality and variation within the country (UNESCO 2016). Children from disadvantaged communities, who most need effective teachers, tend to be taught by the least qualified people (UNESCO 2014). As Chapter 1 has shown, in Bangladesh, as in many developing countries, poor and rural students do less well and have lower completion rates.

Rather than abating, in many countries such challenges will continue to grow, due to increasing demand for quality education that is unmatched by large-scale systemic change in the quantity and quality of teacher supply. Whilst population growth has slowed over recent years in Bangladesh, if policy targets for universal secondary education and PTRs in primary and secondary are to be met, these will dramatically increase demand on teacher supply. The challenge of SDG 4 therefore lays before us several intersecting imperatives in relation to teacher development:

- *quality*, to prepare teachers with the knowledge and skills required to teach effectively; and *relevance* to the needs of their students, recognizing the *diversity* of social and cultural contexts in which teachers serve;
- *scale*, sufficient to meet the rising demand for teacher supply and *urgency* for this demand to be met in years rather than decades. This requires *affordability* as well as quality and scale;
- *equity*, that the supply of effective teachers is developed or delivered where it is most needed; that teachers are not marginalized or disadvantaged because of their gender, geographic location, language or culture; and that teachers learn to improve *social inclusion* within their classroom practice.

It is in this context that common approaches to TD in LMICs are considered, echoing the key messages of the Global Education Monitoring Report. This argues that, if TD policy and practice are to respond adequately to the challenges of achieving the SDG for education, we need 'new approaches, a heightened sense of urgency', and should 'fundamentally change the way we think about education and its role in Human Development' (UNESCO 2016: i).

A critical examination of common approaches to teacher development in LMICs

A note on discourse, context and agency

Because teachers' knowledge and practice are key determinants of students' learning, as noted above, then an improvement in students' learning outcomes requires an improvement in teachers' knowledge and practice, which in turn requires appropriate and effective TD. But relatively little is written about teachers' lives and practices in the context of disadvantaged communities in LMICs, which might inform an understanding of which TD approaches are 'appropriate' or 'effective'. Drawing upon her ethnographic and capability-approach orientated research, Buckler observes:

> There is a need for policy makers in rural education to know more about these
> rural teachers' lives and have a better understanding of personal, environmental

and social contexts that impact on their ability to acquire new qualifications and skills ... there is very little written about teachers' perceptions of how these environments impact on their teaching and learning.

Buckler 2011: 2

The lives of the rural poor are not well understood and policy-making is often not based on a deep understanding of the educational experiences of disadvantaged communities. Huge variations in regional and local circumstances lie hidden beneath national or international statistics and may have profound effects on teacher, student and community experiences of education (Nelson Mandela Foundation 2005). Further, teachers and teacher educators are often themselves products of the poorly performing education (and teacher-education) systems in which quality improvements are being sought. The DFID-funded review commented that:

> If teachers have not seen or experienced a different way of teaching, they cannot be expected to implement it themselves, alone, in their classroom. The limited teaching experience and cultural differences of teacher educators were a stumbling block ... for example where teacher educators selected only the pedagogy they understood and taught [to teachers] using rote learning.
>
> Westbrook et al. 2013: 60

Since teachers' current practices and beliefs are rooted in their day-to-day experience, in order to move beyond this situation it is necessary for TD programmes to create opportunities for both teachers and teacher educators to develop an *experiential understanding* of more constructive and social pedagogies.

Failure to acknowledge both the contexts in which teachers practise and the possible limitations of their prior experiences can lead to a discourse in which it becomes common to frame teachers as 'deficient'.

> A deficit model of teachers characterizes teachers, at best, as passive implementers of inputs and innovations, as just another factor in the production of education 'outputs'. At worst, they are seen as the source of problems of education, as an obstruction to the effectiveness of government and donor intervention.... However, VSO's examination of teachers' own views on what factors inhibit and support their motivation suggests that most teachers remain deeply concerned about the quality of their professional practice as educators, and that they harbour a real desire for practical and pedagogic support in this arena.
>
> VSO 2002: 14 & 31

That many teachers maintain such deep concerns about the quality of teaching and learning is commendable, given the often deeply challenging situations within which many work (Leach et al. 2005; Power 2012). Although much of the infrastructure of classrooms, books and professional support is typically more developed in Bangladesh than in some LMICs, most teachers still face challenges of large class sizes, double shifts, irregular student attendance, long and difficult journeys to training events for primary teachers or, in the case of secondary teachers, an absence of formal professional development structures. There is often little extrinsic reward for innovation or disincentive for poor performance (World Bank (WB) 2013b). Consideration of approaches to TD and associated issues of teachers' knowledge, skills and practice should also attend to the personal, workplace and policy factors that enable or constrain teachers' ability to maintain commitment to their own professional development and to students' learning (Day and Gu 2010).

Forms of teacher development

A common and enduring feature of TD has been the distinction between initial teacher education (ITE or 'pre-service training') and continuous professional development (CPD or 'in-service training'). Although the importance of CPD is increasingly recognized, there remains a historic policy emphasis on ITE (UNESCO 2004). In most countries, ITE receives the greatest allocation of resources, both financial (Dladla and Moon 2013) and academic (Moon 2016). The distribution of time, money and academic contribution between ITE and CPD remains a critical policy question (Bird et al. 2013), yet data on the effectiveness of either ITE or CPD approaches is very limited, particularly from LMICs (Anamuah-Mensah et al. 2013; Tatto 2013; Lawless and Pellegrino 2007; Wilson and Berne 1999).

This section examines common approaches to ITE and CPD through a consideration of the imperatives of quantity, quality and equity. The following section then considers characteristics of TD associated with improved teacher practices and student learning outcomes from an emerging body of evidence.

Initial teacher education (ITE)

The 2005 global monitoring report (UNESCO 2004) identified four models of ITE (see Table 4.1). 'Model 1' or 'Model 2' are most common and are often viewed by policy-makers as a 'gold standard', despite the high costs involved (Anamuah-Mensah et al. 2013).

Quantity

The problem of teacher supply cannot be solved by ITE. Teacher supply through ITE has failed to close the teacher gap during the MDG years and it will not be closed during the SDG years without radically different approaches (UNESCO 2016). In Bangladesh, there is an ongoing but ineffective game of 'catch-up' to put unqualified teachers through 'pre-service' programmes, sometimes decades after they began teaching.

Quality

Pre-service has long been criticized for emphasizing 'academic content' over professional knowledge and skills (Lewin and Stuart 2003; Bold et al. 2016). Multi-country studies have shown such training has little impact on classroom practice or student learning (Pryor et al. 2012), and this is also the case in Bangladesh (World Bank 2013b). Given that the vast majority of investment in TD is apportioned to pre-service training, the return on investment or value for money would appear to be very low.

Equity

As noted above, international and national figures indicating the mismatch between teacher supply and teacher demand hide what can be substantial regional and local variation, with teacher shortages being most severe in rural areas (Lewin 2015; UNESCO 2016). Deployment policy and practices are amongst the chief concerns raised by teachers in LMICs, with many reluctant to be posted to disadvantaged communities because of the additional professional and domestic challenges (Bird et al. 2013); this may exacerbate teacher shortages in such areas. It is often the least qualified and experienced teachers who are posted to the most disadvantaged communities (UNESCO 2014).

Analysis of National Student Assessment data has shown that 'The most important determinant of learning in Bangladesh is the school/institution that one attends. Family characteristics also play a role, but much less so than school-level characteristics' (World Bank 2013b: 17). It has already been shown that teacher quality is the most significant school factor. Therefore, it is imperative that disadvantaged communities are not further disadvantaged by inequitable teacher supply.

Table 4.1 Four models of initial teacher training

Description	Duration	Entry	Curriculum	Teaching practice	Cost per student
Model 1					
College certificate or diploma (e.g. Bachelor of Education)	One to four years' full-time residential	Junior or senior secondary school leavers with or without experience	Subject upgrading, subject methods, professional studies	Block practice of four to twelve weeks in one or more years, sometimes followed by internships	Relatively high
Model 2					
University post-graduate certificate of education	One to two years' full-time residential after first degree	University degree, mostly undergraduates without experience	Subject methods, professional studies	Block practice of two to ten weeks, sometimes followed by internships	Relatively high but for less time
Model 3					
In-service training of untrained teachers based in schools, leading to initial qualification	One to five years' part-time residential and/or non-residential workshops, etc.	Junior or senior secondary school leavers with experience as untrained teachers	Subject upgrading, subject methods, professional studies	Teaching in schools in normal employment	High or low depending on duration and intensity of contact with tutors
Model 4					
Direct entry	Zero to four years' probation	Senior secondary, college or university graduates	None, or supervised induction	Teaching in schools in normal employment	Low

Source: UNESCO 2004: 162, Table 4.9

Is ITE up to the demands of the SDGs?

This message echoes in policy across the world: ITE needs to be more effective in improving teachers' classroom practice (Moon 2016). As evidence in the next section will show, school-based approaches (Table 4.1, Model 3) are intrinsically more practical in focus, more relevant and more contextualized than training outside the school. Closing the teacher 'gap' through innovative and rigorous approaches to Model 3 (school-based, in-service) may be more effective, affordable, scalable and equitable, than attempting to bring Models 1 or 2 to the required scale and impact. In many countries, school-based approaches may be the *only* way in which the gap could be closed within the timeframe of the SDGs (Moon and Villet 2016). Teams within the Prime Minister's Office of Bangladesh have reached similar conclusions and are considering how a rigorous approach to Model 3 might be developed, including alternating blocks of school-based development supported by Open and Distance Learning (ODL), with campus-based provision.

Although 'Model 3' ITE is relatively rare, there are notable examples: school-based and ODL methodologies have been successfully deployed in the UK and China, with hundreds of thousands of teachers supplied through these routes (Moon 2016); whilst in Cuba all teachers enrol on school-based programmes of ITE or CPD (Ness and Lin 2013).

Continuous professional development (CPD)

Successive reports have found approaches to CPD fragmented, incoherent or ad hoc, both in developed economies (McCormick 2010) and LMIC contexts (Pryor et al. 2012). Even in the UK, there is 'a paucity of literature on what happens in ordinary schools and under-theorized work ... in terms of teacher learning' (McCormick 2010: 395). In LMIC contexts, very little evaluation data are available from large-scale CPD programmes (Popova et al. 2016; Tatto 2013). The nature of CPD provision is highly varied; unlike ITE, CPD often goes unreported as there is no common administrative method for data collection (UNESCO 2016). The majority of evaluation data available come from small-scale (around sixty schools and 600 teachers) pilot studies of interventions designed by researchers (Popova et al. 2016). Many such evaluations provide sparse information about programme mechanisms or contexts, treating the link between programme inputs and improved teacher or student learning as a black box (Popova et al. 2016).

For the purposes of this chapter, two broad categories for CPD relating to the main locus of teacher learning implicit in programme design will be considered. The first and most common category locates teacher learning as something that happens primarily in 'out-of-school' workshops. The second category locates teacher learning as something that happens primarily 'in-school', particularly through classroom practice (though this does not preclude additional support activities outside school).

CPD with teacher learning primarily 'out-of-school'

The most commonly reported approach is to send teachers to short, one-off training events out-of-school, with teachers attending eight days of such training a year on average (UNESCO 2016). The dominant model for in-service professional development is a series of 'out-of-school' courses provided through regional centres. These may vary in length from one or two days to two weeks. Specialist staff in the form of advisors and inspectors take responsibility for such programmes. Certification is rare and links to pre-service providers are generally weak. In some countries, the cost of transport and subsistence associated with in-service activity takes up the bulk of resources available. This type of provision is expensive. Millions of teachers have no access to it (Anamuah-Mensah et al. 2013: 202).

Such short courses may need to be organized at very large scale, reaching all schools or all teachers of a particular subject (Pryor et al. 2012). In order to reach large scale, it is common to use a 'cascade' system, involving a number of tiers of 'master trainers' and 'teacher trainers'. DFID highlights a number of problems with cascade training: whilst cascades can transmit simple messages such as a change in policy, content tends to become distorted or attenuated as it passes down the cascade – 'as one respondent said: "the trouble with cascades is that those at the bottom don't get wet, or they get wet with dirty water"' (DFID 1999: 3). The report notes that cascades are especially problematic where training seeks to change practice, concluding that the use of cascade training risks sacrificing quality in order to reach scale. A later systematic review of teacher education in LMICs also found cascade training ineffective, with little evidence of impact on classroom practice or learning outcomes (Orr et al. 2013).

At the start of EIA, the CPD for primary teachers in Bangladesh had no coherent or logical structure, with overly theoretical training being delivered through an 'ineffective cascade approach', and ad-hoc, one-off training events with no follow-up; overall, there was seen to be little effect on teaching quality

(Kraft et al. 2009). Towards the end of the EIA Programme, the national *Teacher Education and Development Plan* for primary education was considered to be more coherent, but there were still large numbers of CPD programmes unrelated to any wider strategy delivered through cascade, with limited academic input or evaluation (DPE forthcoming). The draft design note for CPD post-Primary Education Development Programme III observes that national student assessment data do not indicate improvements in learning outcomes, despite the substantial CPD investment.

CPD that situates teacher learning primarily 'in-school'

Systematic reviews of the impacts of strategies to improve the performance of under-trained teachers (Orr et al. 2013) and of teacher education in developing countries (Westbrook et al. 2013) commissioned by DFID identified a number of CPD programmes that provided evidence of positive impact on classroom practice or learning outcomes; all such studies included aspects of programme design that focussed on teacher learning within classrooms or schools. Orr et al. (2013) found that those with the most convincing evidence of change all had ODL self-study materials for use by teachers in school and regular follow-up visits to schools (as did Westbrook et al. 2013, and Popova et al. 2016), including classroom observations, in addition to regular out-of-school workshops. Effective CPD programmes did not provide workshops as 'one-off lectures' to transmit subject-knowledge, but used initial workshops to introduce the programme approach, whilst subsequent workshops provided opportunities to discuss teaching methods in the light of real classroom experience (Orr et al. 2013). Head teachers may also play a significant role in either encouraging or constraining application of TD to classroom practice in schools (Westbrook et al. 2013).

Is CPD up to the demands of the SDGs?

DFID (1999) signals a tension between *quality* and *scale*. Much of the data that shows evidence of *quality* TD (through positive outcomes) typically arises from small-scale pilots rather than large-scale programmes (Popova et al. 2016). There is scant evaluation evidence from large-scale programmes that rely primarily on teacher learning 'out-of-school'; what limited evidence there is suggests such programmes typically produce little impact on teaching practice or learning outcomes. Programmes that situate teacher learning in school are far less common, yet in recent reviews, evidence of positive impacts from CPD (Orr et al. 2013;

Westbrook et al. 2013) arises almost exclusively from programmes that explicitly support teacher learning in school (e.g. through ODL materials, new technologies, or face-to-face support within or close to schools). Orr and colleagues note that successful programmes do not have a single support strategy (such as school visits alone), but combine multiple strategies into a functional CPD system. Whilst this makes it difficult to disaggregate the effect of individual elements of support, as the next section of this chapter will illustrate, there are some common features of CPD programme design repeatedly identified in studies that demonstrate effective outcomes.

Summary of approaches to teacher development in LMICs

There is limited evidence to suggest that either ITE or CPD, as most commonly found in LMICs, is adequately equipping teachers with the knowledge and skills required to drive necessary improvements in the quality and outcomes of primary or secondary schooling. In many parts of the world there are already large numbers of un-/under-qualified teachers and the challenge of demographic change is likely to dramatically exacerbate this situation. Financial and infrastructure or capacity issues limit the extent to which it may be possible to upscale the quantity of current teacher supply whilst simultaneously addressing issues of quality and relevance.

In many countries, it will not be possible to 'ensure inclusive and equitable quality education for all' (SDG 4) through universal primary and secondary schooling, without the radical re-imagining of TD. Business as usual will not suffice (UNESCO 2016; Birdsall et al. 2005).

Characteristics of CPD associated with improved teaching and learning: towards an emerging consensus?

For the purpose of this chapter, the key findings from the DFID-funded review (Westbrook et al. 2013) are used (headings 'a–d' below) with a fifth and perhaps more tentatively evidenced finding on the use of mobile technology drawn from Power et al. (2014). From 2013 these findings have been used to frame EIA's policy dialogue with the Government of Bangladesh and other development partners, within the institutionalization and sustainability strategy. Because evidence of impact from CPD on teachers' practice or student learning outcomes in LMICs is sparse, findings from wider international literature are also referred to where these resonate with findings from LMIC contexts.

It has already been noted that data on effectiveness of ITE or CPD are highly limited and accounts of TD are often under-theorized. There are multiple research traditions amongst studies of international development and education and differences of opinion over qualitative and quantitative approaches and different preferences for randomized control trials (see Chapter 11). Often quantitative measures fail to say *how* changes were brought about (Tatto 2013) and there is little detail on programme design or delivery, making systematic comparison challenging (Popova et al. 2016).

In considering evidence for this section, the dangers of empiricists on one hand and relativists on the other are avoided (Tickly 2015) by adopting a 'critical realist' position (Pawson 2013), which is interested in the mechanisms of change and how such mechanisms interact with heterogeneous contexts to produce varied outcomes. Therefore, this section draws upon evidence of outcomes from randomized control trials, but also upon other forms of evidence about the processes and contexts of change that enable programme 'effectiveness'.

Peer support and co-learning

Teacher peer support was identified as the primary facilitating factor for improving teacher learning and practice identified by Westbrook et al. (2013), with positive evaluations from eight studies that included peer support for the implementation of improved classroom practices. Four of these studies (including EIA) also presented evidence of improved student learning outcomes (Westbrook et al. 2013: 60).[2] Peer support emerged in the context of interventions that specifically attempted to introduce new pedagogic practices in the classroom, and therefore may also be associated with a focus on classroom practice and follow-up support. Westbrook and her colleagues framed peer support as 'a continuation of the more formal follow-up support ... through informal groups, formal clusters or pairs of teachers at the same school' (2013: 61–2). Therefore, ongoing teacher 'peer support' may be a planned aspect of programme design (as is the case in EIA) but this does not preclude other informal and ad hoc support between peers within or between schools that will affect classroom practice and hence student learning. Peer support was also identified as a common characteristic amongst successful programmes for under-qualified teachers in LMICs, where local support from peers or experienced teachers and regular opportunities to discuss experiences were associated with greater engagement and application to classroom practice (Orr et al. 2013).

In particular, Orr and his colleagues report that TD programmes with evidence of successful outcomes tend *not* to use 'workshops' or similar out-of-school events as a 'means to transmit subject knowledge' (2013: 6), but rather to create a forum for face-to-face peer support between schools, enabling teachers to share experiences of applying new methods in the realities of their schools.

Evidence suggests peer support is valued highly, with teachers and programme implementers identifying it as the aspect of programme implementation most appreciated by teachers (Leach et al. 2005; Popova et al. 2016). However, the use of peer-coaching approaches such as Japanese Lesson Study was shown to have mixed results across a range of settings (Ono and Ferreira 2010, South Africa; Thijs and van den Berg 2002, Botswana; Wang and Lu 2012, China). One possible explanation may be that in schools where many teachers may have low levels of subject and/or pedagogic knowledge, some external stimulus or resource may also be required. The strongest evidence of change was found from studies that combined ongoing peer-support workshops with ODL self-study and school visits to observe practice (Orr et al. 2013), where ODL resources and project staff are likely to have provided inspiration for new practices.

Amongst the wider (non-LMIC) literature the BERA-RSA enquiry found peer support between teachers 'omni-present' in all the studies analysed, helping embed new pedagogies in day-to-day practice through practical and emotional support and shared risk taking (Cordingley 2013: 5). Similarly, Avaolos (2011: 17) found teacher co-learning emerging 'powerfully' from the last decade's literature.

Ongoing support for the application to classroom practice

The Westbrook et al. (2013) review identified *professional development aligned with classroom practice* as one of the four facilitating factors for improving teaching and learning, citing evidence from six studies from four countries across Sub-Saharan Africa and South Asia. These report programmes that set out to change practice through a combination of regular TD meetings facilitated by mentors, regular classroom observations and feedback on practice from mentors or peers. These studies all reported teachers being observed to implement more active and diverse learning activities in the classroom. Three of the studies (Arkorful 2012, Ghana; Leach et al. 2005, Egypt and South Africa; Saigal 2012, India) were also rated by the review team as having the highest standards of both methodological rigour and contextual awareness, providing the strongest evidence of 'highly effective' TD interventions found by the review (Westbrook et al. 2013: 97). Both Leach et al. (2005) and Saigal (2012) explicitly framed their work as 'situated learning' approaches, with the school being the locus of TD. However, these were all small-scale qualitative studies involving teachers from just six to twenty-four schools and two were studies of 'projects' of the same size; none presented quantifiable impact on learning outcomes.

Statistical analysis of impact evaluations from twenty-six programmes in LMICs reported the largest influence on student learning outcomes (+0.47SD)[3] where the primary focus of training was on practical classroom management, with large influences on student learning outcomes (+0.26SD) from follow-up visits to school (Popova et al. 2016).[4] Lesser influences were also found from programmes that had a primary focus on pedagogy or new technology (both +0.18SD) and where a proportion of training was spent practising with other teachers (+0.17SD; Popova et al. 2016).

In the wider international literature, Cordingley found 'All of the research indicates that significant improvements depend upon elapsed time ... that more time secures greater depth ... when teachers participated for at least one year' (2013: 6), highlighting the need for sustained collaboration with colleagues. It is clear that prolonged TD interventions are more effective than short or one-off events, particularly for enabling workplace or enquiry-based learning (Avaolos 2011; Cordingley 2013).

Support from head teachers

Westbrook et al. (2013: 62) identified '*support from the head teacher*' as a facilitator to the effectiveness of TD, citing several studies (Arkorful 2012, Ghana; Geeves et al. 2006, Cambodia; Lall 2011, Myanmar) including one from EIA (Power et al. 2012); most were small-scale qualitative studies of no more than twenty-five schools, apart from EIA, which included data from over 200 schools. Three studies (Arkorful 2012; Geeves et al. 2005; Power et al. 2012) were identified as evidencing moderate-to-highly effective outcomes, whilst the results were mixed in one (Lall 2011). In all these studies, support from the head teachers and through them the wider school community (teachers, school management committees, parents and guardians), was reported as an important enabler for the continued introduction of new methods of teaching. Conversely, ten studies reported the lack of such support as a significant barrier to teachers changing their classroom practices.

Cordingley also drew out the importance of school leadership to effective CPD, particularly in promoting the use or generation of research evidence to improve classroom practice (2013). A systematic review of 'practitioner engagement in or with research' found, in studies of teacher learning, that institutional support was critical to successful outcomes and improved practices. It recommended that school leaders should foster a school culture in which teachers felt safe in taking managed risks and learning from their mistakes whilst developing new practices (Bell et al. 2012). Timperley et al. (2007) argue leadership engagement should involve goal-setting, putting plans into practice, monitoring progress and making adaptations where required. Robinson et al. (2009) identified a number of school leadership activities linked with improved pupil outcomes: of these, promoting and participating in teacher learning and development was linked with the largest effect size (0.84; twice as powerful as the next largest effect) on student outcomes.

Alignment with student curriculum/assessment

Westbrook et al. (2013) identified alignment with the school curriculum/ assessment as an enabling factor, citing five studies mostly orientated to the introduction of new curricula (Altinyelken 2010, Uganda; Holland et al. 2012, Uganda; Vithanapathirana 2006, Sri Lanka; Arkorful 2012, Ghana; and Coffey International Development 2012, Ghana). Popova et al. (2016) found that CPD programmes with a specific subject focus were associated with gains in student learning outcomes, whereas those without direct application to a particular subject were associated with lower student learning outcomes. Similarly, Power et al. (2014) found all the effective CPD programmes identified had a specific subject focus.

There is also evidence of barriers to effectiveness where the alignment between student curricula or assessment and teacher CPD is weak: Westbrook et al. (2013) found six studies reporting that overloaded curricula and high-stakes examinations compelled teachers towards rapid coverage of the curriculum and didactic methods, despite CPD programmes promoting alternative pedagogies.

Appropriate mobile technologies

Although it is not one of the four key findings in the DFID-funded review, Westbrook et al. (2013) identify several studies where the innovative use of ICT was particularly appropriate for rural teachers' professional development. In these, smartphones, mobile phones and mp3 players were all used to bring digital learning resources to teachers and schools poorly served by electricity supply or wired communications networks. For example:

> Leach's 2004 intervention study in Egypt and South Africa [Leach et al. 2005] developed the use of handheld computers and pocket cameras ... Specially devised professional development programmes enabled teachers to integrate a range of ICT-enhanced activities into their teaching of literacy, numeracy and science, supported by school visits and a range of multimedia resources. A total of 74 per cent of teachers reported that their use of ICT facilitated collaborative ways of working, 54 per cent that they had better ways to present materials and 31 per cent that ICT enabled independent learning.
>
> Westbrook et al. 2013: 46

The practical and research experience from Leach's work was a direct contributor to the design of mobile learning for TD in EIA (see Chapters 5 and 6).

The DFID *Topic Guide on Educational Technology* (Power et al. 2014) reviewed almost eighty recent studies from LMICs, identifying several examples with evidence of positive impacts on classroom practice or learning outcomes. However, positive outcomes were always in the context of programmes led by curriculum and pedagogic (rather than ICT) imperatives (e.g. phonics-based early literacy, and communicative English language teaching) and supported by TD programmes, usually at least partially aligned with the key findings discussed previously. Most positive impacts were associated with interactive radio instruction, mobile devices used by teachers, or e-readers/tablets used by students. All positive impacts were associated with appropriate digital materials for classroom use and with supporting teacher professional development resources.

In the wider literature, innovative uses of technology to support professional development, including online forums, the use of video case studies of classroom practice in online discussions and the use of classroom video materials for teaching and learning are common, with the review of a decade of articles in the journal *Teacher Education* concluding: '... combinations of [digital] tools for learning and reflective experiences serve the purpose [of TD] in a better way' (Avaolos 2011: 17).

Lessons learnt

Again, the themes of quality, scale and equity are used to consider the lessons for EIA in the literature on teacher education and how it should be conducted for the situation in Bangladesh.

Quality

Few TD programmes are appropriately evaluated in LMICs, particularly large-scale or system-wide programmes. There is little evidence to suggest that the most common approaches to ITE or CPD are effective in equipping teachers with the knowledge and skills required for quality teaching and learning. Several studies, including studies in Bangladesh, have analysed student learning outcome data and found no significant improvement associated with teachers' ITE. ITE and CPD are often overly theoretical, and lack relevance or application to practice in schools. The quality of TD programme outcomes is strengthened when:

- the programme has a specific subject focus and promotes a clear, practical pedagogic approach;
- teachers are supported through a broad range of strategies, which work together as a coherent system (effective strategies typically include: ODL learning materials; support from peers and head teachers in school; regular workshops/meetings that focus on experience in classrooms; classroom observations; appropriate technologies);
- programmes allow sufficient time for teachers to develop and apply new understandings of classroom practice within their schools.

Scale

The challenge of teacher supply is long-standing and may grow. In many countries, including Bangladesh, teacher shortages contribute to large numbers of out-of-school children, large class sizes, multiple-shift schools and a reliance on under-qualified teachers. Alternative approaches are urgently required to meet the policy goals of the international community in general and Bangladesh in particular.

Common approaches to CPD may achieve scale but risk sacrificing quality in doing so. In order to achieve the necessary scale of CPD whilst trying to retain quality, professional knowledge and practice should not be 'cascaded', but may be embedded in ODL materials and new technologies, and placed directly into teachers' hands. The current Bangladeshi government's design note for primary teacher CPD intends to take such school-based, ODL and mLearning approaches and to build capacity to deliver these at national scale (see Chapter 12).

Equity

The quality and quantity of teacher supply is often not equitably distributed, with disadvantaged communities being the least likely to receive adequate numbers of well-qualified teachers. The most common current approaches to ITE and CPD provision rely on taking teachers out of schools to attend training centres. This can be particularly challenging for teachers from remote rural communities, or for female teachers.

To improve the equity of CPD programmes:

- it is preferable, as far as possible, to bring the training to the teacher in their school and local area, rather than the teacher to the training at a remote centre;
- when the 'quality input' is embedded in ODL materials or digital resources, rather than cascaded through tiers of trainers, it is in principle possible to bring the same quality of input to all teachers, regardless of their location (see Chapters 5 and 6);
- school-based approaches should in principle both increase the equity of teacher supply, by improving teacher quality even in disadvantaged communities, and improve the equity of teachers' access to quality TD.

How EIA endeavoured to meet these challenges is discussed in detail in Chapter 5.

Notes

1 *Access to Information* (A2I) team of the Prime Minister's office and the post-Primary Education Development Project III design note consultants for pre-service, in-service and educational technology. Unpublished data, May 2017.
2 To put this in context, this was the highest number of studies that could show impact in either classroom practices and or student learning outcomes.
3 A difference of 0.5 SD (standard deviations; a measure of the spread of the data) is usually considered a 'medium' effect, whilst a difference of 0.2 SD is considered a small effect.
4 Programme implementers described follow-up visits as a crucial component of TD design and cast doubt on the effectiveness of face-to-face training in the absence of such follow-up.

The EIA Approach to Teacher Development

Tom Power

Introduction

The purpose of this chapter is to provide a succinct high-level overview of the English in Action (EIA) approach to teacher development (TD), thereby supplying contextual information for subsequent chapters whilst highlighting some critical issues and challenges in the implementation of such an approach at scale. The first section touches upon the underpinning theories of teacher learning, previous work and guiding principles that all contributed to initial Programme design, illustrating how these were framed from the outset as a response to aspects of the global educational challenge outlined in Chapter 4. The second section illustrates how EIA implemented this approach in practice, with a brief summary of the roles and experiences of some of the key actors, as exemplifications of the 'features of effective teacher development' identified in Chapter 4. The third section considers the evolution of the EIA TD approach over the ten-year life of the project, examining both the anticipated and un-anticipated changes; it also considers how our conceptual understanding or 'narrative' of the approach has developed over time. The final section draws out the lessons learnt about the principles and practice of school-based, networked and technology-enhanced approaches to TD in LMICs, from the EIA experience, many of which signpost to subsequent chapters of the book.

A principled approach

Chapter 4 identified a number of imperatives for a TD response to the global educational challenges represented in the Millennium Development Goals and subsequently the Sustainable Development Goals: quality, scalability and equity.

The EIA Programme team was aware of, and determined to address, these issues from the outset.

Regarding *quality*, it was an essential prerequisite that the Programme improved student learning outcomes; the project team understood from the outset this would require changes in teachers' understanding and practice (see Chapter 4 for international evidence and prior work). The EIA log frame[1] and the research, monitoring and evaluation framework set out the ambition to provide evidence of the extent and nature of such changes at increasing scale (see Chapter 11). Yet the Programme team were well aware that several prior programmes had failed to realize similar intentions, as explained in Chapter 2. Why should this time be any different?

Teachers do not learn solely or even primarily from teacher educators; they learn as much or more from their practice and from their peers (Bransford et al. 2000). Academics at The Open University (OU), drawing upon the learning theories of Vygotsky and of Lave and Wenger, had for some years been framing teacher learning as a process of creating meaning through *participation* in the social activity of teaching, that is integrated in the dynamics of social interaction (McCormick et al. 2011). Hence, teacher learning had of necessity to be *situated* within the context of practice – teachers' everyday experience of classrooms and schools. Drawing on the work of Engstrom and of Vygotsky, they also highlighted the importance of the use of tools (conceptual, linguistic, physical or technological) as integral to practice, shaping our ways of knowing the world and ourselves (Leach and Moon 2008). Hence a key purpose of the EIA Programme design was to extend 'teachers' pedagogic toolkits', including uses of new digital technologies for professional learning and classroom practice.

This rich, multifaceted view of teacher learning was both applied to, and refined through, a number of previous OU TD programmes (TDPs), including the Open-PGCE (UK), DEEP (Egypt and South Africa)[2] and TESSA (Sub-Saharan Africa).[3] The Open-Post-Graduate Certificate of Education provided a model of working with large numbers of teachers, through a combination of open-distance learning (ODL), school-based teacher development (SBTD), teacher networks (including, but not limited to, online networks) and technology-enhanced learning. The DEEP project explored how such approaches could be adapted for LMIC contexts, through participatory research with teachers from schools in urban slums in Cairo and remote rural communities in the Eastern Cape. It set out four principles (Leach and Moon 2008: 140) that were carried forward into the design of the TD approach for EIA:

1. teacher learning and development are social processes;
2. teachers have the potential to be change agents: proactive and intentionally focused;
3. a social perspective enables us to recognize that the boundaries of learning are limitless;[4]
4. cultural artefacts, tools and technologies mediate learning and are an essential component of agency.

Thereby a theoretically informed, principled approach, together with the lessons learnt from prior programmes, provided the foundation for EIA's attempts to achieve *quality* and *relevance* in the process and outcomes of TD in Bangladesh.

Regarding *scaleability*, the Introduction to this book has set out the increase in numbers over the phases, culminating in EIA being institutionalized into national systems. In order to be sustainable, whilst scale increased, unit costs had to be reduced by similar orders of magnitude, ultimately coming into line with Government of Bangladesh (GoB) norms (see Chapter 13). It was therefore imperative for the Programme's long-term success that the TD approach be conceived as capable of achieving large-scale, low-unit cost, but with high impact. The ODL business model is designed for scale (high initial development costs, followed by very low unit costs for subsequent delivery) with value for money (VfM) increasing with scale. The critical challenge would be EIA's ability to identify, recruit or develop enough educators, distributed across the country in urban and rural areas, capable of providing meaningful support, to facilitate the implementation of SBTD at school or upazila (local administrative) level.

Finally, regarding *equity*, the Programme was required to work across the country, not just in urban centres but in rural and isolated schools, often serving highly disadvantaged communities. The challenge of powering and maintaining digital devices in remote rural settings was an initial concern, but teachers and schools had in earlier initiatives found ways to solve this problem once they understood the value of the digital tools to improving practice – with solutions that were human and social, rather than technical (Leach et al. 2005). Further, DEEP demonstrated the value of school-based, ODL and technology-enhanced programmes for rural educators, where it is much better to bring the teacher education programme (activities, resources and materials) to the teacher in the school, rather than demanding that the teacher is taken out of school. This was particularly important for female teachers for whom domestic responsibilities and practical or social difficulties associated with travel, or accommodation away from home, could present significant obstacles to participation in out-of-school training. SBTD approaches should not issue edicts to follow, but rather encourage teachers to explore and adapt effective practices (finding out together 'what works' for particular purposes, settings and student-groups) and are therefore inherently flexible, adaptive and responsive, improving equity through generating diversity of practices fitted to context.

A practical, school-based, networked and technology-enhanced approach

Outline of the approach

The EIA approach addressed many of the critical issues for TDPs raised in Chapter 4. First, it bridged the theory–practice divide by taking the principles of communicative language teaching (CLT) and illustrating different ways in which these could be implemented in practice, in schools across Bangladesh. These illustrations took a number of forms (including modelling and practice during face-to-face TD meetings at local level), but there was a crucial role played by mediated authentic videos (MAV; see Chapter 6). Second, teachers did not simply 'watch and learn' from such illustrations, but were supported to approach them critically by a narrator in the MAV, by the teacher facilitator (see below) and other peer teachers. Teachers then experimentally adapted and applied the illustrated activities in their own practice before reflecting on the outcome individually and collectively with peers: a reflective practice cycle. This was conceptualized as SBTD with a central focus on the development of new pedagogic activity in classrooms, supported by various people, tools and ODL resources in the classroom, the school and beyond (see Figure 5.1). Third, the ODL materials had an explicit and practical focus on inclusive education, so that as teachers experimented together with new classroom practices, the lenses of inclusion, gender and special educational needs became part of the teachers' 'toolkit' for examining each others' pedagogy and practice (Leach and Moon 2008). Fourth, the development and delivery of the in-service programme was enabled through active engagement from OU staff, drawing upon digital technologies to engage teachers.

The EIA approach incorporated the characteristics of TD discussed in Chapter 4: situated within the school; focused on improving classroom practices; supported over a period of a year or more; with peer support operating informally within schools and formally between schools through regular TD meetings.

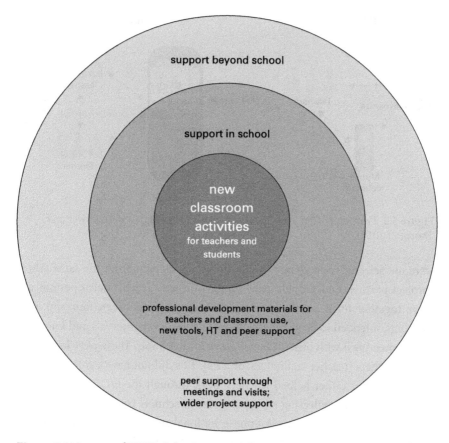

Figure 5.1 Aspects of SBTD (after Power 2015)

Although not initially included in the programme design, after the pilot stage head teachers (HTs) supported and monitored SBTD activity in school. There were explicit links between the TD materials and the school curriculum and textbook content. Though there were no formal online support networks, spontaneous informal teacher networks arose using Facebook or WhatsApp, as well as email, text messages or calls on mobile phones.

In practice, with some variation from one phase to the next, teachers attended an initial orientation workshop (lasting one to three days, usually in the local district), where they received print and digital resources (ODL materials) and practised working through these together. Digital materials were accessed offline on mobile devices (an iPod in Phase 2, a low-cost feature phone provided by the Programme in Phase 3, and their own phone in Phase 4). Over the next nine to eighteen months, teachers explored CLT practices in their teaching, guided by activities within the materials, which they studied at home or at school. Teachers

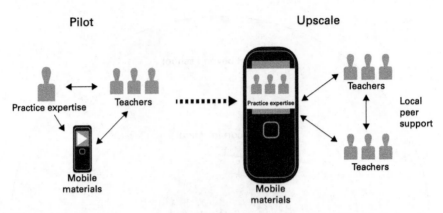

Figure 5.2 Peer-supported, mobile-enhanced SBTD (adapted from Power and Thornton 2015)

were not selected individually from schools, but as pairs from the same school (project partners), to provide peer support on-site. Teachers also periodically came together for a number of local TD meetings (between four and eight meetings, intended to be at roughly four- to eight-week intervals and known as cluster meetings) with other teachers from local schools. These were led by two of the teachers (teacher facilitators, or TFs). TFs did not have a role as 'experts' or 'trainers', but rather helped teachers work through the ODL materials and practical activities, reflecting on experiences in schools (see Box 5.1). This was possible because, during the pilot phase, national and international experts had worked in collaboration with teachers to explore CLT practice in authentic Bangladeshi classrooms; the teachers' experiences of this were then captured in the digital resources, becoming the primary source of inspiration for subject knowledge and pedagogic practice. 'Expert knowledge' was thus embedded, without attenuation or transmission loss, in the ODL materials that teachers had direct access to, rather than 'cascaded' through tiers of trainers (see Figure 5.2 above). HTs encouraged and monitored teachers' progress in school – in terms of teachers' study of the ODL materials and their planning, implementation and review of new approaches to teaching English (see Box 5.2). GoB Education Officers (EOs), EIA Programme staff and OU academics visited many schools to provide monitoring and support on site.

A teacher facilitator's journey

Box 5.1 provides a description of the experience of a teacher who was selected to become a TF in 2010 (during the pilot phase). It illustrates how TFs were helped to develop the confidence and skills to support other teachers through the EIA programme.

Box 5.1: Yasmeen Chowdhury, Jessore

In 2010 Yasmeen was a primary teacher from the semi-rural area of Jessore. Yasmeen had previously taken part in a number of training events on communicative teaching, but like most such teachers, she understood this meant getting her students to 'talk more', while remaining very unsure of how to do that. Her experience of EIA began with attending a three-day workshop, with another teacher of English from her school (her project partner). On the second day of the workshop Yasmeen and her project partner were very excited when all teachers were given an mp3 player and a speaker for use in their classroom. It had videos of Bangladeshi classroom activities and audio that could be used with every lesson. Yasmeen left the workshop eager to try new activities in her classroom and feeling more confident about her English, which she had used more in the workshop than ever before.

At the end of the workshop Yasmeen was invited to play a special role as a TF, helping to run the monthly day-long cluster meetings that would take place over the next year. She would be supported by the Teacher Development Coordinators (TDCs; EIA central or divisional staff). Yasmeen was not sure what this meant, as all the courses she had attended had 'trainers' who acted as 'experts' and told teachers what to do. Over the course of the following twelve months, Yasmeen was supported to develop her identity and practice as a TF by TDCs through a number of 'TF workshops' where they went through the upcoming activities. TDCs also attended many local meetings to support TFs and remained in regular contact by phone, email and social media.

In the first months after the workshop, several teachers had difficulties charging their speakers properly for use in the classroom as their schools had no electricity. Others did not understand the relationship between some of the materials and the textbook. Gradually, teachers overcame these difficulties and helped others to solve their problems together. After one year, Yasmeen felt more confident about using different techniques in her own classroom; both she and her students spoke more English than before and they liked using audio in the classroom. Yasmeen also thought attendance had improved. As well as seeing such changes in her own practice, Yasmeen had enjoyed helping other teachers learn together and felt this had improved her confidence and the respect she received from others. (Adapted from Power et al. 2012)

A head teacher's journey

Box 5.2 gives a description of the experience of a HT who took part in EIA from 2013.[5] Her government primary school is in Bhola, one of many low-lying islands to the south of Bangladesh that constitute the 'Char'. Char communities live hand-to-mouth, fishing and farming; they are exceptionally vulnerable to climate change. Many children work to provide food or are sent to make money in the cities. This description illustrates how a primary HT took part in TD herself, but also motivated others to do so.

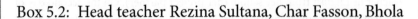

Box 5.2: Head teacher Rezina Sultana, Char Fasson, Bhola

Figure 5.3 Rezina in her classroom

Like many primary school HTs, Rezina taught English language classes, but she and the other teachers felt demotivated by their own difficulties with the language. Rezina was also disappointed with her experience as a HT: she said attendance had been poor and many students dropped out before completing school. She said that when she found out some of her best students had been sent to work as household servants in Dhaka, just the day before the end-of-school examinations, she began to lose her motivation to teach.

In 2013 Rezina and some other teachers from her school began the EIA Programme. Rezina said from the first workshop onwards she started applying what she learnt in her teaching. She was encouraged by the positive responses she got from her students. She felt motivated to learn more and encouraged the other teachers to make similar changes and help each other. She said: 'EIA equips us to take class in an effective way and make lessons interesting . . . I felt that only now have I become a true teacher.' The father of one of her students reported a common response to the changes Rezina had been making: 'My daughter is now eager to go to school. She enjoyed the songs she learns from school. Very often she dances with [sic] the songs at home.' The local education officer said that amongst the fifteen EIA schools in Bhola: 'Teachers reported to me that they are noticing changes in students' interest to learn . . . Now they feel more motivated to come to school.'

EIA field officers

EIA field officers were central to the design and delivery of EIA. Some were responsible for the quality of TD activities and materials, or relationships with central or local government. Others were responsible for finance and administration. Together they became the Programme's core human resource for programme delivery, managing the organization of TD meetings and supporting TFs in leading such meetings. This was particularly important for TFs who felt uncertain of their role, or in districts where matters such as workload and working practices seemed to be particularly sensitive subjects for teachers or education officers.

An evolving approach

Anticipated changes

The project design and funding anticipated a number of broad shifts over the different phases of the Programme. During the pilot phase, the Programme started at relatively small scale, with hundreds of teachers. Yet per-capita funding for this phase would be at the highest level because of the need for baseline and other research to inform programme design as well as the high initial costs for ODL material development and development testing. (During this time, the partnership with the Under Privileged Children's Education Programme was of enormous value, allowing rapid trialling and refinement in their schools: see: Shohel and Banks 2012; Shohel and Kirkwood 2012; Shohel and Power 2010).

There were also high costs for equipment: whilst most teachers possessed mobile phones, these could not play audio or video materials, so iPods had to be provided. There were also extensive contributions from the OU academic team, in leading the research, programme design, TD workshops and building local capacity.

As noted earlier, for each subsequent phase, per-capita funding reduced dramatically. Trends in technological capacity and cost were anticipated, so expensive iPods in the pilot were replaced by much cheaper phones and eventually, by teachers' personal phones, which by the final phase would be capable of fulfilling all the tasks hitherto done by the iPods. It was also anticipated that the balance between OU academic contribution and local team leadership would change, with a more even balance in the upscaling phase, and local leadership in the institutionalization phase. All of these changes were anticipated to enable lower unit costs and increased value for money (VfM) and sustainability (see Chapter 12).

Unanticipated changes

In the pilot phase, EIA treated HTs as 'gatekeepers', recognizing that they needed to consent to teachers' participation in professional development outside and within the school, as well as to the introduction of new teaching and learning activities and resources in lessons; but there was no explicit role or support for HTs. By the end of this phase, it was realized that HTs were keen to play a more active role in supporting SBTD and improved practices. A HTs' programme was developed, delivered through quarterly meetings and support materials, which focused upon the leadership role of HTs in the Programme. In primary, where many of HTs also taught English, they were also recruited directly as teachers of English in the TDP.

EOs had no explicit role in the initial delivery of the Programme, beyond that of gatekeeper (in the selection of schools and teachers to participate in EIA). As the Programme scaled up, EOs were recruited to support monitoring through school visits, filling in an additional form when they went to visit EIA schools (see Chapters 11 and 12).

It was initially anticipated that each year, new TFs would be recruited from teachers who had completed EIA in order to facilitate the progress of future cohorts. However, this was not possible due to the need to progressively increase geographic spread for political reasons. The response, in Phase 3, of developing MAVs for TFs as well as for teachers, was not anticipated but was crucial in enabling large numbers of new TFs to support teachers' work through the Programme, despite having had no prior experience of SBTD.

As the Programme scaled up, EIA field officers had to be decentralized to each district of Bangladesh to enable closer collaboration with, and support of, EOs, HTs and schools. Others took on more specialized central roles, for example, in TD materials development or working on institutionalization with central government bodies.

By the final cohort of teachers in 2017, HTs and EOs were the lead implementers of the Programme, both in schools and through locally managed, but nationally mandated, TD events. EIA divisional teams supported such decentralized and institutionalized 'programme' delivery.

Lessons learnt

These are examined using the themes of quality, scalability and equity, and they have general import to all those embarking on designing such SBTD programmes.

1. The underpinning theoretical frameworks and guiding principles helped shape a TD approach that has achieved impact on teachers' knowledge and practice, and through this on student learning outcomes (see Chapter 9), which have been maintained as scale increased. Whilst core aspects of this were framed from the outset (e.g. focus on practice, school as the locus of teacher learning, support over time, support from peers and the transforming potential of mobile technologies), they have subsequently been affirmed by a number of studies (see Chapter 4). EIA has both contributed to, and benefitted from, this emerging evidence base on the characteristics of effective TD using technology. Thus, where there is a limited evidence base, it is important to initially trust professional experience and develop clear guiding principles, but undertake ongoing examination of initial decisions as research evidence emerges.

2. HTs and EOs can play a crucial role in promoting and encouraging quality SBTD activities and, despite their limited initial role, EIA learnt to make theirs a more central and explicit role (to support and monitor Programme implementation).

3. One of the most challenging aspects of maintaining quality whilst increasing scale was the development of teachers who have the confidence

and competence to lead others through the SBTD activities (i.e. TFs). This is particularly problematic when TFs themselves had not previously completed a similar SBTD programme or experienced (as teachers or learners) the pedagogies being promoted. It is important to provide resources to support the development of TFs' knowledge and practice for them in turn to support TD. As Chapter 6 will show, video has a role to provide TFs support in the same way as it supports teachers.

4. Though many schools had no regular electricity supply, most teachers found the use of mobile phones and rechargeable speakers effective for both TD and classroom use. This has been shown to be capable of successful outcomes in schools across Bangladesh, including urban and rural locations and minority communities, with upazilas representing every quintile of socioeconomic deprivation, thus fulfilling the Programme's contribution to equity.

Notes

1 A log frame (logical framework) sets out the various indicators at different levels to measure the success of a project, and milestones and targets are set for each indicator over the life of the project.

2 www.open.ac.uk/deep (accessed 29 October 2017).

3 www.tessafrica.net (accessed 29 October 2017).

4 Learning is not limited to a particular location (the school building, the teacher training centre) or time (the school day, a training event), but can take place anytime, anywhere, with anyone.

5 Adapted from: http://www.eiabd.com/success-stories–2015/199-eia-plays-an-important-role-in-attracting-students-towards-school.html (accessed 14 October 2017).

6

The Role of Mobile Technologies in Transforming Teacher Professional Development (TPD) at Scale in Bangladesh

Clare Woodward, Bikash Chandra Sarkar and Christopher Walsh

EIA's model for providing over 50,000 teachers with teacher professional development (TPD) to improve their communicative English language teaching (ELT) in Bangladesh over nine years entailed a journey that was both research based and futures oriented. In this chapter, we reflect on this journey, highlighting how the Programme leveraged mobile technologies to offer increased opportunities for teachers' professional learning and English language acquisition. This journey was unique in the extent of the choice enjoyed by teachers in when, where and how they learn.

Setting the scene

As Chapter 4 reminds us, training teachers at scale remains problematic in both developing and developed nations. This is particularly true of English teachers in Bangladesh, where teaching English communicatively is inherently challenging because one in five teachers across the country have no teaching qualification (UNESCO 2006; Shohel and Banks 2010). Thus, conceptualizing and delivering comprehensive English teacher professional development (TPD) at scale via new and emerging technologies was one of the Programme's challenges (Walsh et al. 2013).

At the time EIA started, there were few examples of international development TPD projects using mobile technologies. Any similar projects had been small in scale and generally provided examples of students using their own mobile phones to learn English (Salameh 2011; Cavus and Ibrahim 2009; Thornton and Houser 2005), or explore their attitudes towards using phones to learn English

(Dang 2013). Even today, research around mobile technologies and TPD tends to focus on the development of the awareness of the potential of mobile devices for learning (Schuck et al. 2013), using tablets in challenging educational contexts (Onguko 2014) or changing teacher attitudes towards the use of mobile phones in teaching (Ekanayake and Wishart 2014).

Mobile learning (or mLearning), particularly via mobile phones, for TPD and English language teaching and learning is still an emerging field in both developed and developing countries. Many case studies outside education highlight various benefits of mobile phones, including: entrepreneurial activity among women in Bangladesh (Aminuzzaman et al. 2003; Sullivan 2007); economic development in relation to microenterprises in Rwanda (Donner 2007); and social innovations in health in Tanzania (Mulgan 2006) and India and Papua New Guinea (Biswas et al. 2009). Important to EIA was leveraging the power of mobile technologies, including mobile phones, in similar ways to provide effective and sustainable TPD at scale. The majority of examples of mLearning largely rely on access to the internet (Walsh et al. 2015; Walsh and Power 2011). EIA stands out as both different and innovative, particularly in terms of how the Programme's TPD was *not* constrained by the need for an internet connection or access to a computer, and by the fact that each year the Programme was scaling up considerably, adding thousands of teachers.

Critically, when it comes to mLearning, EIA's work aligned closely with the Government of Bangladesh Prime Minister's Office's philosophy of 'Digital Bangladesh' (see Chapter 1). EIA's approach, situated within existing government initiatives, provided TPD at scale to over 50,000 teachers by using mobile technologies, particularly (in Phase 2) the iPod Touch and Nano (2007–10) and (in Phases 3 and 4) low-cost alphanumeric mobile phones (2011–17), with complementary audio and video resources, supported by local face-to-face meetings, supplementary printed Teachers' Guides and visual resources for both primary and secondary English teachers, and print and video resources for head teachers and local government officials, known as education officers (EOs).

Developmental research on the use of mobile phones to deliver TPD

EIA's developmental research and pilot studies (Phase 1) were carried out with 700 teachers from government schools across twenty-one of Bangladesh's upazilas (sub-districts), as well as some sixty teachers from non-governmental organizations (2010–11). Two-thirds of these teachers worked in primary schools, one-third in secondary schools. Eighty per cent of all EIA pilot study schools were in rural areas with limited or no access to electricity. The developmental research, baseline and pilot studies helped the Programme explore the use of mobile technologies for English teachers' continuous professional development (CPD) and the use of audio resources in the classroom.

As Chapter 1 indicated, computer ownership and access to the internet were low and access to a supply of electricity varied considerably by location; mobile phone access was high, though, even in rural areas, and most teachers had access. However, they had not used audio or video materials to support teaching (EIA 2009h, j). This information was used to inform the decisions made with regard to the use of technology as the Programme moved into the upscaling phase from 2011.

Pilot phase: 2009–11

Technology and resources

EIA's pilot in Phase 2 (2009–11) provided extensive audio and video resources to a total of 700 primary and secondary English teachers on the Apple iPod Nano (for primary teachers) and iPod Touch (for secondary teachers). Although these were more expensive than other mobile devices, such as a basic mp3 player or iRiver, they were chosen for their durability and ease of use. Despite their small screen, they were simple to navigate and use, and functioned well to deliver the TPD resources designed by EIA. Such devices, when used with portable rechargeable speakers, also made it easy to play classroom-based audio resources. Most importantly, audio and video resources could be stored directly on the iPods without recourse to the internet, thus giving teachers zero-cost access to the diversity of EIA's bespoke TPD resources. Other delivery alternatives were explored and rejected. These included FM radio, which was not viable because radio coverage outside large cities in Bangladesh was poor and the majority of the population (three-quarters) lived in rural areas with little or no electricity (Power and Shrestha 2009). It was anticipated that advances in technology over the period of the Programme would bring similar functionality to (cheaper) mobile phones, as was indeed the case by Phase 3 in 2011.

The iPods were loaded with videos of English language teachers implementing communicative language teaching (CLT) practices with their students, together with audio resources for the classroom to match every lesson in the national textbook series *English for Today* (*EfT*) for Grades 1 to 9. This gave teachers and students examples of Bangladeshis speaking the textbook content in English. The time constraints on producing and delivering videos during the pilot phase, together with the Programme's inability to identify teachers able to use the targeted approach to English teaching, meant that the pilot TPD videos were filmed using actors in a Dhaka film studio. (See Chapter 8 for more details.) Table 6.1 shows all the materials distributed in Phase 1.

Secondary teachers received fewer additional classroom resources because they generally had higher levels of English-language proficiency and had received more pedagogical training. All of the materials (Table 6.1) were locally developed in collaboration with Open University (UK) academics and contextualized for use in Bangladesh.

The portable rechargeable speakers could be connected to the iPod to play audio recordings during English classes. Even though most teachers participating in this pilot phase had never used any learning technologies in their classrooms

Table 6.1 Pilot phase resources

Per primary teacher	Per secondary teacher
Ipod Nano with preloaded video and audio resources	Ipod Touch with preloaded video and audio resources
355 audio files of dialogues, readings and songs from *EfT* Grades 1–5	46 audio files of dialogues and readings from *EfT* Grades 6–9
18 TPD video clips illustrating student-centred classroom teaching practices and activities	12 TPD video modules focused on aspects of CLT
A general Teachers' Guide on using the materials	A general Teachers' Guide on using the materials
Activity Guides for levels 1–5 with specific lesson plans	
Per primary school	**Per secondary school**
A set of flashcards aligned with vocabulary from *EfT* 1–5 (per school)	A set of maps
A set of posters	A set of photographs
A set of figurines (per school)	A portable rechargeable speaker
A portable rechargeable speaker	

prior to their participation in EIA (EIA 2009j), they experienced little difficulty using them for both classroom teaching and professional development. Feedback on EIA teachers' use of iPods was collected after six months of the Programme's intervention. The findings revealed that EIA's pilot phase technology kit facilitated 'access to learning', and improved the 'quality of teacher education' (Shohel and Power 2010: 213). EIA teachers believed that their classroom practice had changed as a result of having access to CPD resources available on the iPod:

> Previously, I used to teach them using textbooks . . . Now I can teach the students using a new method instead of traditional methods by selecting from a set of methods given in the iPod. It's also helping the students to increase their listening skill significantly.
>
> Shohel and Power 2010: 206

> That [iPod material] helps me to learn the language and use it in the classroom context. I did not know the language earlier in this way. I knew, but not in this way. I did not even think of talking these to students. I could not think of teaching English of this level to the students! Even we did never learn in this way! We never got tips!
>
> Shohel and Power 2010: 206

However, despite having a positive attitude towards the technology, teachers also indicated significant challenges. These included difficulties in charging the phones and speakers, in addition to their own mobile phones, particularly in rural areas. Teachers also reported the speakers were not always loud enough for all students to hear and some (the heavy 'Block Rocker' model) were difficult to transport.

As Chapter 9 will show, there was an increase in student talk (and in the use of English by both teachers and students; EIA 2011b), and an improvement in English language competence (EIA 2012a).

A qualitative study of classroom practice was undertaken in October 2010, approximately eight months after EIA's intervention (EIA 2011a). The study provided insights into the ways teachers were implementing communicative approaches to English teaching through participation in EIA. The sample for this study was ninety teachers (sixty primary; thirty secondary), and 102 lessons were observed. From this, the forty-six most comprehensive lesson observations, detailing classroom behaviour (twenty-eight primary; eighteen secondary), were selected for analysis. This indicated that Programme materials were being used in 60 per cent of the lessons (primary and secondary), while 40 per cent of the teachers also used non-Programme materials.[1] More primary school teachers were using the Programme materials (82 per cent) as compared to secondary teachers (28 per cent). A further analysis into the type of resources being used revealed that more teachers were using the audio materials provided by the Programme (Table 6.2). Again this could be a reflection of their access to the EIA approach showing teachers how to use the resources through both the iPod resources and face-to-face meetings.

Of all the audio materials provided by EIA, the songs were the most popular amongst primary teachers. These were produced by local Bangladeshi artists in order to make them accessible and they were fun to sing. These were played at the start of the lesson as a warm-up activity, as well as at the end. Even though the songs were usually played using the iPods and speakers, some of the teachers were observed reciting them at times when the technology, as one teacher said, was 'in trouble'. This is perhaps evidence of the motivation demonstrated by the teachers to incorporate EIA approaches into their teaching of communicative English. The study also revealed that teachers used the audio texts to help explain, check student understanding and reinforce language. In this, they used the various functions on the iPod including the pause and play facilities. Many of the primary teachers (57 per cent) observed also used EIA's locally designed and produced posters (Figure 6.1) and flash cards (Figure 6.2) in conjunction with the audio to reinforce students' understanding.

Table 6.2 Type of resources used by teachers

Resource type	% of primary teachers reporting using the materials*	% of secondary teachers reporting using the materials**
EIA audio	68	28
EIA poster	57	N/A (not provided by Programme)
EIA flashcard	14	N/A (not provided by Programme)
EIA figurine	0.4	N/A (not provided by Programme)
Non-Programme textbook	32	28
Non-Programme/ other resources	25	17

*N=28; **N=18

Figure 6.1 A teacher using one of EIA's posters

Figure 6.2 Students using EIA's flash cards

Challenges

Although the pilot phase was successful in terms of the iPods being used for TPD, there were considerable challenges reported. As noted earlier, a significant technological challenge was that many teachers found it extremely difficult to charge both the iPod and portable speaker because of the intermittent availability of electricity across Bangladesh. In the later phases, the use of SD cards in mobile phones relieved this extra pressure. An equally significant challenge pedagogically was the questionable authenticity of the videos used in the pilot phase. It became obvious that a different, more authentic approach to video would need to be developed.

Budget constraints of 6,000 Bangladeshi Taka (BDT) per teacher (£60) mandated that EIA construct multiple kits to field-test and pilot for the upscaling phase (Phase 3: 2011–14). At the same time, it was also thinking about post–2015, when there would be much less funding available for the more than 50,000 teachers who would still require a robust programme of TPD with access to digital resources. Two low-cost alphanumeric mobile phones with 4GB micro-SD cards and portable rechargeable speakers and an SD card and portable rechargeable speakers were chosen to pilot as three separate kits from March to September (2011) in two rural upazilas (Walsh and Power 2011).

Phase 3: up-scaling (2011–14)

The Programme selected the Nokia C1–01 mobile phone and Maximus M45i with 2GB micro-SD cards and different portable speakers and field-tested them with a group of teachers who had used the iPod-based technology kits. Feedback was exceedingly positive for the Nokia C1–01 mobile phone, which was considered better than the Maximus on almost all criteria, in particular ease of navigation, compatibility with the speaker, and being able to play the audio recordings. Some of the teachers' comments regarding the use of mobile phones included:

Nokia C1–01 mobile phone

> The navigation of the Nokia phone is easier than the iPod Nano. It is easy to recharge the mobile phone and I take it all the time to use in the classroom. It takes one hour to charge the phone (Nokia) and the speakers. The new speaker is easy to carry and use. Now I can do many things with the mobile, which I can't do with the iPod Nano.
>
> Teacher of Grade 4, Rangamati

> The mobile phone is much better than the iPod Nano and also the speaker. I can keep it in my pocket and can charge it from anywhere. It takes only 30 seconds to connect the mobile phone to the speaker and about a minute to play the audio file.
>
> Teacher of Grades 3 and 5, Pangsha

Maximus M45i

> Maximus takes more time to find any dialogue or song.
>
> Teacher of Grades 1, 4, and 5, Pangsha

> The iPod is easy to play, but the Maximus mobile is not easy to use. The Maximus mobile phone has some disadvantages. It takes time to find the files.
>
> Teacher of Grades 2 and 4, Rangamati

The teachers indicated the Lane SH–120 amplifier was easier to use and more reliable than the 'Block Rocker' speakers used in the pilot phase:

> The Block Rocker is too heavy to carry; the new speaker is portable and able to carry anywhere. I can place it anywhere in the classroom.
>
> Teacher of Grades 2, 3, and 4, Pangsha

The field test indicated mobile phones would work with all of EIA's classroom and TPD resources. A new mobile phone-based technology kit was assembled consisting of the Nokia C1–01 with 2GB micro-SD card and the Lane SH–120 amplifier costing £59 (Figures 6.3 and 6.4).

Mediated Authentic Video (MAV)

Although generally positive, teacher feedback on the audio and video resources used for TPD during the pilot phase indicated, as noted above, that certain aspects of these materials lacked 'authenticity'. Teachers quickly recognized that the 'teachers' in the videos were in fact actors and commented: 'I couldn't do this in my classroom'; 'I have too many students to do this activity'; 'I have to use the course book every day' (Woodward et al. 2014). There was also a concern that the

Figure 6.3 EIA's new mobile phone-based technology kit

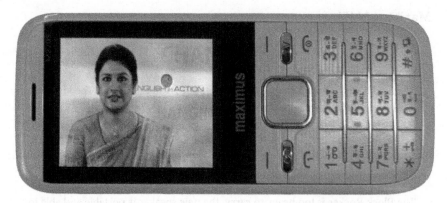

Figure 6.4 EIA's narrator, or 'Natasha apa' ('Sister Natasha'), explains which activities will be presented

extra classroom resources shown in the videos were not available to most teachers. Most teachers saw a significant gap between the practice advocated in the videos and what they believed was possible in their own context – ironic when the purpose of the video was to help bridge the gap between their current beliefs and practices and the 'new' practices being demonstrated. These criticisms, together with the need to revise the pilot materials after trialling them with the first 700 teachers, led to the redesign of the video materials for Phase 3.

Following discussions with many teachers in the pilot phase, it was clear that video materials were popular but the examples shown needed to be of real classrooms and teachers, illustrating the same lack of resources, large classes and government textbook as the viewing teachers themselves experienced. Fortunately, by 2011, the EIA team had access to teachers who had successfully been through the pilot phase. What was required was to show active and participatory language classes, where teachers were using the core textbook in the way it was designed: for communicative, personalized and active learning.

The aim of using video was to show examples of a communicative approach to ELT in action. It was important to choose a small group of teachers for the video filming who had participated in the pilot phase and who represented a cross-section of ethnicity, gender and age, so that all viewers would identify with at least one of the filmed teachers. Filming therefore took place across the whole country. It was also essential that the teachers in the video should be proficient (but not exceptional) teachers successfully using the *EfT* textbook with a more communicative and student-centred approach to learning. Classroom visits carried out in June 2013, mid-Phase 3, found teachers using approaches demonstrated in the videos. Monitoring data showed that the TDP videos were rated as 'very important' by 65 per cent of teachers, just a slightly lower proportion than cluster meetings and classroom activities (EIA 2015c).

The videos needed to be of professional quality. For the filming therefore, two fixed cameras (one capturing the teacher and one the students) and a hand-held, roaming-boom camera were used, together with ceiling microphones and a microphone attached to the teacher. A small local film crew, together with a Bangladeshi director from the Programme, and OU ELT academics, filmed in all locations. In the first location, a director experienced in filming in schools with the OU worked with the crew and local director as a part of the capacity-building element of the Programme.

Zhang et al. (2011) describe the use of video as a 'window into practice' and this was the approach that the team took. It was clear, though, that a video of classroom practice alone would not result in adequate TPD. There needed to be a narrative to mediate it, since observation does not necessarily lead to learning (Miller and Zhou 2007). In the absence of structural input from colleagues or mentors, teachers' learning is limited by their tendency to view videos through the lens of their background experience; the role of experienced teachers and mentors in guiding this observation process is important. A narrator was added and the MAV approach, which encouraged teachers to adopt new practices by both challenging and allowing them to build upon their existing understanding of their classroom, was developed.

The scripted narration supported the teachers in their reflection on what they were seeing and how to apply it to their own teaching. The narrator (Figure 6.4) takes the place of a mentor in face-to-face TPD. Before the teachers watch the video, she sets a 'viewing task' and then poses reflective questions for them to consider and respond to *after* viewing, and after practising similar techniques in their own classroom. The narrator highlights particular sections of the video so that features of teaching and learning can be addressed. The video at times is 'frozen' to focus on critical moments and the narrator asks the viewer to reflect on what had or had not been done in the midst of the action. As Whitehead and Fitzgerald (2007) suggest, this can result in teachers seeing 'deeper'. This 'mediated video deconstruction technique' (Woodward et al. 2014) enabled the materials to be more self-guided and better supported EIA teachers in improving their practice.

This expert voice of the virtual narrator also enabled the Programme to move away from a cascade model of large-scale professional development where information is passed down from the original author through a succession of master trainers, eventually reaching the teacher often in a 'diluted' form

(Robinson and Latchem 2003; see also Chapter 4). In the MAV model, each teacher, regardless of how many there are, has direct contact with the key messages through the presence of the video narrator. In Phase 3 of the Programme, when the original videos on the *iPod* were replaced by MAV on the Nokia phones, the new materials were also mediated in face-to-face cluster meetings (i.e. one-day bi-monthly meetings held locally for twenty teachers – see Chapter 5) and could therefore be further and more deeply explored; however, in Phase 4, with more limited support, the role of the narrator was particularly crucial in encouraging reflection.

For the filming, as well as using teachers with whom the Programme's teachers could easily identify, it was also important to choose teachers with good interpersonal skills, who engaged warmly with their students and were comfortable taking direction from the filming team. In order to achieve a natural and realistic view of the classroom, the activities could not appear practised or over-prepared. The teachers therefore were not given the opportunity to prepare the lesson until the afternoon before filming; indeed frequently the focus of the lesson would be changed after discussions between the teacher and production team as filming was taking place, and meant that most of the videos were almost completely spontaneous. The interaction between teacher and students also impacted on the activities that were filmed, often with unexpected results. Elements of the teacher's engagement with the students, and the particular strengths of each teacher and class, were highlighted through the shaping of the video in the editing studio in the UK, by academics who had been present at the filming. This joined-up way of working meant that the script for the video narrator grew out of the authentic classroom footage rather than the footage being scripted to fit the narrative. The video narrator was then filmed in Bangladesh with scripts recorded in both Bangla and English so that decisions could be made in partnership with the Programme Team on when and where Bangla language support was necessary. As with the filming, there was a significant element of capacity building during post-production.

Between June 2012 and September 2013, using the new mobile phone-based technology kits ('the trainer in your pocket'; Walsh et al. 2013), the Programme launched the up-scaling phase with 12,500 teachers. Initial workshops began a 16-month intensive support cycle of one-day, bi-monthly cluster meetings. Joint viewing of the MAV at cluster meetings (Figure 6.5) offered teachers a common framework for reflective discussion (Barnett 2006). As noted in Chapter 5, video materials were also developed to train the teacher facilitators (TFs) who ran these sessions. Several pairs of TFs were filmed running cluster meetings and, as

Figure 6.5 Teachers in cluster meetings working in groups using the mobile phones

with the teacher MAVs, the video narrator device was used with the authentic classroom filming to explain and encourage reflection on the activities of the TFs on video. The key aim of the TF resources was to demonstrate that their role was one of supporting and managing teachers rather than being trainers.

Each teacher was provided with printed guides, posters and flashcards as well as the Nokia C1–01 mobile phone with a micro-SD card with all of the Programme's audio and video resources. The SD card came preloaded with the following:

- 452 audio files for use in primary classrooms and 227 for secondary;
- thirty-eight primary and twenty-four secondary video clips for TPD;
- twenty-six primary and seven secondary video clips on additional classroom techniques.

The TPD materials were centred on the MAV, supported by the printed Teachers' Guide. Different sets of material were developed for primary and secondary teachers, with each divided into eight modules and each emphasizing all four skills of listening, speaking, reading and writing while having a focal topic, for example, in secondary module 2 'Active Reading'. Each of the MAVs included a section entitled 'Teachers Talking', which consisted of recordings of small groups of Bangladeshi teachers discussing specific issues relevant to English language teachers. The final element of the MAV comprised an audio file of classroom language, linked to the language covered in the classroom video. Throughout the MAV, the teacher was encouraged to try out approaches and techniques shown in the classroom video in their own classrooms through applying them to whatever textbook lesson they were currently teaching. The approach therefore is not one of copying activities but of reflecting on techniques used and using a similar approach in their own teaching. As well as these MAV materials, also included were audio files for a specially developed English course, English Language for Teachers (see Chapter 9 and Leelen and Shaheen 2012).

Use of Bangladeshi artists and musicians

The EIA materials were designed to be in keeping with the Bangladeshi context, using local-style music, and local artists and actors in designing and producing materials. Music used familiar melodic and rhythmic styles, and was accompanied by traditional instruments such as sitar, harmonium, tabla and bamboo flute. The classroom audio used Bangladeshi actors, including children, to produce dialogues and stories from the *EfT* textbooks. Clear pronunciation was maintained through a sequence of critical feedback using a studio-based language supervisor, the EIA Dhaka-based Materials Development Team and OU academics. (See Chapters 8 and 9 on the choice of a local model of pronunciation.) For classroom audio, a large number of songs were written and recorded.

In Phases 2 and 3, A2-sized glossy posters were designed and produced by local artists, illustrating textbook content in rural and urban Bangladeshi contexts (Figure 6.1). All artwork reflected an inclusive gender perspective, cultural sensitivity and concern for children's rights. The posters were based on themes appropriate for students and could be used in a number of ways, following guidance in the teachers' materials. In the later stages of Phase 3 and into Phase 4, these posters were digitized as the availability of projectors in Bangladeshi classrooms rose and the need to reduce the cost of materials became important.

Phase 4: institutionalization and sustainability 2014–18

As the Programme moved into the final stage, institutionalization and sustainability, for cost reasons (see Chapter 13) most materials were in digital form. They were redesigned to encompass elements of the support which previously had been provided in print format. The classroom video was re-edited (and supplemented by additional filming) and the narrative for the video narrator rewritten and refilmed to include a greater focus on reflection and practice. MAV sequences were 'chunked' into around forty clips, for both primary and secondary, under eight thematic units. Examples included: 'Use of English in English lessons', 'Make your lessons fun' and 'Reading with understanding'. Video units under the theme 'Let your students speak in English', for example, included: controlled speaking practice; speaking practice for accuracy; helping students with pronunciation; speaking tasks for fluency.

The final phase SD card contained the following material:

- 551 audio files for use in primary classrooms and 167 for secondary;
- eighty-seven digital posters for use in primary and thirteen for secondary;
- forty-eight primary and thirty-seven secondary video clips for TPD;
- forty-three primary and thirty-eight secondary video clips on additional classroom techniques;
- fifteen primary and twenty-seven secondary audio files for classroom language;
- thirty units of primary and secondary self-study audio files 'English Language for Teachers'.

In this final phase of the Programme, EIA provided only an SD card (at a cost of £4 each) to 38,000 primary and secondary teachers containing all the audio and video materials for teachers, to be used in their own mobile phones. In addition, all TFs who facilitated the Programme at local level, received the EIA AV teaching and learning materials as well as the TF facilitation materials on an SD card together with a mobile phone.

The government officials (EOs), who provided follow-up support to primary teachers, were given a low-cost mobile phone together with an SD card preloaded with all the EIA primary materials and a printed 'Implementers' Guide'. In 2016, video-based materials developed specifically for the EOs, consisting of discussion on topics relevant to a communicative approach to language teaching, were added.

The EIA Programme was implemented over approximately half the area of Bangladesh. In order to enable non-EIA teachers to benefit from EIA's approach and assets, a DVD-based 'Digital materials kit', containing all the primary materials and an instructional manual for EOs, was produced. EIA created a hub in each upazila where any teacher could copy the material onto their own SD card and use it in their personal phone. Local EOs were encouraged to enable face-to-face peer-managed meetings to take place, to support learning from the digital resources but, where that was not possible, teachers at least had access to the video and audio materials, mediated by the narrator. In this phase, 3,016 EOs were provided with a phone and SD card. The materials are also available for teachers to download from government websites such as those of the Directorate of Primary Education and the National Curriculum and Textbook Board.

EIA materials were embedded into the government mainstream with teachers encouraged to use the EIA approach to ELT by both the pre-service and in-service education systems. For the English subject specialism within the Diploma in Primary Education (DPEd; see Chapter 12), EIA worked on the development of Subject Knowledge (SK) and Pedagogical Knowledge (PK) units, re-versioning EIA materials and including them in core training materials.

Conclusion

The findings from internal evaluation studies over the various phases of EIA suggest teachers' participation in EIA resulted in changes in their classroom practice and an increase in students' and their own English language competence (EIA 2011b; 2012a; 2014a; 2015a). This was achieved through exploiting mobile devices for individual use, with the support of face-to-face meetings. The MAV approach delivered through a mobile phone allowed teachers to engage in self-directed learning 'anytime' and 'anywhere', mediated wherever possible at a local level. As a result, through showing authentic examples of good practice and encouraging reflection, EIA provided local solutions to a much-debated problem: how to implement TPD at scale in a LMIC. This chapter demonstrates how the use of mobile technologies and a mediated approach to authentic classroom video can provide the basis for a model of TPD that is able to achieve large-scale reach with a significant degree of impact.

Lessons learnt

- In pilot phases of a programme, use the technology most appropriate to the target aims of the programme in order to trial the key concepts. As the programme scales up, however, make use where possible of the technologies that the target stakeholders already use.
- A programme of this kind, with a significant media component, provides many opportunities for capacity building of local technical stakeholders such as film crews, directors, audio production agencies, project support team members and academics.

- Authentic material is vital to ensure 'buy-in' from teachers and other professionals; teachers and students need to be recognizable to the participant teachers.
- Filming needs to be embedded in the local context and suited to the needs of the teachers, taking into account such things as assessment demands and processes, class size and available resources.
- Wherever possible, AV resources should be supported through local face-to-face meetings.

Note

1   Note that these figures are approximate and should be treated with caution, as the original report makes clear (EIA 2011a).

7

The Organizational Imperative

Sustaining Locally Appropriate Ecologies of Innovation at Scale

David Pedder

Introduction

Chapters 4, 5 and 6 consider different facets of a highly ambitious research and development project – English in Action (EIA). The project aimed to develop a model for providing 50,000 teachers in primary and secondary schools in Bangladesh with professional development to improve their communicative English language teaching (ELT) over a period of nine years. Against a backdrop of disappointing student learning outcomes reported by UNESCO in 2016, it has been all too easy for popular commentators and politicians of different persuasions to scapegoat teachers as inadequate and portray them as the problem to be solved. Such naïve analysis distracts attention from evidence-informed priorities, policies and strategies of improvement that are required in order to enhance the quality of learning experience of students in classrooms worldwide and the quality of support that teachers can offer them. This is why projects such as EIA are so important. They bring a much-needed recasting of the problem of low student attainments in terms of the adequacy of teacher development, and teacher development supports, rather than the adequacy of teachers per se, and this is an argument that is forcefully made in Chapter 4.

The project foreshadowed the Sustainable Development Goal (SDG) 4, 'to ensure inclusive and equitable quality education for all'. The three broad teacher development principles that shaped the design, focus and aspiration of the project (and later articulated in the SDGs), namely quality, scalability and equity, are threads that run through all three chapters. These principles bring both cohesion and specificity to the overarching question addressed by the teacher development strand of the English in Action project: How can teachers in low-to-middle-income countries be supported to improve their professional knowledge and practice?

The project team's thinking and assumptions about what might characterize effective teacher professional development (TDP) associated with improved teaching and learning were in line with the conclusions of Westbrook and colleagues (2013) in their authoritative DFID-funded review of research into teacher education in developing countries, which was published around the beginning of Phase 4. Four teacher development characteristics associated with enhanced teaching and learning were identified as follows: peer support and co-learning; sustained forms of teacher learning support that are well aligned with classroom practice; leadership and school support for teacher development; and clear alignment of teacher development with curriculum subject and assessment systems. In addition to these four characteristics, the innovative use of mobile technologies, not reported in the Westbrook review, provided an additional fifth assumption and an integral strand of the innovation and scale-up achieved through the EIA project design. Chapter 6 elaborates an account of how the particular use of mobile technologies was leveraged to increase opportunities for TDP at the remarkable scale of 50,000 teachers throughout Bangladesh, especially in rural and often remote areas of the country. These five characteristics were used to frame the policy dialogue that developed between the EIA team and the Government of Bangladesh and other development partners. Together with the three teacher development imperatives of quality, scale and equity, the five teacher development characteristics summarize the principles that guided the aspirations and processes of the EIA teacher development model reported in Chapters 4–6.

Of Westbrook and colleagues' four teacher development characteristics associated with enhanced teaching and learning, leadership and school support for teacher development appears to be the characteristic least emphasized in the EIA project design and implementation. While there was a clear focus on teacher learning, EIA did not recognize sufficiently 'school learning', although head teachers explicitly supported and monitored school-based teacher development (SBTD) activity in school as reported in Chapter 5. Furthermore, while there were clear moves in the EIA approach in the direction of leadership and school supports, these moves could have gone considerably further.

In the remainder of this chapter I would like to focus on the importance of the organizational imperative for sustaining locally appropriate ecologies of innovation at scale – an embracing theme that arose from my reading of Chapters 4, 5 and 6, and which necessarily includes leadership and school support.

Building capacity for leadership and organizational learning

Asking teachers to shift from a traditional mode of English teaching to Communicative ELT approaches represents a significant transformation of their practice world in terms of the knowledge, beliefs and dispositions that underpin how they teach and how they learn. Teachers cannot be expected to make such transformative pedagogic innovations alone. They need to be supported by their schools. And schools themselves need to look critically at their organizational cultures and systems, as well as prioritizing the cultivation of supportive ecologies for innovation as an intrinsic purpose and priority in the life of the school. Such cultivation is a collective enterprise to support both teachers and students in their learning and growth and involves learning and leadership at all levels of the school.

The pre-eminent leadership challenge in cultivating supportive ecologies for sustained innovation at scale within and between schools is to embed and sustain school cultures, routines and systems for teacher professional learning. Pedagogic innovation can only happen at scale within and between schools if schools themselves recognize the significance of the professional challenge faced by teachers in transforming their practice (e.g., Pedder and MacBeath 2008). The focus of practice transformation in this project was the incorporation by teachers of the social and constructivist practices that undergird communicative approaches to teaching and learning English language.

School leadership teams need then to take seriously the importance of establishing school conditions and cultures in which processes of professional learning can thrive and grow as the basis for genuine and locally appropriate practice change at scale (e.g., Pedder 2006). School leadership teams also need to acquire the capacity and know-how to lead and sustain cultivation of new supportive ecologies for innovation in their schools through teacher professional learning. This is a leadership and organizational learning task which should develop in interaction with teachers' professional learning. In this way, teacher learning is best understood and planned for as a dynamic process that is embedded within, rather than separated from, the environments in which teachers work and learn. This argument runs beneath the comparisons between out-of-school and in-school teacher learning in Chapter 4. This is why from the outset, leadership and organizational learning capacity-building needs to be planned for, and properly resourced, as an intrinsic feature of all projects that aim to sustain and embed locally appropriate pedagogic change and professional learning at scale. Such leadership and organizational learning capacity-building can then be recognized as a central feature of the ecology for innovation of a school or a network of schools.

The influence of school-level beliefs and values on teachers' learning

In order to understand the importance of organizational learning and leadership capacity-building elements to projects, such as EIA, which aim to promote and support optimal quality, scale and equity of teachers' professional development, we must consider how school-level beliefs and values about learning exert considerable influence on the equitable distribution and scale of high-quality teacher learning. Even when English provides a specific curriculum focus for professional learning and pedagogic change in classrooms, as with EIA, school-level beliefs and values about learning carry a vital influence and are an important source of leverage for change. The social and constructivist practices at the heart of communicative approaches to English teaching promoted through EIA also have their application in every other curriculum subject. A whole-school approach to change across subjects can involve subject and school leaders in encouraging and supporting cross-subject learning from and adaptation of successful social and constructivist practices developed in different subject contexts. The value for pupil learning would be the nurturing and growth of social and constructivist experiences, dispositions and mindsets across the curriculum.

Organizational values affect teachers' individual and collective practices by establishing norms of action (Sampson et al. 1999). Coleman's work on the social theory of normative control (1985, 1987 & 1990) confirmed that a group of teachers will exert influence on an individual teacher to change her practice when that practice violates group pedagogical values and beliefs. New or inexperienced teachers are particularly vulnerable to making changes to their practice to align with collective pedagogical values and beliefs (e.g., Chester and Beaudin 1996; Woolfolk Hoy and Burke Spero 2005).

As well as their collective pedagogical norms, expectations and practices, schools also have collective awareness of their capacity for learning and growth. Goddard states that 'Teachers have not only self-referent efficacy perceptions but also beliefs about the conjoint capability of a school faculty' (2003: 184). Bandura argues that 'an organization's beliefs about its efficacy to produce results are undoubtedly an important feature of its operative culture' (1997: 476). This collective sense of capacity directly affects the diligence and resolve with which a school chooses to pursue its goals.

Thus, while individual teachers have their own values and practices about teaching and learning (e.g., Pedder and Opfer 2013), school-level beliefs (including collective sense of capacity), values and practices are equally important starting points for promoting sustainable innovation in pedagogy and teacher learning (e.g., Opfer et al. 2011). Chapter 5 is surely right to focus on the practical school-based approach adopted by the EIA project. Schools can play a substantial approach in supporting the kinds of organizational and teacher learning that together are intrinsic to fruitful ecologies for innovation needed for the successful shift from traditional to more communicative approaches to English language teaching in primary and secondary schools in Bangladesh. Those schools that support learning create continuous learning opportunities that are well aligned to classroom, curriculum and assessment contexts, promote enquiry and dialogue, encourage collaboration and team-learning, and establish systems to capture and share learning – all of which improves the learning of individual teachers and also the school itself.

Nevertheless, creating these systems is difficult, and many schools fail to provide the systems and supports necessary for teachers to engage in effective professional learning and practice change. Just as with teachers, placing the blame at leaders' doors is to miss the wider point and policy imperative. Programmes of leadership and organizational learning need to run in interaction with those of teacher professional learning, and indeed with pupils' learning (e.g., Jull et al. 2014; Malakolunthu et al. 2014). To maximize scope for leadership and organizational learning that is relevant to context and culture, the starting points need to be focused on helping leadership teams 'see' their organizations afresh. For example, leadership teams can be supported in 'seeing' their school through the lens of its collective elements such as the school's collective values about teacher learning, prevailing teacher learning practices, current systems and supports for teacher learning, and perceptions of current collective capacity for learning.

Promoting pedagogic innovation at scale through organizational, leader and teacher learning devolves considerable autonomy to the school and to groups of teachers within the school. On the one hand, the development of local appropriately contextualized approaches to professional learning and ways of realizing the tenets of communicative approaches to teaching English language in teachers' routine classroom practice are well served by such a devolved system, which sows the seeds of innovation so to speak in the particular ecology of the local school, and indeed amongst local subject teachers. On the other hand, the risk can be an unhelpful splintering and fragmentation of pedagogic and professional learning practices through which a sense of policy and practice coherence (related to both pedagogic and teacher learning innovation) is lost. Upholding policy and practice coherence within and between different subject groups is a key leadership task for which leaders themselves need professional development support

It is in this respect that the EIA team's technology-enhanced approach is so important and well developed. The very helpful and informed account of the role of mobile technologies in transforming TDP at scale in Bangladesh is presented in Chapter 6. The use of locally appropriate, cost-effective mobile technologies facilitated the scale-up imperatives of the project by enabling the large number of teachers nationwide (including teachers in rural, professionally-isolated regions), to have professional development opportunities from which they would otherwise have been excluded. The use of technology provided the basis for ensuring a balance within the overall project strategy of promoting and encouraging local models of innovation in teacher learning and classroom ELT while at the same time ensuring coherence and comparability of approach across the different ecologies for innovation in schools and networks throughout Bangladesh.

The organizational imperative and ecologies of innovation

In this chapter attention has focused on the importance for schools of creating supportive ecologies for innovation in the fields of pedagogy and teacher learning. I have argued that leadership and organizational learning capacity-building needs to be an intrinsic element to any project with ambitions to promote pedagogic and teacher learning innovation at scale. A supportive ecology is one where relationships between school-level practices, beliefs and values for organizational and teacher learning are a focus of a school's critical self-evaluation and organizational learning processes. A supportive ecology enables both individual and collective teacher learning and organizational learning. However, schools and their leaders need to be supported in developing critical self-evaluation and organizational learning processes as a basis for creating policies and strategies for establishing supportive ecologies for innovation. Although there was some attempt in EIA to provide such support with participating head teachers, a more systematic and pro-active approach to leadership and organizational learning capacity-building could have been planned from the outset.

Leveraging values–practice dissonance and alignment for creating policies and strategies for building supportive ecologies for innovation at scale

If – as I have attempted to argue – organizational learning and leadership are central dimensions of any successful strategy for creating policies and practices for supportive ecologies of innovation at scale, then EIA could have worked with local leaders in Bangladesh to plan and implement a more proactive organizational and leadership strand to further build on the success of their programme of innovation and pedagogic change at scale. But to build an effective organizational imperative into programmes of innovation such as EIA is to engage with a set of challenging complexities.

A great deal of research in developed country contexts suggests that organizational cultures of professional learning are multi-voiced, heterogeneous, and plural. This points to the inadequacy of single labels for capturing this aspect (and perhaps any aspect) of a school's culture. It also points to the need for leadership teams to develop the sophistication required to engage constructively with such plurality. They need to reflect, in their policies and professional learning approaches, a sensitivity to the different professional learning needs and orientations of different teachers, including different teachers of the same subject. Supporting leadership teams to develop such constructive engagement with diversity among different groups of teachers is an important element that needs to be planned from the outset in programmes such as EIA.

Related to this plurality of a school's culture of professional and organizational learning, the concepts of dissonance and alignment have been very strong themes that have run through a number of large-scale research projects in England: 'Learning How to Learn in Classrooms, Schools and Networks' (James et al. 2007; Pedder 2006; Pedder and MacBeath 2008) and 'Schools and Continuing Professional Development in England of Teachers – The State of the Nation Study' (McCormick 2010; Opfer et al. 2011; Pedder et al. 2010; Pedder and Opfer 2013).

In any school, values–practice dissonance or alignment can act as liminal spaces in which transformational learning, including the organizational learning of schools and the professional learning of teachers, can take place in ways that are relevant to, and generative of, the development and establishment of supportive ecologies for nurturing pedagogic innovation in schools. Underpinning this argument is the idea that awareness among school leadership teams of conflicting interplay between teachers' perceptions of school practice and their values can result in a 'change-provoking disequilibrium' (Woolfolk Hoy et al. 2009) if such conflicting interplay is handled sensitively by school leaders as resources for change and innovation instead of threats to an organizational status quo that may have run its course. The question for leadership teams is what kinds of strategy can they develop to engage constructively and sensitively with such conflicting interplay?

A strategy of collecting data from teachers at a school and then feeding back the values and their perceptions of organizational, leadership and teacher learning practices of a school's staff to those schools individually reflects principles of school self-evaluation as a continuing process of organizational learning embedded in the day-to-day life of classrooms and schools (e.g., MacBeath 1999). Here local ecologies of innovation begin to grow through the collective interpretive work of school teachers and leaders working directly with data that reflects their practices and values. Through the sense-making that is achieved during reflective conversations among school staff, the full richness and school relevance of the data becomes apparent and more nuanced. Asking teachers and leaders to make sense of gaps between teachers' perceptions of school practices and the values they place on those practices was a useful means for leadership teams and groups of staff to develop more penetrating, critical and reflective understandings of current organizational practices at their schools (Pedder and MacBeath 2008). Helping school leadership teams develop such data and then develop locally appropriate collective processes of school self-evaluation and organizational learning provides one possible though challenging framework for building leadership capacity-building opportunities in projects such as EIA. Such collective processes support development of whole-school approaches to policy and practice change, and whole-school approaches are important because they involve all staff and foster whole staff buy-in to policy and practice change.

Leadership capacity-building needs to interact and articulate as closely as possible with opportunities for teacher development supports, including technology-enhanced opportunities of the kind built into English in Action, in order to authentically embed and sustain pedagogic innovation at scale. Again, helping school leadership teams investigate patterns of values–practice dissonance among their staff and then to develop school self-evaluation approaches in working with the data to change and adapt current policy and practice is an important dimension of the organizational imperative outlined in this chapter.

Single- and double-loop learning in schools

Schools differ in how their leadership teams interpret and engage with change-provoking disequilibria reflected in gaps between teachers' perceptions of school practice and their values. Some leadership teams and their schools are more settled in an uncritical single-loop learning mindset (Argyris and Schön 1978, 1996). They not only avoid development of rigorous self-evaluation processes that make such disequilibria and their underpinning values–practice dissonance visible, in some cases they also view such disequilibria as a risk, jeopardizing the stable state of prevailing operational efficiency. Such schools might be simply unaware of contradictions and disequilibria or they might simply choose to live with the underpinning values–practice dissonance. The problem arises when school staff act on the basis of different and unexpressed values–practice perspectives in relation to key purposes of a school's life; then discontinuities and conflicts can solidify into forms of systemic incompetence (Pedder and MacBeath 2008). Such schools are disabled from growing ecologies of innovation, and unable to support fruitful change. Indeed in some cases they resist further change, preferring instead to cultivate and hide behind organizational learning disabilities (Senge 1990) and defensive routines (Argyris 1993; Argyris and Schön 1978, 1996) that inhibit development of the mindset, tools and strategies for constructively and critically engaging with values–practice dissonance as a resource and growth point for a school's ecology for innovation. Helping school leadership teams understand such organizational processes would be one important strand of a leadership of change capacity-building strand to a project such as EIA. It is, however, in the more critical second-loop learning practice that reaches into a school's underpinning values that organizational learning deepens, becoming genuinely transformative (Argyris and Schön 1978, 1996). This way a school's ecology for innovation is replenished by embracing a more critical reflection and introspection on the values and practices of school staff as the basis for planning future action and change. It is through such organizational processes that tensions between scale and quality discussed in the previous chapters can begin to be resolved. The quality, purpose and scope of innovation related to pedagogy and professional learning are subject to ongoing critical local test and examination in double-loop school learning cultures.

Schools that adopt double-loop learning strategies are prepared to face up comfortably or uncomfortably to the challenges of learning individually and collectively about themselves, and this raises the question of how do we as a school organization learn? Engaging critically with this question is a necessary stage in the growth of an ecology for innovation. More specifically, this challenges a school to see itself less in terms of a tidy, conveniently homogenous school culture of learning that is easily managed. Instead, schools should be prepared to see themselves in terms of a far less convenient complex of multiple contrasting preferences, practices and values of learning reflected in distinctive values–practice profiles of different groupings of teachers. Schools willing to learn and grow with a double-loop critical approach are willing to adapt and develop strategies that enable distinctive groupings of teachers among their staff to be recognized and heard. Such schools have evolved systems, cultures and a mindset for embracing multiple perspectives of teachers and leaders, as a resource for developing more differentiated policy directed at catering to a diverse range of professional learning needs within and between schools. A school's differentiated strategy for professional learning and change needs to articulate with, and respond to, the specific mix of orientations of particular groups of teachers in its particular organizational learning culture and ecology. Using a dual scale format survey instrument, such as the those used in the Learning How to Learn and Schools and CPD State of the Nation studies, as part of a school's self-evaluation processes is one useful strategy for enabling schools to develop diagnostic data as a basis for developing such more differentiated and responsive strategies of professional learning supports. This provides arguably the best scope in which schools and networks of schools may nurture supportive ecologies for innovation.

Conclusion

The strategies and ideas presented in this brief chapter can inform development of the kinds of explicit organizational learning and leadership capacity-building strand that can and should be attempted and adapted for use in local contexts as part of projects such as English in Action. I have argued that the organizational imperative is an intrinsic element of TPD and pedagogic change projects (such as EIA) aimed at promoting innovations in professional learning and classroom practice at scale.

Nevertheless, the prospect of building school self-evaluation and organizational learning approaches to developing, embedding and sustaining enhanced professional learning and classroom practices of teachers and the learning of their pupils, presents schools anywhere in the world with profound leadership and organizational challenges. The work of developing data related to the practices and values of members of a school community, developing systems that enable the individual and collective critical interpretation and reflection based on such data, adopting a school strategy of policy and practice change that constructively engages with the interpretations, values, commitments and priorities of all members of the school, and a preparedness, in light of such learning, to re-invigorate the prevailing school culture with an ecology of innovation, present considerable challenge.

This work also carries enormous potential. Change strategies based on collective self-evaluation processes and the critical examination of practice–value differences not only assume a collective and individual sense of agency (of school and teacher); such strategies promote its constructive development. The constructive development of agency is a pre-condition of innovation at scale if such innovation as described in this book is to be successfully realized as a lasting feature of the educational landscape. Incorporating the organizational dimension as an imperative feature of project designs such as EIA is one constructive way of fostering the agency needed to sustain locally appropriate ecologies of innovation at scale.

Part Three

English Language Teaching

The first part of the book examined the context of Bangladesh, and its education system in particular, including teacher professional development. The second part examined teacher professional development, both through the international evidence and how this was realized within EIA. All the chapters of Part 3 address matters of English language teaching.

Chapter 8 outlines core features of the model adopted by EIA, and ways in which it developed over three implementation phases in response to the realities of teachers' existing beliefs and practices, of the classroom and of the curriculum, including the examination system. It argues for the importance of promoting an approach seen by teachers as authentic and outlines the reasons for adopting a 'weak' model of CLT, in which, to ensure understanding, some use of the students' first language is encouraged. In Chapter 9, the implications for the Programme of the low level of English proficiency of many teachers are considered in terms of both students' learning outcomes and of teachers' own proficiency development. Further, it seeks to understand the apparent discrepancy between teachers' low proficiency scores and observations that their use of English in the classroom was often fluent and competent. At the heart of both chapters is the question: how were improved English language teaching practices envisaged, developed and supported through EIA?

In the concluding critical chapter of Part 3, Amol Padwad considers EIA's approach to English language teaching (ELT) to have been 'context-sensitive and pragmatic' and recognizes the benefits of a practice-based intervention that teachers perceived not to be adding to their workload. He sees the development of teachers' proficiency through classroom English as effective in meeting immediate goals, but has reservations about it as a long-term strategy, since in his experience, English teachers are very concerned to improve their general proficiency. He does, however, clearly approve of allowing the use of Bangla in the English classroom, a step he describes as 'decriminalization'!

8

Empowering Teachers and Learners through EIA's Approach to English Language Teaching

Clare Woodward, Malcolm Griffiths and Mike Solly

Introduction

This chapter sets out a detailed account of English in Action's pedagogical model as it developed over the course of the Programme's implementation and looks at the changes that have taken place in EIA classrooms.

One of the distinctive features of the Programme is the consideration of the views of teachers and other stakeholders, formally through monitoring and informally mostly through contact in cluster meetings (CMs) and on classroom visits. Feedback from teachers in particular allowed the Programme to develop iteratively over its lifespan. While the principles remained constant, details of the model changed as the Programme team learnt more about what was working and what needed to change.

English language teaching and teacher development before EIA

Chapters 1 and 2 set out the context and pedagogy of a typical English classroom in a Bangladeshi government school prior to the EIA intervention. Little English was to be heard in lessons that were based on repetition, copying and translation of the textbook. The teacher dominated and students played little active part. English lessons focused on teaching *about* the language rather than using it communicatively (Chowdhury and Ha 2008; Hamid et al. 2009; Hamid and Erling 2016). The overwhelming majority of students failed to progress in communicative ability year-on-year (EIA 2009a), while a majority of teachers had to teach at levels of proficiency higher than their own.

To develop teachers' practice, several donor-funded projects had been implemented, the most recent being the English Language Teaching Improvement Programme (ELTIP) which ran from 1997 to 2012. Like its predecessors, ELTIP had promoted a communicative methodology, very different from traditional grammar and translation-based methods. The principles guiding the Communicative Language Teaching (CLT) approach underlying the Programme's advocated pedagogy are set out in the Introduction. There is, however, more than one form of CLT:

> There is, in a sense, a 'strong' version of the communicative approach and a 'weak' version. The weak version which has become more or less standard practice in the last ten years, stresses the importance of providing learners with opportunities to use their English for communicative purposes and, characteristically, attempts to integrate such activities into a wider program [sic] of language teaching ...
> The 'strong' version of communicative teaching, on the other hand, advances the claim that language is acquired through communication, so that it is not merely a question of activating an existing but inert knowledge of the language, but of stimulating the development of the language system itself. If the former could be described as 'learning to use' English, the latter entails 'using English to learn it.'
>
> Howatt 1984: 279

While our experience of talking to former ELTIP teachers suggests that their training had promoted a 'strong' form of CLT, in point of fact the knowledge that they had acquired very rarely emerged in classroom practice (Hamid 2010; EIA 2009c; Hamid and Erling 2016). This fits our experience: many teachers we spoke to were able to describe in some detail what might be expected of a communicative approach, but the practice we observed remained traditional.

Furthermore, our conversations with participants in earlier projects revealed that:

- training consisted of one-off theoretical sessions with limited or no practical elements;
- project activities were often perceived by teachers to be an extra burden;
- teacher professional development (TPD) in communicative English language teaching (ELT) was perceived as irrelevant to the practical issues encountered by Bangladeshi teachers;
- teachers felt that the practical realities of their school militated against many of those techniques;

- there were no Teachers' Guides or manuals to assist in implementing the lessons in the (ELTIP-designed) *English for Today* (*EfT*) textbook, despite the authors' intentions;
- there was no support to help teachers apply the techniques advocated.

Whatever the reasons, most teachers had not formed a clear understanding of teaching communicatively as a way of working practically in their classrooms (Hamid and Baldauf 2008; EIA 2009c).

The evidence (including the Programme's own) available as EIA began was that teachers were using ineffective practices and that substantial and long training programmes had failed to make any impact on those practices. While lessons could undoubtedly be learnt from earlier projects, it seemed that many of these would be of the 'what not to do' variety. Finding an effective 'what to do' was the challenge that faced the EIA team.

EIA in the classroom

The EIA Programme recognized the realities of the context and the need to address them pragmatically. Rather than present teachers with a story to tell about 'good' English language teaching, it set out to harness teachers' professionalism and agency, to ensure that they would feel motivated and enabled to change their classroom practice. How teachers were supported to adopt new pedagogies can be linked to their changing understanding of classroom practice.

Table 8.1 is taken from the guidance materials for head teachers and education officials to support their classroom observations, and it aims to give an idea of what they should look out for in English lessons. It therefore provides a summary of EIA's approach to ELT.

There is a strong emphasis on practical and personal engagement by the learners: they are using English, talking to each other and about themselves and what they know. There is also challenge, experimentation and excitement for the learners: errors are seen as an essential part of learning, and fear of them should not deter students from making their contribution in pair, group and class work. Students have opportunities to express themselves in open-ended activities, which allow them to approach a task in various ways.

Meanwhile, the teacher is making things happen in a lesson: she or he plans, manages and monitors activities. By promoting fluency as well as accuracy, and by appearing relaxed and confident the teacher creates a positive environment

Table 8.1 Changes in the classroom

Student actions	Teacher actions
Students using English more within a lesson than before the Programme.	The teacher is using English more than they did before the Programme.
Students are talking more and in a wider variety of ways than before the Programme.	The teacher is using mainly English to manage the lesson (classroom language).
Students sometimes work together in pairs or groups.	Some classroom routines have been established.
Students may talk about their real-life experiences when practising English: they are not just repeating words and phrases from the book.	The teacher is including more students in classroom activities.
Most students seem to follow what the teacher is saying.	The teacher may sometimes use gestures and body language to enhance the communication.
Students may make some mistakes in order to express themselves in English, for example, in role plays, or answering open-ended questions.	The teacher is allowing for some mistakes in accuracy, in order to promote fluency.
Students are reading in a variety of different ways, including silently.	The teacher is monitoring the learning of individuals, at least for some of the time.
Students are sometimes practising different skills together in an integrated way (reading, writing, speaking and listening).	Some evidence that the lessons are planned in a logical sequence of 'stages'.
Most students are clearly engaged and enjoying the lesson.	The teacher appears relaxed and confident.

Source: Extract from *English in Action: In School Support Guide* (for head teachers; translation)

for active learning. She or he consistently uses English as much as possible, while ensuring that the language used to give instructions and support learners is kept clear and comprehensible, occasionally, where necessary for understanding, supplemented by a few words (and sometimes more) of Bangla. In this respect the Programme's approach differs from a 'strong' CLT approach.

Naturally, teachers use the EIA resources. Audio recordings help bring the *EfT* texts alive, while the sing-along, and act-along, songs and rhymes proved to be highly popular and motivating for learners in many schools (EIA 2014c). EIA action songs are still frequently performed by hundreds of children in primary school assemblies across Bangladesh, and owing to popular demand several of the more popular primary songs are now available in the secondary school audio package as well. However, beyond the attractiveness of the songs, the TPD materials place a strong emphasis on their pedagogic value. Teachers are encouraged to use songs as a means of teaching vocabulary and grammar structures in a systematic way and to focus on meaning and understanding, just as they would with any other text, and the EIA evidence showed that they did and that almost all students enjoyed them (EIA 2014c).

The evidence of use of the TDP and classroom materials was strong, as these figures[1] show:

> three quarters (78%) of primary teachers reported using the teacher development videos every week and almost two thirds (64%) used the 'English language for teachers' (EL4T) audio course every week. In the classroom, almost all (94%) primary teachers reported using EIA activities during teaching every week; most teachers (86%) used EIA posters and flash cards every week and almost half of the teachers (47%) reported using the audio resources every week.
>
> EIA 2015c: 4

Through the CMs and resources, teachers have been guided to maximize the potential visual impact of posters, flashcards and also the pictures in their textbooks for practising language in meaningful and motivating ways. By showing teachers how to take these visual materials beyond the limits of pointing at a picture and asking 'What's this?', the TPD videos and supporting print materials promote a communicative use of language. Teachers are encouraged to develop personalized, imagination-based activities for reviewing and reinforcing previously learned language, for example, in meaningful grammar extension 'chains', role plays and stories, true/false games, all of which can be derived from a few simple images.

Learners have been supported to understand and use the grammar, vocabulary and pronunciation of English more effectively through using English in a meaningful and purposeful way – rather than learning 'about' the language, as they had done previously. This has been done by textbook-based activities involving a contextualized approach to language use, often through games and playful, non-threatening activities. The use of pair and group work was encouraged not only because it enables frequent, active and meaningful use of English, but also because it acts as a strategy for managing large classes and giving some autonomy to learners; again there is evidence from them that they overwhelmingly report using these exercises (EIA 2014c). This resulted in a substantial increase in the use of pair and group work (over the baseline) and almost a quarter of all student talk being observed in these activities (EIA 2012c).

Through the Programme, teachers were guided on essential classroom management strategies, for example, how to quickly organize a class into groups, how to lead discussions and give feedback, thus ensuring that any activity in the classroom would be productive. The Programme also supported the development of teachers' English for classroom management (see Chapter 9), and successive studies of classroom practice showed an increase of pair and group work (EIA 2015b).

Through the use of a wide range of interactive techniques, English became motivating, non-threatening and enjoyable to the students (EIA 2011c, 2014c). Literacy tasks became communicative and interactive, through for example, the use of scaffolded reading activities, a process approach to writing and meaningful pair and group work. As well as listening to their teachers (some of whom were not, in fact, well-equipped to offer a good model), students listened to audios which featured recognizable local pronunciation, natural speeds and authentic elements of spoken language such as elision, ellipsis, stress and associated vowel reduction. However, despite the above evidence of the use of audio in the classroom and the general enthusiasm for this by students, early evidence (Phase 2) indicated that for students one of the three things that they mentioned negatively was difficulty in following the audio, either because it was too fast or the content was too difficult (EIA 2011c). For Phase 3 this was addressed in the revision of materials.

The principles of the EIA classroom – active learning, communicative use of English, encouragement to take risks and so on – were also to be found in the TPD sessions. The Programme introduced a practical, learning-by-doing approach, with teachers asked to try techniques explored in the sessions in their own classroom. Table 8.2 gives an example of how teachers' TPD experience mirrored the approach advocated for classroom implementation.

Table 8.2 Teachers' and students' learning through EIA

Learners	Teachers
Learners are exposed to near-authentic local examples of English in meaningful contexts through a combination of:	Teachers are exposed to authentic models of classroom practice through a combination of:
• the basic *EfT* texts in the EIA-produced audios;	• videos of authentic classroom situations;
• the teachers' confident use of English in the classroom;	• supporting print materials, and resource banks;
• the teachers' confident use of effective teaching methods.	• facilitated face-to-face peer-group meetings.

Developing pedagogy through Mediated Authentic Video (MAV)

Chapter 6 set out the principles underlying the Programme's use of video and how MAV developed. MAV gives teachers the opportunity to build a wide repertoire of engaging pedagogical activities and techniques designed to promote effective learning of reading, writing, speaking and listening in English. The videos feature serving teachers (who had been members of earlier EIA cohorts) and thus show real classrooms with typical resource levels, usually difficult seating arrangements and very high (up to seventy) pupil numbers. Even facing these constraints, the teachers were able to demonstrate collaborative, interactive lessons in which students were very actively and enjoyably engaged, as the following examples in Box 8.1 illustrate.

Box 8.1: Video example activities

Example 1: Primary, Class 1

The teacher points to a particular letter on the board and calls out a word which may or may not begin with that letter. If the learners think the letter and word match up, they call out 'yes'; if not, they all call out 'no'. This is repeated several times with both the teacher and learners in animated mood: the learners seem to be excited by the chance to rise to this gentle challenge and at the same time the teacher is able to assess the learners' knowledge of letters and sounds.

Example 2: Primary, Class 4

The teacher works systematically with an action song. She 'teaches' the song by scaffolding various stages: first she gives the overall idea to engage students' enjoyment; then she focuses on key vocabulary items with a board drawing and a quick antonyms activity; then the students listen and perform the actions without singing; finally, she and the class sing and repeat each line separately. Viewing teachers see how song or rhyme, attractive for its motivational qualities, can be an effective vehicle for learning, not just a pleasant time-filler.

Example 3: Secondary, Class 7

After an initial focus on a reading text, the teacher has the learners practise the present perfect tense using the following structures: 'Where have you been?' and 'Have you ever …?' to talk and ask about personal experience. He begins by

---

asking the class 'have you ever been to Khulna?' and then asks various students where they have travelled in Bangladesh, eliciting a range of transport options. He then invites different students to suggest questions, which he writes on the board: 'Have you ever been to ....?'; 'Have you ever seen a ....?'; and 'Have you ever eaten ....?' After some whole-class practice, the teacher invites a pair of volunteers to come to the front of the classroom. Girl A asks the class 'Have you ever been to Khulna?', 'Have you ever eaten ice-cream?', 'Have you ever seen a tiger?' etc., based on the prompts on the board. The class, in response to the questions, stand up if they have done the thing mentioned in the questions. Girl B counts the number who stand up and records these on the board, gradually building up a class survey. The activity goes at a reasonably brisk pace, the students are all seen to be actively engaged, following with mild amusement throughout, and giving personally true responses. The sequence shows a communicative activity being managed smoothly with a large class, and the teacher gauging the learning taking place. He makes a mental note of grammatical inaccuracies particularly with reference to past participles and drills them at the end of the activity with the whole class.

Video sequences such as these were not offered as models to be followed to the letter, but as examples to be considered in the context of each teacher's own classroom. Rather, they were encouraged to adapt and apply similar techniques in their own classes. Thus each video had relevance for every teacher, regardless of the teaching content of the lesson shown.

Reflection was fostered in facilitated peer-support group meetings (CMs) by a regular activity in which teachers were supported in planning how to apply the ideas derived from the EIA materials and develop them into *EfT*-based classroom activities, and encouraged to use their professional agency. This was followed by a practical session where these activities were undertaken in the relatively low-stress environment of their peer group. Teachers were able to reflect on all aspects of the lesson, including the instructional phrases, grammatical structures, vocabulary sets, language skills and classroom management techniques required to successfully carry out the activity in the classroom.

Cluster meetings provided an opportunity to discuss challenges and successes, and to reflect on progress with these new techniques. These meetings were also a valuable opportunity for teachers to adapt, invent and share their own versions of these techniques, thus building a community of practice. They were consistently seen by teachers as the most important element of EIA: 98 per cent thought they were either 'important' or 'crucial' (55 per cent in the latter group; EIA 2011d).

Alongside the videos, the teachers had printed guides (digitized in Phase 4) which encouraged them to engage with the content of the video and which also contained a bank of resources containing additional activities (e.g. games) each of which could be used to teach many different language elements, classroom language glossaries and classroom management advice (including advice on working with large classes).

Teaching, learning and teacher development in a Bangladeshi context

Much of the pedagogy described in the previous section will be as familiar to experienced communicative language teachers as it was, initially, alien to the EIA teachers. One of the key strategies of the Programme was to ground its approach in the context of Bangladesh and Bangladeshi schooling.

For example, the Programme's posters depict urban and rural Bangladeshi environments, recognizable to teachers and students, and the audio-recorded songs use familiar local instruments and rhythms. It was assumed that using familiar cultural features would make the materials more attractive and readily acceptable to both learners (earlier evidence showed it was), and teachers (who might have felt disoriented or even alienated if the materials were situated in a foreign-looking and sounding environment). This proved to be the case, and the materials were embraced by schools, teachers and students.

The variety of English used in the audio recordings was chosen to be compatible both with the need to equip students with the kind of English that would be useful to them (for example in the workplace) and the kind of English regularly used by teachers. Speakers used a clear, easily understood Bangladeshi variety of English (see Chapter 9). The Primary audios used this variety exclusively, while the Secondary audios also included a few examples of other varieties, including Standard British English and Australian.

Possibly even more important was to match EIA materials and training to the curriculum that teachers saw as closely guiding their teaching. Throughout the Programme's life, teachers used the national *EfT* textbooks and followed the Government curriculum. With EIA, however, the teacher used the kind of communicative approach intended by the authors, but which, because of a lack of appropriate training, support and resources, teachers across the country had failed to discern or adopt.

EIA teachers were equipped with a range of effective techniques that could be applied to help the learners engage with the textbook curriculum effectively and meaningfully. Learners worked with the same dialogues, stories and other texts as other learners across the country. They explored the same language-focused examples and did the practice activities contained in the textbooks. However, in well-functioning EIA classrooms, the learners were listening to the dialogues and stories on a professionally produced audio recording, which provided valuable opportunities for learners to develop flexible listening skills in a wide range of contexts and which also provided the learners with appropriate and consistent models of spoken language. Because all the audios were verbatim reproductions of texts from the course book (*EfT*), they were seen by the teachers as helping with their lessons rather than overburdening them with extra resources. (In Phase 2 the Primary audios had attempted to scaffold the textbook language with vocabulary from earlier lessons, an initiative to which many teachers responded negatively.) The audios have also been identified as a factor in the improvement of teachers' own English (see Chapter 9), and were appreciated by students, as noted earlier.

Related to this issue is that of the teachers' use of Bangla. Early observations of classrooms by the EIA team showed that in some classrooms the low use of Bangla (a contrast with the situation pre-EIA) threatened students' ability to understand. An effort was made in CMs to correct this. The systematic evidence subsequently indicated a more balanced use of Bangla (EIA 201a). Attitudes indicated something of a dilemma for primary teachers (Phase 3, cohort 3):

> when asked whether Bangla should be used frequently in English classes for students' better understanding ... 51% of the teachers disagreed (31% agreed), higher than in cohort 1.
>
> EIA 2014c: 20

At the same time 43 per cent of them thought students preferred Bangla. Secondary teachers were slightly less polarized: 57 per cent disagreed while 27 per cent agreed the use of Bangla was better for understanding (EIA 2014c: 31). Nevertheless, English has predominated throughout for teacher talk (In Primary 70 per cent in Phase 1 and 80 per cent in Phase 2, and around 86 per cent for secondary in both phases; EIA 2015b).

The EIA classroom approach aimed to bring the national curriculum to life and to optimize the conditions to achieve its goals as a communicative language learning programme. Head-teachers, parents, local education administrations and learners themselves had no reason to see a threat to the achievement of national standards for learning outcomes and competencies, by which each of the stakeholder groups has at some stage to be assessed and/or be held accountable.

Throughout the Programme's life, EIA sought to promote a communicative approach in a way compatible with the realities of Bangladeshi schools. This is not to say, however, that there was always agreement between stakeholder groups over the details of implementation. Three areas of debate were:

- the models of English language provided;
- the balance in emphasis accorded respectively to listening and speaking skills, and reading and writing;
- the extent to which classroom activity was, and should be, linked to formal assessment (principally the national examinations) and a related emphasis on teaching languages as a systems of rules; i.e. the importance of grammatical accuracy, precision in pronunciation and so on.

While the Bangladeshi variety of English used in most of the audios caused little comment, some teachers questioned the quality of spoken English used by the teachers filmed in some of the classroom videos, especially when the teachers in the MAV came from a different part of the country. This is somewhat ironic, given that the reason for filming around the country was to enhance the degree to which teachers identified with the teachers they saw on screen. Members of the Programme's support team found ways of responding constructively to such reactions, often by directing attention towards the core pedagogic messages.

Another concern expressed by members of a number of stakeholder groups related to a perceived bias towards oral/aural skills. Early on, EIA team members and facilitators quite frequently reported that some teachers, head teachers and education officials believed that the Programme was promoting only listening and speaking and was not concerned with reading and writing, and that the EIA materials and approaches promoted fluency only and ignored aspects that had been traditionally central to the examination system such as formal writing and grammatical accuracy. In the team's experience, most teachers in both primary and secondary schools felt under pressure to focus on reading and writing and it was not surprising that they worried that activities focused on speaking and listening diverted precious time away from these (examined) skills. However, teachers quickly saw that listening and speaking were rarely practised in isolation and that most activities led to opportunities to integrate all four skills. Again, the materials and training made these principles of integration completely explicit and observers, such as head teachers, were guided to look out for logical staging of different, but related activities within a lesson. Teachers were also persuaded that vocabulary and grammar soundly learnt through meaningful and purposeful spoken activities provide a firm foundation for reading and writing.

It was a key principle of EIA to ensure that the project was fully endorsed by the government and aligned to the resources and curriculum. While the matter of keeping the government course books central to the classroom practice of EIA's teachers was dealt with through devising supportive activities and resources, it was more challenging to incorporate the demands of the national-level assessment which could be seen as a rather separate 'activity' from the classroom practices of EIA. For their assessment in English, students sat two papers annually: one focusing on the course book and the other on grammar and structure; in Years 5 and 8 these papers were standardized national examinations. Teachers and students often saw these areas as quite separate, with greater efforts usually going into preparing for the grammar paper, the questions in which reflected a very prescriptive attitude to language structure, while not always being consistent with Standard English. Sometimes a question would have several possible answers (depending on potential contexts), only one of which would be accepted and marked as correct. The 'course book' paper required much rote learning of reading passages, though there was also some misalignment between what was tested in the examination and the textbook contents. What was recognized at government level as being essential to improve students' English, namely the skills of listening and speaking, were not tested at all.

That the assessment system perceived grammar as a body of knowledge to be studied separately from English communication was an issue EIA's approach tackled head-on, as it was deemed counter-productive to ignore it with the teachers. Activities in EIA (in both primary and secondary materials) were consistently built around the *EfT* course books, and grammar was specifically acknowledged and practised in a communicative way, while teachers were offered opportunities to analyse the grammar. The secondary materials, for example, have a specific area of 'grammar focus' in each of the modules. In addition, teachers were, through the face-to-face sessions in EIA, encouraged to reflect on the relationship between grammar and communication and to encourage their students to become more confident and better equipped to perform well in the assessments as well as in their communicative abilities in English. Nevertheless, teachers exhibited some conflict in their views regarding both agreement with grammar as a separate study, and their positive agreement with a communicative approach to grammar (EIA 2011c).

Related to this was the point made earlier about teachers' demand for content-specific textbook activity for any given day. Initially several teachers appeared reluctant to accept the notion of practice activities, perhaps using posters, dialogues or songs that included content (such as vocabulary from an earlier lesson) that they considered to be a diversion from the syllabus, which they felt had to be adhered to in order to prepare students for government examinations. This proved to be an extremely valuable learning point for the EIA team. A principle widely accepted within CLT – that of revisiting and building on previously learned language – could not be taken for granted. It highlighted the need to develop strategies that acknowledged teachers' different perceptions and beliefs about what was good teaching.

These issues were addressed in a number of ways. The teaching videos and later editions of the printed materials included explicit guidance on techniques for teaching and practising essential syllabus items such as advanced grammar structures, often in enjoyable and creative ways, which teachers came to welcome. Such activities also benefited learners in terms of fluency and confidence. Additionally, as the number of teachers who were adept at leading suitable classroom activities increased, it became possible to capture on video a range of assessment-oriented activities. Teachers then had the opportunity to see, try out and reflect on techniques which satisfied their requirements for formative assessment in all skill areas (something that qualitative research showed they did not do; EIA 2011a), including speaking and listening. Both teachers and learners were then receptive to strategies they would not have considered in the early years of the Programme (EIA 2011a).

Changes in practice

Over the lifetime of the Programme there have undoubtedly been important and measurable changes in participating teachers' approach to their classroom practice (EIA 2015b). An observer entering the classroom of an EIA teacher in the later phases would have seen many of the elements listed in Table 8.1 above:

- learners and teachers using English frequently;
- successful pair and group work;
- grammar taught as a language component to use, rather than simply as something to know about;
- inclusivity: teachers involving students from the whole class;

- integration of reading, writing, speaking and listening;
- clearly established classroom routines;
- activities that were enjoyable for both students and teachers.

In its later stages, more than 150 teachers from all stages of the Programme spent a year engaged in action research projects to gather evidence about learning and teaching in their own classrooms. Their many reflections include:

> Making groups with mixed-ability students worked better and I think, all should get chance to be group leaders by turn.
>
> Teacher GPS. Khulna Sadar

> I can try to develop myself alone but professional development gets coloured with the help of a peer teacher.
>
> Teacher GPS, Brahmanbaria Sadar

> Peer assessment is a great tool to let students support their peers, especially in a large class and it is my best learning from my classroom research.
>
> Teacher, Secondary school, Bola Sadar

> From my study I have learned that role-play is one of the best techniques to let students speak English.
>
> Teacher, Sutrupur, Dhaka

In the case study in Box 8.2, Shamima shows how she has not only changed her pedagogy, but also how she perceived her role as a teacher.

Box 8.2: Shamima

Shamima has worked as a teacher in a Government Primary School in Noakhali since 2007. Teaching had not been her initial ambition for a career and for some time she 'was working like traditional teachers'. After working with the EIA approach for some time, she now considers herself to be an 'extraordinary teacher'.

She aims to use English as much as possible and has even made a study, along with three other teachers from nearby schools, into how she can continue to improve her own level of English. At the same time she is passionate about how to make her lessons enjoyable and fun in ways that include all learners. So, as well as EIA audios, she makes a point of including games, and using visuals. Her classroom is a lively engaging environment: there are pictures, and colourful posters based on learners' work on the walls, she makes frequent use of pair and group work and role play and acted dialogues and singing are common features of her lessons.

Shamima also tries continuously to improve the quality of her teaching through her own constant evaluation. In her words: 'I think I need to evaluate my own teaching: how am I doing, how are my students progressing?' Her recent study also included a component on the effectiveness of fun and inclusion-oriented activities, and she used a range of different research techniques: video clips, questionnaires, 'smiley surveys', peer observation and a reflective journal. While this approach has helped her to apply new techniques, she also thinks that it has helped bring her closer to her learners, even to the extent of revealing barriers to their learning that she had previously been unaware of. Having initially been something of a 'reluctant' teacher, Shamima now happily describes herself as a teacher-researcher and 'I am the classroom changer and I am really proud of that'.

Shamima's case illustrates how far some teachers have progressed in realizing their own professional agency. Her practice is a far cry from that of traditional teachers who see their role as simply to 'teach' the textbook pages through repetition and translation. Shamima has taken control of the teaching and learning process in her classroom, trying new techniques, evaluating them and building her own successful pedagogical repertoire. Box 8.3 gives a student's perspective.

Box 8.3: Mim, from Bogra

When we were in Class 3 I was very weak in English. But my friend Sristy always got good marks – I did not have any interest in English. Always I wanted to go far from English.

Some days ago we were introduced to new ways of learning lessons by our English teacher. It gives me much pleasure because it removes my fear of English. When our teacher plays lesson-related audio on speaker, we get a clear idea about correct pronunciation. It improves our listening, speaking, reading and writing skills. We also learn new words from various games, such as bingo, silent mouthing, miming, acting etc. We learn new grammar by chain drill and by throwing paper balls with our class friends. We learn rhymes with action. We enjoy when we hear various greeting songs and action songs.

So I am much more confident in English. Even now I can compete with my close friend Sristy and I believe I will get high marks in English.

Lessons learnt

The initial model for the pilot phase (Phase 2) was developed on the basis of lessons learnt from the baseline studies (EIA 2009a, b, c) and the Programme team's understanding of the strengths and weaknesses of earlier projects. The assumption that it was important to develop a model that closely met the needs and opportunities offered by the local context was quickly borne out by experience, and many lessons about how best to work with the local context were learnt over the course of implementation.

Working with a context is often seen as a matter of accommodation, and one of the most important elements to accommodate was the nationally determined curriculum. The Programme team very quickly learnt, for example, that their analysis of the language content underlying the textbooks was much less significant than what was actually on the pages, which teachers saw as their responsibility to teach. While that led to some frustration (e.g. some early primary lessons covered little more than four letters of the alphabet and four associated words), the benefits in terms of teachers' readiness to see EIA materials and methods as things which would make their job easier with improved success, more than outweighed such shortcomings. Similarly, while the team did what it could to lobby for changes to the national examinations, the Programme had no choice but to acknowledge the examinations' influence on teachers and work.

Moreover, sometimes it proved necessary to counter objections that the context is not being respected. As noted earlier in this chapter, the Programme's emphasis on classroom interactions led some teachers, head teachers and administrators to the conclusion that reading and writing – the examined elements of English that they considered vital – were being neglected. It was important that these objections should not be ignored, so the emphasis in training materials for all stakeholder groups on showing how the Programme dealt with the four skills of reading, writing, speaking and listening in an integrated way, was enhanced.

A policy of formally researching, monitoring and informally listening to the views of teachers and other stakeholders enabled progressive improvement of the materials in order to better meet the needs of teachers.

One of the key lessons regarding pedagogy can be summed up as 'show, don't tell'. Earlier projects had shown that telling teachers about CLT produced teachers who can talk about CLT. By showing a range of ELT techniques in action (using MAV), teachers were able not only to quickly understand how they worked, but to see that they could be enacted by teachers like themselves with classes like their own. By asking teachers not simply to imitate what could have been seen as model lessons, but rather to plan carefully to implement the techniques themselves, teachers took ownership of the pedagogy and learnt to implement it in a way that suited them and their students.

The approach to CLT that emerged in EIA classrooms was 'weak', rather than the 'strong' model (Howatt 1984) adopted by earlier TPD projects. Ninety per cent of teachers named communication as their focus in English classes (EIA 2014c). They felt comfortable with an approach that allowed them to foreground meaning and purpose, for example, by making appropriate use of Bangla to support understanding rather than losing students' attention in an 'English only' environment.

Note

1   The corresponding secondary teacher percentages are: 64 per cent use of video, 59 per cent EL4T audio, 69 per cent for EIA activities, 72 per cent for posters and flash cards and (surprisingly) 69 per cent for classroom audio.

9

Raising Standards of English

Questions of Proficiency

Ian Eyres and Rehnuma Akhter

Introduction

English in Action began in a challenging context. Students' and teachers' levels of proficiency were extremely low (EIA 2009a), and prevailing traditional pedagogies ineffective and uninspiring. Teachers' understanding of their craft seems to have been based on a combination of a view of language as 'a system of structurally related elements for coding meaning' (Richards and Rodgers 2014: 23) and a behaviourist conception of learning based on copying and repetition. An emphasis on linguistic form was maintained through culture and practice and reinforced by national examinations. Such a view of English recalls the 'autonomous' conception of literacy (Street 2003) and the idea of autonomous subject knowledge (Ellis 2007), each existing free of social or cultural considerations, with learning a cognitive exercise of mastering component parts. Relatively little English proficiency is required of the teacher, just the words and phrases of the textbook, to be presented and explained in Bangla. The overwhelming majority of the classroom talk observed in the EIA baseline study was in Bangla (EIA 2009c).

In the international context, this unpromising situation is far from exceptional. Reviewing studies around the world (Nunan 2003; Wedell 2008, 2011), Wedell concludes that 'there are relatively few state school classrooms anywhere in which most learners are developing a useable knowledge of English' (Wedell 2011: 3). Reasons identified include teachers' inadequate English proficiency, ineffective pedagogy, the examination system and a mismatch between initiatives' goals and classroom realities (Nunan 2003). The last of these is often attributable to a 'native speakerist' (Holliday 2013) perspective, which roots language pedagogies in western culture, and sees native English speakers as the ideal teachers and conflicting aspects of local culture as something to be 'corrected' (Holliday 2013). Factors obstructing effective innovation include policy-makers' failure to support teachers and recognize the demands being placed on them, the ways in which teachers and teacher educators are trained, a failure to engage influential members of the wider ELT 'culture' (including examination designers), and inflexible modes of implementation (Wedell 2008).

English in Action's challenge was to overcome shortcomings in teachers' subject knowledge (proficiency) and pedagogy, whilst avoiding alienating teachers and promoting harmony between the Programme's aspirations and the demands of the national system. Most of these matters are addressed in detail in other chapters and the focus of this chapter is on teachers' English language proficiency, the very low level of which (EIA 2009a) was considered one of the major challenges to the goal of raising students' attainment levels.

The common-sense assumption that English teachers require a high level of English proficiency is rarely challenged (Chambless 2012) and target-language competence underlies language education policies around the world (e.g. Qi 2009; Nunan 2003; Butler 2004). The target language competence of English teachers is reported to be inadequate in many countries (Sešek 2007) and calls for it to be improved are frequent (Butler 2004). Moreover, teachers themselves often judge their competence to be inadequate (Barnes 2006).

However, whilst the improvement of teachers' proficiency is an important driver in many teacher professional development (TPD) programmes (Butler 2004), there is some acceptance of the idea that a lower degree of proficiency may sometimes be sufficient. For Modern Foreign Language (MFL) teaching in English primary schools, for example, it has been argued that a class's own teacher may be more effective than an outside specialist even though her/his command of the target language may be rudimentary (Cable et al. 2010). In Italy, Level B1 of the Common European Framework (CEFR) (Verhelst et al. 2009) has been deemed a minimum level for primary teachers (Bondi and Poppi 2007). The view that 'very good language teachers may not necessarily have the top levels of language competence according to the CEF' (Kelly and Grenfell 2004: 49) challenges the position that improving teachers' proficiency will necessarily improve their effectiveness.

The issue of teachers' proficiency becomes especially salient in the context of a communicative language teaching (CLT) approach, since the target language must be used with flexibility and facility to conduct each lesson (Banegas 2009).

However, the proficiency even of university language graduates may be inadequate, thanks to a focus on general and academic language, rather than the language of the classroom or even of communication (Elder 2001).

Meeting the needs of English teachers in their training has been seen as an example of English for specific purposes (ESP) (Sešek 2007; Elder 2001). Using English, teachers need, for example, to be able to manage classes, introduce lesson topics, give explanations, make presentations, initiate and moderate discussions and carry out assessments (Sešek 2007). All these activities require the use of particular forms of language.

Elder (2001: 153) identifies six language functions over which English teachers must have command:

- presenting information and explaining subject-specific metalinguistic concepts;
- extracting meaning from multi-way discussion (with two or more speakers);
- discussing a problem/expressing an opinion;
- summarizing/paraphrasing simplifying/disambiguating information;
- formulating questions;
- issuing directives, setting up a classroom activity.

If (as CLT approaches assume), interaction underpins language learning, then teachers must be able to use English to 'shape learner contributions and mak[e] strategic decisions in the moment by moment unfolding of a lesson' (Walsh 2006: 133).

Moreover, the English demands on teachers will vary according to context (e.g. students' age, purpose for learning English, level of study) (Sešek 2007).

The above discussion can be seen in terms of teachers' professional knowledge. The idealized form of English (usually gained in earlier study), and the particular subset of it which is codified as 'curriculum knowledge', are held by teachers as 'subject content knowledge'. The version of English used for teaching is part of 'pedagogical content knowledge' (Shulman 1986, 1987) and may result from teachers' application of their previously learnt proficiency to classroom purposes (Loewenberg Ball et al. 2008). Alternatively, the integration of English proficiency and pedagogy in teacher training has been advocated (Sešek 2007; Banegas 2009), though practical initiatives such as ELTeach (Young et al. 2014) and the University of Joensuu's 'Classroom Language' course are 'still a rarity' (Sešek 2007: 412).

It makes sense to consider classroom language, rather than classroom English, since teachers must strike a balance between their use of students' first language and the target language. This element of pragmatic competence has been called 'code-switching' (Sešek 2007) and, in more recent literature, 'translanguaging' (e.g. García and Wei 2014). The question of the appropriate use of Bangla and English was an important consideration in the development of EIA's materials and played a significant part in the way the Programme played out in practice (see Chapters 6 and 8).

So far, the question of the kind of English that teachers seek to teach has been left unexamined. With English increasingly seen as an international language (EIL) and a lingua franca (ELF) (Young and Walsh 2010), the wisdom of referencing to any one national standard (be it British, USA or whatever) is questionable, as is the very notion of invariable models of a language. There is certainly a Bangladeshi variety of English, instanced by a thriving English language press and heard when an international language is required. If Bangladeshi students progress to using English in the workplace (one of the outcomes envisaged by the Programme), this will be the variety they encounter.

The traditional pedagogies identified in the baseline study (EIA 2009c) take an autonomous view of English and focus mainly on the English of the textbooks (curriculum English), taking no account of the kind of English specifically tailored to teaching. Communicative approaches prioritize the use of the target language, but many of EIA's teachers had a low level of proficiency. The remainder of this chapter will explore the ways in which the Programme developed teachers' proficiency alongside their pedagogy and considers the impact on student outcomes.

Gains in teachers' proficiency

Pedagogy and proficiency

This chapter is concerned with the place of 'proficiency' in a programme that set out to raise students' proficiency primarily through improving teachers' pedagogy. In light of this, the effects of the EIA Programme on teachers' proficiency were in some ways surprising.

English language proficiency assessments (EIA 2012a) were conducted with teachers at the beginning and end of the pilot presentation (2010–11), and at the end of the first presentation of Phase 3 (EIA 2014a). Data from the start of the pilot (2010) were used as the baseline. Assessments were carried out by an external agency, Trinity College London, using their Graded Examinations in Spoken English (GESE) syllabus (Trinity College London 2009). Full details of sampling and data analysis can be found in the respective research reports (EIA 2012a, 2014a), while the assessment methodology is set out by Trinity (Trinity College London 2009). The GESE scale maps to the Common European Framework of Reference (Verhelst et al. 2009), but is finer grained, with usually two GESE levels corresponding to one CEFR level (e.g. GESE Levels 2 and 3 correspond to CEFR Level A1).

English language proficiency: primary teachers

In both 2011 and 2013 the English language of the Programme's primary teachers showed statistically significant improvement. Figure 9.1 shows the comparison of these two cohorts with the baseline (EIA 2014a: 23).

In contrast to the baseline, no primary teacher failed the assessment in 2011 or 2013 with the great majority (97 per cent in 2011, 92.7 per cent in 2013) achieving Grade 2 or above. This level corresponds to the proficiency required by the Class 3 textbook.[1] In both years, more teachers achieved Grade 4 and above (44.9 per cent in 2011, 35.7 per cent in 2013), representing improvements over the baseline of 7.9 per cent and 9.2 per cent respectively. While improvements in

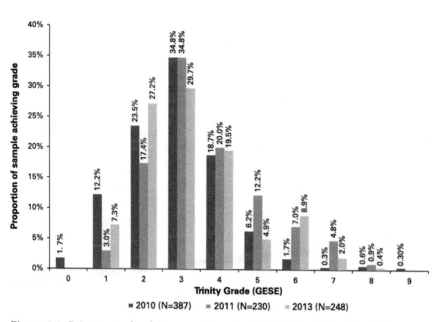

Figure 9.1 Primary teachers' EL competence in 2010, 2011 and 2013, by EL Trinity (GESE) grade

both years were statistically significant, those in 2013, with a much larger cohort, were not quite as high as those achieved in 2011.

English language proficiency: secondary teachers

The picture for secondary teachers is more complex (Figure 9.2; EIA 2014a: 27). Statistically significant improvements were registered in 2011. However, the results for 2013 showed no statistically significant difference between either the 2010 baseline (p=0.475) or the improved results of 2011 (p=0.238).

In 2011 there was a statistically significant improvement (p<0.05) across all the pass grades up to Grade 6, but this was not repeated in 2013, where the greatest improvement was in the numbers attaining at Grades 3 and 4 and in all grades above Grade 2.

Although the 2013 secondary teacher results were in part disappointing,[2] more attained at or above the grade (Grade 3) that maps to the language demands

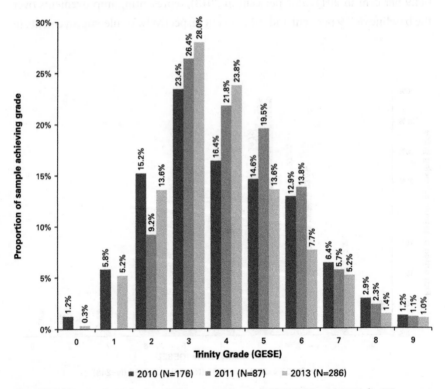

Figure 9.2 Secondary teachers' EL competence in 2010, 2011 and 2013, by EL Trinity (GESE) grade

of the first secondary textbook (Class 6), and at Grade 4, which gives access to a significant proportion of the Class 7 textbook. As will also be seen, the performance of the students who were taught by these teachers did show statistically significant improvement.

Gains in students' proficiency

The focus of this chapter has so far been on the development of teachers' English language proficiency. The question of the impact on students' learning is more difficult to answer as it is impossible, from these studies, to separate the effects of improved pedagogy from those of improved proficiency. What is clear, however, is that EIA students' proficiency *did* improve.

English language proficiency: primary students

In each year in which their proficiency was assessed, primary students showed statistically significant improvement ($p<0.01$ in each year) over the 2010 baseline (Figure 9.3).

The proportion of students passing the assessment rose from 35 per cent at the baseline to 50 per cent in 2010 and 70 per cent in 2013 and 2014. After 2010,

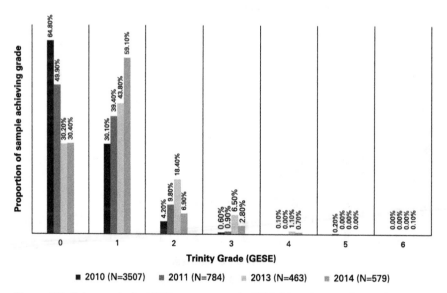

Figure 9.3 Primary students' EL competence in 2010, 2011, 2013 and 2014, by EL Trinity (GESE) grade

most students attained at Grade 1, with a steady increase in the number attaining Grade 2 falling back to 6.9 per cent in 2014, a figure still above the baseline level.

English language proficiency: secondary students

As with primary students, secondary students showed statistically significant improvements (2011 $p<0.001$; 2013 & 2014: $p<0.01$) over the 2010 baseline in each successive cohort (see Figure 9.4).

Again, progress centred on the number of students achieving any kind of a pass grade, a proportion ranging from 90 per cent in 2011 to 83 per cent in 2014. In both 2011 and 2013 the proportion attaining within the Grade range 2–7 was greater than in the baseline study, but this was not the case in 2014.

For both phases then, the major achievement was in terms of a substantial improvement in the number of students passing the assessment, while appreciable improvements at higher levels occurred in some years but not others.

The place of English in English in Action

Over the life of the Programme, EIA's prime focus has been on students' proficiency and overall the impact has been positive. There have also been improvements in teachers' proficiency and, while these might be linked to

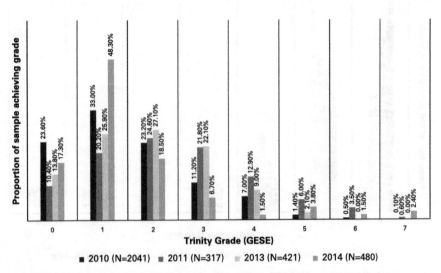

Figure 9.4 Secondary students' EL competence in 2010, 2011 and 2013, by EL Trinity (GESE) grade

specific initiatives such as English Language for Teachers (EL4T) or the 'Classroom Language' resources (see Chapter 6), one of the tenets of EIA is that language always has a context. This section examines the context in which EIA teachers experienced English. First of all, consider what happens at a cluster meeting (see Box 9.1).

Box 9.1: Inside the cluster meeting

Vignette 1: Cluster meeting 1

Azad and Mina, two teacher facilitators (TFs), have started the first day of a cluster meeting. It is 9:15 a.m. and about twenty-five teachers are present. Mina conducts the first session in English, using an ice-breaker activity from the Facilitators' Guide. The participants take part in English. They do not need to be excellent English speakers to participate and they enjoy the short interaction with their colleagues. Some look shy but they still manage to play a full part.

Next, Azad supports teachers to study Unit 1 from the Teachers' Guide and shows the link between the Guide and the audio-visual materials. Together they watch a video of a classroom activity. The presenter explains in Bangla the techniques shown, then summarizes them in English. Next, Azad asks the teachers, in small groups, to discuss (in English) the techniques, using questions given in the Teachers' Guide. The four or five teachers who usually teach English in Class 4 and 5 seem quite confident in speaking English. Azad had to explain the questions to the whole group in Bangla because most of the teachers are hesitant to use English during the group work. In the plenary, the confident English users are chosen by the group members to present their group work. Their answers are quite vague and abstract, so the TFs elicit more detail by asking questions. At one point, a member of the central EIA team, who is observing, encourages teachers to use both English and Bangla during their discussion. A few teachers who are quite proficient in English are still in favour of using only English, but many have become spontaneous and active once they know they can use Bangla.

In the next activity, teachers develop a lesson plan; they interact mostly in Bangla. This is a very practical session where they are consulting the textbook and Teachers' Guide to see how they can apply new techniques seen in the videos in their own classroom and go on to plan a lesson they will lead in English. Teachers demonstrate the activities in small groups and provide constructive feedback to each other, mostly using English, like the teacher in the video.

Next Mina plays an EL4T audio activity and teachers work in pairs following the instructions given by the audio. Teachers practise simple language that can help them use effective English in the classroom. They can see that the theme and vocabulary of the activities are similar to the content of the textbook they use in their classrooms.

During the final session of the day, Azad summarizes all the activities in English and participants share their action plans and learnings of the day in English and Bangla.

Vignette 2: Final cluster meeting

In the first session of the meeting, Mina identifies that some participants could not understand the theme of the previous unit and about five teachers could not follow their lesson plans properly. Another ten are ready to share reflections on their lessons. Both TFs try to create an environment for open discussion where teachers can share their positive or negative experiences. One teacher shares that now she feels more confident to speak in English in the classroom because she knows the frequently used classroom phrases. Her students also understand them because she uses them regularly. Last month a government high official praised her practice after observing her English class.

In this meeting, the teachers study the last few units of the Teachers' Guide. In discussions that take place after watching the videos, the extent of English use is considerable. The participants seem more confident compared to the first meeting. Their use of English is not always accurate but they are more fluent. Now they are quite comfortable in switching languages from Bangla to English. When they feel they are unable to express their opinions, they often switch back to Bangla.

Another teacher shares a recent initiative, establishing a weekly English-language club for teachers, using the EL4T materials. The teachers say they want to continue with EIA-style activities after this final meeting, so Mina asks participants to identify ways they can do so. Teachers come up with several promising ideas and plan to meet up informally.

The vignettes in Box 9.1 show that teachers experienced cluster meetings as a language-rich environment. Teachers do a lot of listening, but also a lot of talking, engaging with each other and the session's facilitators. Much, but not all, of the language used is English (there is some code-switching) and there are examples of curriculum English, classroom English (both explicitly taught and arising from planning and presenting lessons) and English used in context for the teachers' own purposes. The TFs encourage and scaffold the use of English ensuring all teachers take part and that everything is understood. Understanding is essential if the meeting is to achieve its purpose of developing teachers' understanding of pedagogy.

In fact, much in the cluster meeting embodies the principles of CLT set out in the book's *Introduction*. There is a communicative purpose to all the language used and a great deal of interaction, in which all teachers are supported to participate. Although the TFs have key themes that they emphasize in each session, the group sessions are highly participant-centred. Teachers use speaking, listening, reading and writing in a naturally integrated way, as they work together on lesson plans, for example. Correction of teachers' English was not part of the TFs' role, and certainly not correction to any Standard form. The language of cluster meetings is English as spoken in Bangladesh and, it is inevitably concentrated on language to use in or talk about classroom teaching.

Bangla is used judiciously to both support understanding and maintain participation, thereby helping develop teachers' English; the technique of explaining a video sequence in Bangla then summarizing in English has resonances with the ways in which the two languages are used together in the EIA materials.

Similarly, the EIA materials expose teachers to a great deal of English. Video materials for both phases show local teachers using English to teach and manage their classrooms in English (see Chapter 6). The classroom audio materials are mostly in English, but include some use of Bangla, especially in material for younger primary classes to scaffold understanding. The print, audio and video materials include many opportunities to read and hear English, with printed documents for secondary teachers drafted in a clear and accessible variety of Standard English. Because the English of many primary teachers was relatively weak (EIA 2009a), all primary print materials were in Bangla.

English, whose English?

A local variety of spoken English was used in all digital materials, not only to support comprehension, but also to ensure audio examples harmonized with the English used by the teacher. Primary teachers heard several minutes of recorded English in each EIA-based lesson they teach and secondary audios were exclusively in English. During Phase 2, all secondary teachers followed a Masters' level TPD course, with sessions led in English by local tutors. The majority of participants opted to complete their assignments in English.

Perhaps the most important English learning opportunity was teachers' own use of English as they taught. Numerous formal and informal observations provide evidence of teachers making effective use of English to teach and manage classes. Most teachers could draw on linguistic resources developed previously,

Table 9.1 Evidence of interaction and use of English in primary and secondary English lessons

	Teacher talk % of lesson		Student talk % of lesson		% of student talk in English	
	Primary	Secondary	Primary	Secondary	Primary	Secondary
Phase 2 (pilot) cohort 1	34	33	27	23	88	88
Phase 3 cohort 2	45	48	27	24	91	92
Phase 3 cohort 3	47	53	27	24	94	92

Sources: EIA 2010a, 2011b, 2015b

and all had the opportunity to apply the classroom language offered in print and audio form in a contextualized and purposeful way.

Systematic studies of teachers' use of English in the classroom in each phase (EIA 2010a, 2011b, 2015b) showed lessons where the majority of teacher and student talk was in English (Table 9.1). A qualitative study in Phase 2 (EIA 2011a) provided evidence of the interactive and purposeful nature of classroom talk, with students no longer spending most of their time echoing and copying as they did in the baseline classrooms (EIA 2009c).

EIA teachers reported that they enjoyed teaching English and were confident in their level of proficiency (EIA 2011c).

Learning English in action

English in Action's research suggests that progress to students' improved attainment has followed the Programme's theory of change (see Chapter 13): TPD activities have led to changed classroom practices, which in turn have led to students' improved proficiency. There is fluctuation in student outcomes over the life of the Programme, but overall, that 'results chain' holds, particularly at the lower end of competency. The picture for improvement of teacher proficiency, while generally positive is less consistent.

Teachers' proficiency is a key component of their improved pedagogy, and in their effective use of classroom language, proficiency and pedagogy are combined. Many observers, over the life of the Programme, have commented that teachers' use of English for teaching appears to be at a higher level than the Trinity assessment results suggest, and this raises questions about the suitability of applying a general assessment of English to the language of teachers. An alternative approach, considering 'English for teaching' to be an example of English for specific purposes (ESP), has been advocated (Elder 2001; Sešek 2007; Bondi and Poppi 2007).

EIA teachers experienced English in two ways. On the one hand, they had plenty of exposure to objectified, autonomous models of language – what Ellis (2007) calls 'knowledge-as-thing' – for example in the language of the textbooks, in the English of their earlier studies, and in some elements of the EIA materials. This kind of knowledge has obvious parallels with teachers' (unenacted) knowledge *about* pedagogy, discussed in Chapter 8.

On the other hand, a good deal of EIA teachers' experience of English involves using the language for dynamic engagement: with peers, EIA facilitators, students, EIA materials and the curriculum. In classroom use, teachers' proficiency is entwined with practice and is thus both subject content knowledge and pedagogical content knowledge. Rather than simply being an inert, invariant object, subject knowledge can be seen as 'emergent within complex and dynamic social systems' (Ellis 2007: 455). Ellis further contends that subject knowledge is not fixed, but a form of collective knowledge held in common by teachers and therefore can be changed. Realistically, the subject knowledge of non-native language teachers is changing all the time, as they develop personal models of the target language. Such an understanding supports EIA's adoption and acceptance of locally developing varieties of English in both materials and teacher development.

In the EIA classroom there is a place for examples of an autonomous (idealized and decontextualized) understanding of English, for example the *English for Today* textbooks, and even EIA's lists of classroom language. However, EIA's approaches to teacher development and pedagogy provide many opportunities to transform this knowledge through contextualized and purposeful interactions. It seems quite likely, for example, that the improvement in many teachers' proficiency involved bringing into active use linguistic knowledge originally rote-learnt for examinations.

Acceptance of the value of previously held understandings is in keeping with both a dynamic, contextualized view of teaching and learning and with the steps EIA took (outlined in Chapters 6 and 8) to recognize and build from context. The perceptions studies (EIA 2011c; 2014c) show how teachers retained beliefs and techniques associated with traditional pedagogies, while fully subscribing to the principles of the communicative pedagogies promoted by the Programme. This included the use of Bangla where appropriate to ensure students' full understanding (something EIA encouraged but previous CLT programmes may have discouraged) and a continuing preference for explicit grammar teaching (EIA 2014c).[3] Teachers were not asked to abandon old ways, but rather to enact their existing professional knowledge in new ways.

All this entails an approach to teacher development which requires more than a simple handover of 'all the necessary new knowledge' in a single training event. EIA's initial workshops were not an introductory lecture but the beginning of a conversation. And since that conversation was largely in English, the English of the participants was improved.

Lessons learnt

Whilst initially emphasizing English language pedagogy, EIA's approach revealed the important role of proficiency in English teacher development. Along the way, a number of valuable lessons were learnt.

The Programme's teacher development materials assumed the importance of both proficiency and pedagogy, initially catering for the two elements separately. However, in practice the close relationship between them has become very clear as has the fact that teachers have developed their competence in the two in tandem. Similar initiatives in the future would be wise to embrace the dynamic and complex nature of teacher development, for example by building on the concept of 'English for teaching' and fostering proficiency and pedagogy together. This would entail a strong focus on classroom English to accompany the development of both pedagogic knowledge and pedagogic subject knowledge.

The materials, largely in response to the baseline finding that little English was to be heard in English lessons, emphasized the need to use English as the classroom language. In practice, even though English became predominant in EIA classrooms, English and Bangla were used together in both schools and training events. Similarly, the strategy of mixing Bangla and English in the primary materials (digital and print) appears to have succeeded in ensuring understanding. It may be that the Programme could have been more forthright about the value of such an approach from its earliest days.

Some lessons have been learnt in connection with the proficiency assessments themselves. First, no suitable alternative could be found to expensive face-to-face assessments of communicative English. Costs were kept to a minimum by careful calculation of sample sizes and by using the same (2010) baseline throughout the pilot and upscaling phases. It was reasonable and realistic to assume that classroom practice and outcomes would not change significantly in schools outside the Programme, but there were demographic changes to the Programme's schools (notably an increasing emphasis on working in the poorest areas) which may have skewed results. Establishing a baseline for each cohort would have yielded more reliable results.[4]

Second, as already noted, many researchers looking at EIA classrooms perceived a gap between a teacher's assessed grade and their use of language in the classroom. It may well be that a general test of communicative English does not do justice to teachers' specialist professional language and therefore it would have been advisable for the Programme to adopt, or develop for itself, an ESP assessment based on 'English for teaching'. Chapter 11, however, argues that pressure on time and resources constituted a significant barrier to the development of such an instrument.

Teachers' perceived inadequate proficiency has been widely identified as a significant barrier to national success in English language teaching. The problem is often presented as a cycle of failure, with low numbers of linguistically competent school leavers becoming over time, lower numbers of competent language teachers producing even fewer competent school leavers in turn. English in Action has shown that it is possible to break this cycle, working from the existing capacities of local teachers. Thus, an important lesson is that teachers with relatively low proficiency can improve the performance of their students and, in the process, improve their own proficiency.

EIA was able to demonstrate significant progress from a starting point where almost two-thirds of primary students and a quarter of secondary students could not demonstrate any knowledge of English at all. It should, however, be recognized that despite some spectacular improvements in the primary phase, the resultant levels are not always high, a case in point being the final Phase 3 cohort results for secondary students. EIA's major achievement has been to raise the attainment of a very large number of students, especially improving outcomes for those who previously would have demonstrated little or no proficiency. The success of language education lies not only in raw attainment, but in the development of successful language learners. School leavers who are willing and able to develop their proficiency further will do so when required to use their English in vocational and other contexts. Improvements in attainment, although sometimes modest, together with the enthusiasm for English evidenced throughout the Programme can, it is to be hoped, go a long way towards breaking the previously dominant negative cycle.

Notes

1   To aid the interpretation of the Phase 2 proficiency results, an analysis of the *English for Today* textbooks, showing the GESE level expected to be attained by the end of each school year was undertaken by a senior Trinity College assessor.
2   The Research report (EIA 2014a) considers possible reasons, including the fact that by this stage the Programme was concentrating its efforts on relatively disadvantaged upazilas, where a baseline study may have shown lower attainment, and the small size of the secondary teacher sample.
3   Though this may be mainly a response to examination requirements.
4   The QE study (see Chapter 11) showed that, though the EIA school results were parallel to those in past cohort studies, the control group performed better than was assumed from initial baseline (EIA 2017). The result was that there were few statistically significant experimental differences between control and intervention (EIA) groups.

10

English Language Teaching

Critical Comments

Amol Padwad

Introduction

Undertaking any large-scale educational change initiative is a hugely complex and challenging process. The complexity and challenge are innately connected with a fundamental dilemma. The change process operates, or is at least expected to operate, at two levels – change in thinking and change in practice. The dilemmatic question concerns which one should lead the other. Massive system-wide teacher training programmes, which are a typical way of operationalizing change in many education systems, often focus efforts on changing the thinking and perceptions of teachers, hoping they will translate into change in practice. So, funding, time and resources are spent on 'orienting' teachers on a new policy or approach, with occasional reference to what it may mean for their classroom practice, assuming that once teachers understand the new policy or approach, they will be able to find ways and means of putting it into practice. This should not be surprising since it is easier and cheaper to conduct series of orientation sessions for teachers and tell them about what is new than actually working with them 'in the field' to evolve an understanding of the new and ways of putting it into action. (The evidence presented in Chapters 1 and 2 illustrates this in the initiatives prior to EIA.) Usually education ministries do not have as much time and resources as are necessary for the latter, which is essentially a long-term and resource-intensive process.

The EIA Programme therefore stands out primarily as different from the conventional mass-training-cum-orientation models of educational change implementation. It has clearly built on the useful insights and lessons from the shortcomings of the previous projects in Bangladesh. The comments of the teachers on the previous projects listed in Chapter 8 show how they were largely theoretically oriented, preparing teachers to talk about change rather than implement it, disconnected from the curricula and textbooks that teachers were tied to and unmindful of the local contextual realities. EIA has visibly made attempts to avoid these basic pitfalls by focusing on direct practice-based interventions, closely linked with the prescribed curriculum and textbooks and clearly situated in the local context. The capacity-building initiatives, training and classroom interventions and pedagogic orientation were built around the prescribed textbooks, which raised the chances of the proposed change being translated from training to practice. Since the training and teacher development materials largely use texts from the prescribed textbooks, teachers are able to find an immediate relevance and practical connections between them and their regular work. An important additional advantage is that the training and preparations for change are not seen by teachers as adding extra burden to their workload, a common complaint in conventional theory-oriented training programmes, but are perceived to contribute to their routine work.

One key weakness of many conventional change initiatives is that they often focus on the teacher alone, perhaps assuming that changing the teacher is enough to ensure the proposed overall change and neglecting to involve other stakeholders in the process or to target related aspects of the system for change. It is true that the teachers are pivotal change agents, but they do not work in isolation. Within the bounds of norms, policies and regulations they have little control or authority over most things and have limited voice and role in planning or decision making in the school. It is not uncommon to see even long-term and large-scale teacher training programmes or change initiatives exclusively targeting teachers without any involvement from head teachers, school managements, education officials or other figures of authority to whom teachers are subordinate. This leads to several problems. Unaware of the change plans which teachers are being prepared for (and asked to try out), head teachers and administrators do not provide adequate scope and support to them, sometimes discouraging them in their efforts to implement any change. Unaware of these plans, head teachers and administrators not only fail to see the potential gains to be made from them for the whole school, but also miss out on opportunities to monitor, support and guide change implementation to the school's benefit. One key reason why teachers go back to their old ways of working despite a long and intensive change orientation is a lack of understanding, consideration and support, especially in the school. In this scenario, the EIA Programme does extremely well to actively involve head teachers and education officials, along with teachers as partners in the change process. They are informed about the change and are trained and involved in classroom observations of the change in practice. This enables them to see not only what is being planned in terms of change, but also how it is being implemented in the classroom. The support material developed for head teachers and education officials shows that they are encouraged to take a constructive and considerate position while observing teachers' attempts at trying out new things. Potentially, such a stance will make teachers feel supported and encouraged, while opening up non-judgmental and practical ways of observing change for the observers themselves.

A key challenge in planning and implementing educational change initiatives is the status of teachers' English proficiency. Needs-analysis surveys regularly show that teachers' own English proficiency is one of their topmost concerns. The examples from East Asia (Nunan 2003) or South America, Africa and the Middle East (Wedell 2011) of poorly proficient teachers bringing extremely limited English to the classroom, thus leading to students using hardly any English, are not very different from the scenarios in the Indian subcontinent. Ironically, large-scale teacher training projects do not seem to treat this seriously, perhaps because the amount of time and resources such a treatment would normally require does not fit into their plans. Not adequately addressing the concerns about teacher proficiency eventually negatively affects the impact and sustainability of such projects.

It is therefore significant that EIA explicitly recognized teacher language proficiency as an important concern and also tried systematically to address it. There are many useful insights to gain from the way complex issues like 'what kind of proficiency is needed' and 'how its development may be integrated into the overall project work' have been handled in the EIA. Two lines of approach taken in the EIA Programme to address language proficiency issues need to be highlighted as pragmatic and sensible. The first of these relates to combining proficiency development with pedagogic improvement, rather than dealing with it as an independent matter of teacher development. This is not only practically and logistically realistic within the constraints of time, resources and priorities that projects normally work with, it is also more relevant and purposeful, and hence more impactful, than addressing proficiency per se. Setting aside for a while the questions of which kind of proficiency and how much of it is needed, it can still be said that tying up proficiency development with pedagogic improvement is an effective way of situating the former in the local context and consolidating the latter by strengthening a means of it.

The second line of approach relates to conceptualizing English proficiency more as an Education for Special Purposes (ESP) requirement than a general language enhancement need for Bangladeshi teachers. This way it becomes easier to specify the frame of operation in terms of content, material and methods of proficiency development and undertake targeted efforts towards clearer proficiency goals. Moreover, the general proficiency needs of participating teachers are likely to be much more heterogeneous than ESP needs and more challenging to address within the project. This position in EIA seems to be informed by a view, drawn from Butler (2004), that 'a lower degree of proficiency may sometimes be sufficient (Ch. 9: p. 130), and the argument of Kelly and Grenfell (2004: 49) that greater language proficiency does not automatically guarantee more effective teaching. In other words, language proficiency development in a change-project environment may be more productively focused on ESP for pedagogy than on overall general proficiency.

This, however, needs to be seen against the backdrop of the actual reports on teacher proficiency development over the lifetime of the Programme. The EIA research on teacher proficiency development (EIA 2014a) does not show hugely significant proficiency gains for teachers. However, research reports (EIA 2014b, 2015b) show a remarkable increase in the use of English by teachers (and learners) in the classroom settings. This clearly suggests that whatever may be the gains in teachers' English proficiency, there are significant gains in their confidence in using English. One may consider this as a kind of validation of the EIA stand that even lower degrees of proficiency may still be exploited to improve teaching (or at least classroom interaction in English). However, it also points to a complex issue. It seems that teachers' actual language proficiency may not by itself work as a strong influence on their classroom performance; it becomes an influential factor in combination with their perceptions of their own proficiency. In other words, besides their actual proficiency, how negatively or positively teachers perceive it determines to what extent it is going to contribute to or hamper effective teaching. This implies that an effective strategy would be to work on both improving teachers' proficiency and increasing their confidence in their proficiency (for example, by strengthening positive perceptions of it). In the EIA Programme there are some examples of this dual strategy. The cluster meetings, where teachers could risk using English in psychologically-safe environments, seem instrumental in hugely boosting teachers' confidence, while initiatives like English Language for Teachers (EL4T) and classroom language resources supported their language enhancement. Thus, it may not be wrong to expect that increased confidence should lead to teachers producing a greater quantity of English, while increased proficiency should lead to English of higher quality. The results of the perception studies (EIA 2011c and 2014c) showed that confidence improved and that more English was used in the classroom (Chapter 9).

However, some concerns about taking an ESP approach as a solution to teacher proficiency needs still remain. Such an approach should be seen as only a short-term solution to specific needs within a project framework. While it would be unrealistic to expect a teacher training project (or even a long-term change project) to work towards improving general proficiency, it would also be unreasonable to assume that achieving adequate ESP proficiency will solve all problems. 'ESP for Teaching' may seem a workable and manageable strategy from the project designers' and education authorities' perspective, but it may not be so from the teachers' viewpoint, since they may find it inadequate in the long run. Though this issue is almost un-researched, anecdotal evidence and my personal experience of working with teachers in India suggest that in many cases teachers are more concerned about their general proficiency. They also appear to show more confidence in using English required to transact their business in the classroom ('ESP for teaching') than in using it outside. In other words, they seem to be less concerned and more positive about their ESP proficiency than about general proficiency. One may hypothesize that while teachers do need and benefit from improved ESP proficiency, general proficiency is their eventual need/interest. Needs-analysis surveys rarely distinguish between the two and hence do not bring much useful information on which kind of proficiency is a greater need. In the absence of such information, it makes better sense for a project to focus on ESP proficiency improvement. But, following from the hypothesis mentioned above, it could be seen as only a stage in overall proficiency development, as a short-term situation-specific intervention aimed at specific ends, which does not undermine the value of general proficiency improvement.

There are several culturally embedded and sensitive issues which pose a challenge in a change initiative. In the context of EIA, some of them have been identified early and addressed in context-sensitive ways. One challenge was related to the tension over prioritizing between listening-speaking and reading-writing. Even though a communicative approach was fundamental to the Programme's philosophy, and developing communicative competence a crucial goal, EIA recognized the premium placed by education authorities and school administrators (as well as the high-stakes national examinations) on reading-writing and ensured that these skills were not neglected. The use of first language in English classrooms is another tricky issue mired in numerous pedagogic and socio-political myths and beliefs. The EIA approach to the role of Bangla in teaching and learning English is constructive in the sense that it seems to acknowledge the presence of Bangla not as a reconciliation with something that cannot be wished away, but as a useful resource that can be fruitfully exploited. With a risk of overstatement, EIA may be appreciated for 'decriminalizing' the use of Bangla in Bangladeshi English-language classrooms.

There are some other culturally embedded issues which it wasn't easy to properly address, as the chapters suggest. One may see, for example, some tension between local culturally rooted beliefs and practices about language teaching and learning and some of the 'modern' or 'Western' ones implicit in the Programme's principles and plans. Learner autonomy, for example, was considered desirable and was actively promoted in the Programme, although the discussion in the chapters hints that the efforts to make learners autonomous did not go much beyond group- and pair-work in classrooms. This is likely to be related to very different understandings of 'learner autonomy' from the Western and Bangladeshi perspectives. Not only is it important to reimagine the notion of learner autonomy drawing on home-grown notions of teachers and learners, built over several centuries of teaching and learning languages, it is also essential to re-examine whether learner autonomy is desirable, to what extent and of what kind. Several teachers from a similar project in Maharashtra, India, reported that their students felt disappointed after a few rounds of activities and group/pair work because 'it was all activities and no teaching' (personal communication). Many of these students would frequently report home to their parents that they had taken part in a lot of activities on the day, but no studies. Teachers, students and parents apparently felt unhappy about 'everything being left to the students and the teacher not teaching them'. It is thus quite possible that learner autonomy may have some negative shades of perception attached to it.

Apart from these, some other issues appear to have remained unaddressed for various possible reasons, which could have a strong bearing on the impact and success of the envisaged change. One issue relates to the assessment regimes and practices in Bangladesh. As acknowledged in Chapter 8, examinations, especially high-stakes national examinations, strongly influence teacher thinking and action, i.e. their plans and practice. The discussion in the chapters gives an impression that, while a considerable change in attitudes, approaches and practices in English language teaching (ELT) pedagogy was planned and expected, and a considerable investment was made to implement it, there was little corresponding change planned in the assessment regime. Though it may be appreciated that the Programme's activities were built around the prevalent textbooks and assessment patterns, in order not to be too disruptive of the established demands on teachers, they might have suffered from the limitations of a mismatching assessment regime. Including assessment in the change process was, in all probability, practically and logistically not feasible, as indicated in Chapter 12. But this yet again points to the common plight of change projects which fail to work to full potential because they (have to) leave some key systemic aspects out. Similarly, it is also often seen that change initiatives in English language teaching do not take into account teaching and learning of other subjects and languages, and work in isolation from them. Many teachers are not just teachers of English; they teach other subjects, such as social sciences, too. Similarly their students attend a variety of classes, not just English. So, it is possible that both teachers and students get very different, sometimes conflicting, kinds of experiences and messages in English and other classes. It is crucial to take into consideration how (new) approaches, policies and practices in ELT correlate with those in other subjects, and also with those in other domains like recruitment, appraisal or employment norms. It is not hard to imagine, for example, how a strong emphasis on learner-centred teaching in English classes may get watered down by heavily teacher-centric science or social studies classes. It is similarly not hard to visualize how recruitment norms (such as entry qualifications and language proficiency levels) or appraisal criteria (such as student performance in examinations or teachers' extra-curricular work) have a direct bearing on ELT policies and practices.

Conclusion

The EIA Programme had the luxury of a long lifespan of ten years, which is not common in state-supported projects. In terms of envisaging and promoting better English language teaching practices it has tried to make the best of the opportunities and resources at its disposal and to avoid the pitfalls identified from the previous projects, as Chapters 8 and 9 show. It recognized and engaged with the systemic constraints which teachers routinely face, such as the need to follow prescribed textbooks or prioritize reading-writing or train students for traditional examinations. It also took a context-sensitive and pragmatic approach on two crucial issues in ELT: teachers' own English proficiency and the role of the local languages in the classroom. The efforts to change teachers' thinking and practice in ELT have been backed by substantial material support (Teachers' Guides and notes, English enrichment resources, pedagogic resources, etc.) and affective support (cluster meetings and teacher groups). While, understandably, some aspects like assessment could not be addressed as directly as teacher thinking and classroom practice, EIA has succeeded in bringing about many tangible and intangible changes in the teaching and learning of English in Bangladeshi classrooms.

Part Four

Strategic Issues

Moving on from the details of the EIA and how the teacher development and English language teaching and learning approaches were implemented, this part of the book addresses the strategic issues of the Programme. Whatever the specific focus of any particular project whose goal is to change teaching and learning, there are at least three general requirements to ensure its success: some kind of evaluation and monitoring; a way of ensuring that the initiative of the project is sustained; and that it can show that it is good value for money. The first three chapters of this section cover these three quite different, though related elements, which brought EIA from a pilot project to an institutionalized 'programme'. First, any project, and especially one of such long duration, must show both that it is learning from its experience, through rigorous data collection and analysis, and that its outcomes are worth the funding invested. The research, evaluation and monitoring programme of EIA provided the evidence necessary to inform strategic decisions as the approach was developed phase by phase to meet the demands of increasing scale. With this increase in scale also came the development of sustainability, through embedding and institutionalizing, and this is the subject of Chapter 12, which shows how any project must work within the existing education system and with a variety of agencies to bring about a sustainable approach. Finally, increased scale cannot be achieved through a simple scaling up of costs, and Chapter 13 examines how a sustainable scaled-up programme was achieved within a value for money (VfM) framework. The question the three chapters address in their different ways is: which issues were critical for any programme that wants to institutionalize and sustain its approach?

The critical comment chapter by Ahmed Shamim (Chapter 14) examines these strategic issues in the light of his long experience of education in Bangladesh.

Part Four

Strategic Issues

11

Research, Monitoring and Evaluation (RME)

Foundational Cornerstone or Luxury Addition?

Robert McCormick and Rama Mathew

Introduction

The title of this chapter reflects the fact that RME thinking and practice within EIA changed over the life of the Programme from the work on initial needs assessments, to pilot work, and the subsequent up-scaling and institutionalization that have been discussed in earlier chapters. From these developments over time we draw out several lessons:

1. the need for RME to respond to the changing environment along the following dimensions:
   a. the EIA Programme phases over the nine years up to its institutionalization phase;
   b. the developing country context where the requirements for evaluation and monitoring have changed over time;
   c. the development of academic thinking about evaluation over time.
2. as a development project, not a research project, evaluation resources (human and financial) were a challenge to enable, for example, extensive instrument development or to conduct sufficient capacity development for Dhaka-based staff.
3. the need to match RME activity to existing capacity and hence to develop that capacity, both within country and within the EIA Open University (OU) team.

The chapter will firstly examine each of the three parts of the first lesson above, drawing out the second and third lessons as this is done. Inevitably the issues are interwoven, and hence there will be some forward and backward references.

The changing environment

Programme and RME developments

The early days

The highest priority initially for EIA was the development of a new approach to teacher in-service training and associated material for English language teaching and learning (including classroom materials). Evaluation had a lower priority because the focus was on developing and implementing new ideas as part of the Programme. The initial concern for evaluation was to find out information of use to the Project development, and hence to carry out studies of the technologies available and the situation of English language teaching and pedagogy in Bangladesh (e.g. EIA 2009h, j, f, c). Nevertheless the role of evaluation and monitoring was clear from the beginning.[1]

The bid for the Project (ABMB 2007: 91) outlined the basis for this evaluation and monitoring strategy, putting forward two measures of success, only the second of which the bid proposers thought could be measured:

1. enhanced learning;
2. changed patterns of behaviour (e.g. teaching practices; support structures within schools and between schools – their teachers and heads – and different levels of administration).

The bid stated that the actual 'evaluation strategy' would be determined during the Project, but indicated the use of: external summative evaluations (at particular milestones); a quantitative and a qualitative longitudinal school and student survey (to survey the same schools or students every year with new cohorts being added each year); quantitative longitudinal cohort studies (using the GoB, Education Management Information System for completion rates); and single action-research studies of sub-components of the Project (ABMB 2007: 96).[2]

The first RME strategy during the early period of Programme development reflected a focus on learning outcomes: 'evaluation will provide the means to assess the extent to which the Project is able to impact on people's ability to communicate in English (the project purpose)' (EIA 2009e: 2). The focus of the Programme was on the 'purpose' level of the log frame which, as Chapter 2 indicated, was developing the English language competency (ELC) of the population to improve the Bangladeshi economy. However, the role of EIA in improving English language learning in the Programme schools became more important and, despite the bid's pessimism about measuring this learning, was the subject of rigorous measurement. Although there was a clear understanding of the need to show that EIA 'works' (the bid even citing DFID on 'impact evaluation'),[3] the strategy cast its net widely in terms of what would be evaluated, including a 'wide set of studies and investigations that aim to contextualize the EIA intervention activities or to inform the development of intervention outputs' (EIA 2009e: 9).[4] Although there was no explicit discussion of the evaluation design, the basic evaluation model was a 'before' and 'after', that is, to measure 'pre-treatment' (baseline) and compare with 'post-treatment'; i.e. a cohort observational-analytic study (DFID 2013b).[5] This followed the 'results' idea set out in the log frame (a baseline set of values for indicators, then a series of milestones and targets for these indicators). As we shall show, DFID confidence in this model reduced and the requirements on EIA to move to more 'rigorous' designs increased.

Nevertheless, the 'results' idea required baseline studies, to provide both a more systematic basis for the development of the Programme and a baseline to compare the effects of the intervention, something routine in development projects of the time.

Baseline studies

The EIA baseline studies prior to the pilot year covered a variety of areas: assessment of student and teacher English language competence (EIA 2009a); motivations and attitudes to English of teachers and students (EIA 2009b); classroom practice of teachers (EIA 2009c); the demand for English language in the workplace and in post-school education (EIA 2009d); an audit of materials for teaching English in Bangladesh (EIA 2009f); an audit of the range of English language teacher training and adult provision (EIA 2009g); the technology environment in Bangladesh – infrastructure and supply and access, and familiarity and use (EIA 2009 h, j). In the situation of launching a number of extensive studies at a time when the preoccupation was with getting the Programme off the ground, the resources (human and otherwise) to develop instruments and methodologies specific for the needs of the evaluation of the Programme were limited. Thus, for example, the classroom observation (to study classroom practice) used the Teaching Quality Improvement in Secondary Education Project (TQI-SEP) approach and instrumentation.[6] This required observation of how the teacher starts and ends the lesson, the rating of various elements of the lesson, and also observations at five-minute intervals during the lesson, noting the occurrence or not of specific teacher and student behaviours (see EIA 2009c, for details). It was a generic approach not directed specifically at the English language (EL) classroom. Although some adaptations were included to remove references to irrelevant behaviours and to add 'an estimate of how much English the teacher had used during the lesson and the proportion of pupils who had the opportunity to speak English in class' (2009c: 5), there was no comprehensive measure of the use of English by the teachers and students. The full outcomes of the EIA intervention would not have been evident if the TQI-SEP approach had been repeated for the post-treatment study (its focus was, in reality, too wide). EIA was concerned to improve the nature of the pedagogy relevant to language development (e.g. the amount of use of pair and group work) and the amount of English spoken by students and teachers, as required in the log frame. The observation for this baseline study was undertaken by the English language specialists who were to be supporting teachers in the pilot (EIA Teacher Development Coordinators). The study of motivations and attitudes to English language was, on the other hand, adapted by the EIA OU team from an English-language-focused instrument with which it was familiar. A research consultant was employed to organize and conduct the field work, and carry out the analysis.

In contrast, the use of Trinity College London to undertake the assessment of spoken English, and of listening comprehension, by direct 'interviews' of students and teachers, matched exactly the expected outcomes of EIA; i.e. a focus on a communicative approach to English teaching and learning (as explained in earlier chapters). The problem became the relatively high costs and the logistics of repeating it at the end of the pilot and for subsequent cohorts of teachers who underwent training.

As with the other aspects of the Programme at the time, the political and social unrest restricted the samples that could be used (to Dhaka and surrounding areas) in the baselines, which continually proved challenging in enabling comparisons with the post-intervention situation and across the years of the Programme. In the case of the baseline studies of classroom practice and ELC, this meant that additional studies had to be conducted to try to correct the sample biases.

The pilot

Before the materials were finalized for this stage, some testing of them had been carried out (developmental testing) along with such things as checking the translations of Bangla recordings in the audio-visual material. Government delays in the implementation of the pilot meant that a start had to be made in

2009 in the Under-privileged Children's Educational Programmes' (UCEP) schools to gain some experience of the materials and teacher training approach (Chapter 12).

The initial preoccupation with implementation of the EIA Programme led to new 'baseline' data being collected four months into the pilot using a new classroom observation schedule to reflect the English learning classroom, an issue for making future comparisons (as we will show). Some of the normal steps of instrument trial and analysis were reduced. The EIA teacher facilitators (TFs), who were local and relatively skilled in the needs of EIA, were trained to use this observation schedule.[7]

Other instruments were developed to investigate the attitudes and perceived behaviours of students and teachers towards the EIA approach (rather than the general attitudes and motivations towards English), again, at a stage that did not enable a baseline to be established (EIA 2011c). One of the important aspects of the 'perceptions' study was what it was able to reveal about the conflicts between teachers' practice and beliefs, the importance of which Pedder articulated in Chapter 7. It showed, for example, that despite teachers' agreeing with EIA's communicative approach to grammar (teaching it only in context), they wanted to explicitly teach it as a 'subject' in itself.[8] In addition, a qualitative element was added to this study by way of interviews with teachers and focus group discussions with primary and secondary school students (EIA 2009c). The RME strategy overall then focused on the needs for 'results' evidence (for the log frame milestones and targets) to match the resources available, and hence de-emphasized some of the more 'research-oriented' studies.

The end-line evaluation on completion of the pilot (post-treatment study) involved the repeat of the English language competence (ELC) assessment and the newly developed classroom practice observation (at that time at twelve to sixteen months of the intervention).[9] A longer-term solution to data collection was created with the Programme's partnership with the University of Dhaka, Institute of Education and Research (IER). Such an arrangement allowed the IER students to learn about research methods and conduct their own individual studies, while at the same time they were provided with experience of fieldwork under the supervision of EIA. This represented significant capacity building in terms of the numbers and levels of training that, in later years, extended beyond data collection to include data analysis and reporting. (In addition, these MPhil students were used for studies of EIA teacher and student lives; see later in this chapter.)

Thus, by the end of the pilot well into 2011, there were substantial data on improvements in ELC, the nature of classroom practice (in the early stages, and at the end of the treatment), and a snapshot of perceptions at the end of the treatment. Earlier chapters have indicated the results of these studies (EIA 2010a; 2011b, c; 2012a), so here the focus will be on the methodological issue of comparison with the baselines and the effective 'new' baselines they formed. We have already indicated the challenges of the baseline studies (sample issues caused by restricted access to areas of Bangladesh; instruments not being ideal and requiring reworking). Although the ELC baseline was seen as sound, the measures of classroom practice were less sound in terms of validity (as the link with the evaluation of EL teaching and learning was insufficient). The attempt to re-establish a baseline for the observation of practice with a more appropriate instrument, meant that it was three to four months into the treatment and hence, when compared to the end-of-treatment observations, there was little change. Thus the comparison for classroom practice had to be with the original 2009 baseline (EIA 2009c), which precluded statistical comparisons because it used a different observation schedule.[10]

The design of a programme of evaluation and monitoring that could be ongoing was then envisaged, not just to establish the outcomes of the Programme at the end of the pilot (after some sixteen months), but to prepare for the up-scaled 'versions' of the Programme that would enable the reproduction of the findings of the pilot in subsequent years, as explained below.

Up-scaling and the need for evidence

Evaluation evidence

The pilot had shown that the Programme worked when the OU team were in direct contact with those supporting teachers (including national EL experts). But as scale increased, this moved to TFs supporting teachers directly, with much less intervention by EIA central staff (OU and Cambridge Education), and hence the need to evaluate how successful the Programme was with this new condition, as well as to explore any new elements required in the scaled-up intervention (e.g. revised video). Some of this was done by monitoring. As noted earlier, the evaluation approach had to ensure that each cohort could achieve the same end-of-treatment outcomes as those in the pilot: thus to show that, even with an increased scale (i.e. changes from 700 to 4,000 teachers and then to 8,000 teachers), the same levels of classroom talk and ELC had to be achieved. This acted as a 'health check' for each cohort (i.e. just a post-treatment study), rather than a pre- and post-treatment model of evaluation for each cohort (as with the pilot). This assumed the baseline would not change over time; not unreasonable as there had been little change in levels of English and classroom practice over a long period of time prior to EIA (Kraft et al. 2009), including during the concurrent Second Primary Education Development Programme (PEDP II).[11] Also pre- and post-treatment studies each year could not be sustained within the budget, nor supported by the IER students. Overall this was not altogether a sound rationale, as the original baselines were not perfect (as has been indicated), neither in terms of samples being truly representative of the Bangladeshi populations of teachers and students, nor the differences in instruments used (for classroom practice) and hence the lack of statistical comparisons. Nevertheless, it was obvious from reactions to presentations of the evidence to government and NGO audiences in Bangladesh (Stakeholder meeting, March 2011) that EIA had established 'robust' evidence to show changes, which reflected pre- and post-treatment learning outcome performance, seen as significant progress for evaluation in the 'development education project' world.

But things were to change, as DFID responses to the Global Monitoring Report of Millennium Development Goals were indicating; something we will shortly examine.

Monitoring evidence

As EIA scaled up, there was a reliance on monitoring evidence. From late 2010 a quality assurance (QA) system was introduced, to improve the quality of EIA activities (EIA 2010b). This involved all those delivering EIA activities in collecting data (e.g. from Cluster Meeting participants), making sense of that evidence and taking action if appropriate. This was ambitious and not altogether successful in the latter two aspects. For example, in Cluster Meetings (CMs) participants would complete a simple questionnaire to rate whether the objectives were met, whether they felt they could use the EIA activities from the CM in their classrooms, the helpfulness of the sessions, and being able to share views with other teachers. The TFs running the CMs then tallied the responses to identify problems to be addressed, before passing on the information to the EIA core trainers (CTs). These issues could be discussed at quarterly meetings attended by both the TFs and the CTs. Central collection of data allowed system problems to be detected and suitable action taken. Well, that was the theory! In practice it was difficult for core trainers to understand quality assurance and to be confident to encourage teacher facilitators to do it. The result was that it was just a 'monitoring' data-collection exercise, with a focus on central data analysis and reporting. Action was only taken centrally and, inevitably, not in a timely fashion. Nevertheless, the system produced very useful and regular data, as Chapters 5 and 8 have shown. As part of the scaling up, Upazila Education Officers (UEOs) were required to visit classrooms and use a 'classroom use' observation form (see Chapter 12), rather than CTs doing so (as was true initially).

An additional monitoring instrument used a form similar to that advocated by Pedder (Chapter 7) to investigate the amount of use of various elements of the EIA package (e.g. the video material) in teachers' learning and practice and compared it with how important teachers thought these elements were (i.e. how much they valued them). This was effectively a low-level investigation of the practice-belief differences of teachers in relation to the EIA approach.[12]

To cope with scaling up, EIA in the latter years moved to divisional teams, who needed to understand how the Programme was running, and plan local responses. It was also important to share information, experiences and action plans across divisions and the Programme, to get a holistic picture and learn together. A *review* ➜ *feedback* ➜ *revision* process was activated in every division on a regular basis, leading to improvement in each division. By 'making meaning' of the evidence, all those involved (including UEOs) took 'ownership' and responsibility, as opposed to just passing on evaluation data for the central RME staff to analyse. This was problematic on at least two counts. First the core trainer team was overworked and saw this work as 'extra' and RME staff's responsibility. Second, RME staff were seen as 'outsiders', who did not seem to value insider-oriented evaluation (i.e. that done for insiders' benefit). Capacity-building of the CT team in this model remained an unfulfilled objective.

The role of qualitative studies

Throughout the life of the Programme there were qualitative studies that: complemented the quantitative elements (e.g. classroom practice study using qualitative observation and analysis methods focusing on English language teaching strategies; EIA 2011a); explored new conditions (studies of new elements of the EIA Programme after the pilot; EIA 2014d); were intended to be longitudinal (teacher and student lives; EIA 2012b); and gave EIA teachers a voice in the research. These aimed to overcome the limitations of the quantitative studies and provide a methodological 'balance' to the picture emerging from the RME work. The teacher and student lives were initially seen as longitudinal studies (i.e. following the same teachers and students over a period of time), but the curtailment of much of the qualitative work towards the end of the pilot, to focus on 'results', meant that this work was shelved. However, the work on teacher voice did take place (see the *Final Reflections* chapter), though it took time to come to fruition.

The work leading to a Teachers' Voice conference came from a human rights perspective (as opposed to a human capital perspective) and focused on teacher professionalism and teacher agency, something argued for in Chapter 4. In this, the following questions are relevant:

1. did teachers have adequate opportunities to confront (and contest) held beliefs and practices and to 'experiment' with new ideas in the classroom?[13]
2. had they been enabled to articulate, reflect on and share with others what the experience of the Programme had been for them?
3. had we provided an opportunity for a bottom-up, grass-roots approach to more holistic and meaningful change?

For this to happen, EIA needed to get teachers to 'tell their story in their own words'. Teachers documenting and narrating their understanding of what the Programme meant for them helped EIA understand their perspective from the 'inside', and gave them a voice and ownership that helped to sustain learning from the Programme.[14] The resulting activity will be examined in Chapter 15, as an indication of life after the 'project'.

Changes in donor views on evaluation

Pre- and post-testing

As noted earlier, in the log frame of 2010, the focus was on 'purpose' levels ('outcome' level as this became), which included improvements in English language competence of the Bangladeshi school population of teachers and students. The actual improvements in the EIA treatment schools were treated as 'outputs', expressed as the *reach* of the Programme (numbers of students and teachers), *practice* improvements (e.g. amount of classroom talk and amount in English) and *English language competence* improvements. As indicated in the previous section, to judge the effectiveness of classroom practice, the aim was to reach particular levels of student classroom talk (in total and in English) as a result of the EIA intervention. For ELC, particular levels of performance were set for specified increased percentages of teachers and students to reach at the post-treatment assessment above the baseline (e.g. for primary teachers, an increase of 10 per cent reaching Trinity Graded Examinations in Spoken English level 2 and above; see Chapter 9 for an explanation of these assessments).

All of the evaluation reports, however, included statistical comparisons of the post-treatment measures of classroom and ELC assessments with the assumed baselines (whether the original 2009 one for ELC or the pilot 'early treatment' observations in June 2010 for CP; the latter 4 months into the EIA intervention). This effectively was taken as the pre- and post-treatment model, though strictly it was not this beyond the pilot year.

At the end of 2011 DFID seemed happy with the evidence being produced, as witnessed by the Head of Business Development[15] at the OU reporting to the Vice-Chancellor on a recent visit to EIA:

> DFID representatives attended the strategy meeting and they said it was the most innovative programme within the whole of DFID, and the most senior person from DFID told us that the research, monitoring and evaluation was the most robust, rigorous and comprehensive produced in any DFID programme.
>
> email 14 December 2011

However, such DFID responses later became more cautious as its staff sought to 'raise the bar' of RME performance.

The role of different individual DIFID education advisors varied over the life of the Programme. By the latter part of 2013 (the second cohort of EIA), DFID wanted stronger evidence of learning outcomes, through an experimental approach such as a randomized control trial (RCT). RCTs require matched control and treatment groups through randomized allocation of schools to these groups, which undergo pre- and post-treatment assessment and observations, to establish whether the treatment (EIA) has a significant effect over the counterfactual (i.e. no treatment).

Concerns for learning outcomes

Chapter 4 has already examined the international concern with the quality of education that resulted in a focus on improving student learning outcomes. DFID had signalled such a concern in its strategy document of 2010 (DFID 2010), albeit in the context of being a means to an end (e.g. of economic benefit). This document published guidance on measuring of learning outcomes; a later position paper on improving learning stated that the 'focus on learning runs throughout DFID's work in education' and that this 'focus on learning does provide a clear measurable indicator of education quality and impact' (DFID

2013a: 3). It noted, however, that 'robust evidence on what works to improve learning remains limited by a lack of good measures, available data and sound research and evaluation' (DFID 2013a: 4). As EIA was able to show learning outcome improvements it led to EIA emphasising them in the log frame and, in 2014, a move of them up from output to outcome level (upon which EIA is ultimately judged), even suggesting learning outcomes at impact level (not implemented).[16]

The international focus on learning outcomes was manifest in DFID policy, for example: in its support for the Strategic Impact Evaluation Fund (SIEF); the £20 million ESRC-DFID Raising Learning Outcomes Research Programme.[17] This changing climate, welcomed by the EIA team, combined with particular views about the nature of evidence and the experimental studies that DFID in Bangladesh came to advocate.

Experimental approaches become fashionable

By 2013, evaluation in the development community was moving to experimental approaches, with DFID education advisors in Bangladesh interested in EIA conducting such an exercise. This led to a request for a randomized control trial (RCT), although as indicated earlier, the 2014 AR pointed to a quasi-experimental study.[18] Informal conversations with the 2014 AR team indicated that DFID staff were being sent on courses with J-PAL,[19] and DFID-supported 3ei, a similar kind of organization.[20] Much of this was promoted almost as a 'new enlightenment' to the field of educational evaluation, despite the long history of controversy in this field, as the next section will show.

Changes in the field of evaluation

Many of these discussions have also occurred a number of times over the years in the general field of evaluation. Here we examine these, to indicate 'there is nothing new under the sun' and that new generations of evaluators and policy-makers do not seem to learn from previous ones. In education, several phases of experimental approaches (e.g. RCTs) and reactions to them have taken place over the years.

In the 1970s, it was argued that experimental approaches (then referred to as the 'agricultural-botany' approach, i.e. an RCT, reflecting its origin) would not inform those who adopted a new project's methods. Illuminative evaluation was proposed to qualitatively examine the interaction of a 'treatment' and the environment (context) in which it operated (Parlett and Hamilton 1972). There were equally criticisms of this approach, and the argument and discussion concerning the strengths of both approaches, were re-enacted thirty years later.

In the early 2000s, there was a 'counter-attack' to the prevailing approaches in education from the US Department of Education, which decided Federal money could be used to fund only RCTs, to determine 'what works' (DoE 2002). This drew a large negative response from the educational research community (e.g. Berliner 2002; Cobb et al. 2003) with counter-arguments (Slavin 2002) from those advocating experimental approaches. This controversy was in the context of funding bodies' control of research; for evaluation the control by donors is even stronger as they are focused on results and, for the likes of DFID, with 'impact'.

Using the same watchwords of 'what works', DFID's policy on evaluation another decade later, saw rigorous evaluation that 'enables DFID to test, innovate and scale up' (DFID 2013c: 2). In the push for both 'impact evaluation' and robust evidence DFID seemed to be favouring RCTs, though it recognized the role of qualitative evaluation (e.g. DFID 2013b). In a working paper for DFID, Woolcock (2013) argues that RCTs are often seen as the 'gold standard' for evaluation evidence,[21] but he advocates the use of case studies in evaluation, to enable the context to be represented and scaling up problems to be understood. This is reminiscent of the 'illuminative approach', which often resulted in case studies. Thus, the kind of approach that DFID promotes in relation to experimental approaches (impact evaluation) may not help in this desire to 'improve' interventions, something recognized by an EIA Annual Review (AR) in 2015 (DFID 2015). From the changing discourse with DFID (including the personal emphasis of its advisors), and an awareness of the history of controversy, it was difficult for EIA to steer a way through, and to plan evaluations that would satisfy DFID (and its AR teams), particularly within the finance available.

Despite the advocacy and predominance of RCTs within the development education evaluation world, worries remain, many that echo the earlier discussions. Fundamental challenges to 'generalizability' exist. Evaluation is often pushed to provide a 'generalizable result' independent of context, for which randomization is seen as central in RCTs. But such randomization ignores the importance of context, as Bold et al. (2013) demonstrated. Pawson and Tilley (1997) mounted a convincing critique of RCTs, similarly arguing for the importance of context: 'causal outcomes follow from mechanism acting in contexts' (Pawson and Tilley 1997: 58).

In the next section we examine more directly how EIA tried to respond to the changing conditions over time, both those within the Project and those outside it.

The changing environment and the impact on the EIA evaluation

The account of the evolution of the RME component of EIA, and the changes and pressures on it, resulted in changes in the RME strategy over the years, which can be roughly summarized as:

- in the pilot phase (first cohort, 2010–11), establishing baseline measures (ELC, classroom practice and perceptions of English) and measuring these again at intermediate milestones and at the end of the Programme, while at the same time establishing the Programme, producing the materials and approaches, and training local and national staff.
- in subsequent years, rationalizing the range of studies with more effective monitoring, and evaluation limited to cohort testing, and a focus on checking that outcomes at scale were the same as for the pilot (i.e. not just comparing against baseline).
- pressure from DFID to show EIA's economic benefits, but also a more definitive outcome evaluation based on a pre-test/post-test study of one cohort (operating at scale) especially for learning outcomes. At the same time AR recognition that EIA was producing good outcome evidence (e.g. student ELC improvements).
- finally, in the institutionalization phase (2015–16), pressure from DFID for experimental evidence of the EIA outcomes, resulting in a quasi-experimental study.

There was also advice and recommendations of the AR teams over the years with a more variable set of pressures. Throughout there was a concern for dissemination, particularly recognizing the importance EIA was having in the international discourse (as an example of a successful project with good evidence, as Chapter 4 implies). In the narrative of the 2014 AR report, but not in the recommendations, the following was noted:

> In general, a limitation of EiA [*sic*] is the lack of a counterfactual or a quasi-experimental design. This could be described as a 'legacy' issue – when EiA was being developed, there was less focus on the need for a counterfactual. Strength of evidence within education interventions has been a rapidly growing field over the last ten years, for example, through the work of the 3ie initiative. However,

the lack of a counterfactual makes it difficult to fully attribute pupils' English language learning gains to the EiA intervention.

DFID 2014: 4

This led to an EIA request to DFID to fund a quasi-experimental study for the year 2015–16, the penultimate year of the Programme. (This was problematic, as at this stage the Government of Bangladesh was implementing much of the Programme and the model had changed from earlier years when EIA was the prime implementer.) The limitations in funds restricted the sample, especially with little room for teacher attrition within the study. The implementation resulted in sampling problems (60–80 per cent of planned samples), contamination of the control group, and limited intervention time caused by political and social unrest. This resulted in little measurable effect size (EIA 2017),[22] meaning that there was a marginal return in conducting the study.

Reflecting on the change in the environment for EIA, both locally and internationally, it may be that the RME team should have been more responsive at an earlier stage to the possibility of conducting an experimental study. The limitations of funds and the required change in the evaluation strategy were part of the resistance to this. Had it been done earlier, some of the technical issues noted above could have been avoided (except for the continued unrest in the country), but in part the resistance was because it seemed an unreasonable demand on a programme evaluation.

The Programme, as a long-term endeavour, was working in a constantly changing environment of views about evaluation and its role in providing measures of efficacy and hence if it was a worthwhile investment. In addition, under these conditions, to provide such evidence of use to the Programme, and to the 'world' more generally, was indeed demanding for a programme evaluation, as opposed to a separately funded research study. Despite this challenge, and set against the kind of evidence that existed internationally for projects, there can be no doubt that EIA made a significant contribution to the evidence base, as Chapter 4 illustrates.

Notes

1　As will become evident later, 'evaluation' is geared to establishing whether a programme is effective over a long term of one or more years, whereas 'monitoring' attempts to provide quick and relatively crude information to help the programme improve as it progresses from month to month.

2 Qualitative studies gather information that is not in a numerical form; for example, diary accounts, open-ended questionnaires, unstructured interviews and unstructured observations. Qualitative studies are typically descriptive or interpretative and as such are harder to compare, contrast and aggregate than quantitative studies.

3 Such an approach considers that any changes (e.g. in student ELC) can be attributed to the Programme, with improvements in ELC being a measure of the effectiveness of the Programme.

4 These elements are part of the reason that 'research' is included with evaluation and monitoring (RME), but also to indicate the approach to ensuring quality and sustainability of the Programme (ABMB, 2007: 88), not least through the rigour of the methods employed.

5 The two terms, 'treatment' and 'intervention', are used interchangeably.

6 https://www.adb.org/projects/26061–013/main#project-documents (accessed 31 October 2017).

7 Designed to minimize the amount of judgement to be undertaken by the TF by focusing upon specific behaviours (who was talking, in what language).

8 Part of this conflict can be explained by the requirements of the examination system.

9 The range of months reflected the different phasing of school and public examinations in primary and secondary schools.

10 For statistical comparisons, the instruments should be identical (at least for the specific elements that are compared).

11 The quasi-experimental study done in 2015 (see a later section) confirmed this assumption.

12 It did not, however, investigate specific EL teaching and learning issues where conflicts might occur; this was done indirectly in the attitude studies (EIA 2011c & 2014c).

13 Again these are the issues that Pedder was calling for (Chapter 7) in asking for practice–belief conflicts to be confronted.

14 http://eiabd.com/tvc.html (accessed 30 October 2017).

15 The department responsible for the International Development Office that administered EIA within the OU.

16 Subsequently the Teacher Development Programme in Nigeria (2012), using the same model as EIA, put learning outcomes at impact level.

17 http://www.esrc.ac.uk/research/international-research/international-development/ esrc-dfid-raising-learning-outcomes-in-education-systems-research-programme/ (accessed 30 October 2017).

18 A quasi-experimental approach compares control and treatment groups, but the control is chosen to match a sample of the treatment group. An RCT is similar except that matched control and treatment groups are achieved through randomized sampling of which schools receive the treatment and which do not (i.e. the control

group); the GoB could therefore not be involved in which schools to include in EIA, something that was politically difficult.

19 Abdul Latif Jameel Poverty Action Lab (J-PAL), based in MIT, has a strong economics disciplinary approach to research methodology with a focus on RCTs: https://www.povertyactionlab.org/ (accessed 30 October 2017).

20 International Initiative for Impact Evaluations: http://www.3ieimpact.org/en/ (accessed 30 October 2017).

21 Not a case advocated explicitly by the DFID documents cited above, where the criterion of 'appropriateness of the design' is valued, with experimental studies to reveal causality, and observational studies to explain this causality.

22 Statistically there was no 'difference in differences' between the control and treatment groups on the main measures of ELC and classroom practice.

12

Ensuring Sustainability

Collective Ownership, from Project Implementation to Institutionalization

Sharmistha Das and Marc van der Stouwe

Introduction

UNESCO declared the period 2005–14 to be the decade of Education for Sustainable Development (ESD) (UNESCO 2017). The objectives of ESD required that learners be empowered to take informed and responsible decisions, while its closing Aichi Nagoya Declaration explicitly emphasized the empowerment of learners and the importance of systemic thinking and called on governments to pay special attention to:

> ... system-wide and holistic approaches and multi-stakeholder cooperation and partnerships between actors of the education sector, private sector, civil society and those working in various areas of sustainable development.[1]

It goes on to make specific reference to the role of teacher development in ensuring sustainable development. The principles and objectives of the ESD are clearly reflected in the Sustainable Development Goals (SDGs) that were adopted in 2015. SDG 4 ('Ensure inclusive and equitable quality education and promote lifelong learning opportunities for all'; UNESCO 2017: 6) in particular, implies both learner empowerment and education systems should be strengthened for sustainability. SDG Target 4.7 specifically addresses sustainable development issues that were emphasized throughout the ESD initiative.

Despite the progress made, the ESD decade also observed a disconnect between the aim of education for sustainable development and the way education and training initiatives are designed and implemented (King 2007). Intervention programmes that supply ad hoc quick fixes to raise academic results without an accompanying strategy for building the education system's capacity, through the institutionalization of their innovations, provide a good example of this disconnect. Moreover, even where capacity-building does feature in the design, and large-scale practices are collectively owned and sustainable, quality may still be an issue. To ensure effective and lasting outcomes, guiding principles and a framework for practice, on the one hand, and flexibility of approach on the other, are essential elements. Working in partnership with all relevant organizations, and ensuring that the programme design is suitable to the local and national context, are equally indispensable. Without these elements, even interventions that make a measurable impact during their lifetime risk leaving little trace after only a few years (Hamid and Baldauf 2008; Hamid and Erling 2016).

In the light of the experience of the primary and secondary education sectors in Bangladesh, contextual relevance and sustainability were vital considerations in the evolving design of the EIA Programme. This chapter will provide an account of how EIA worked towards sustainability through collaborative work at many levels and with numerous institutions, seeking to embed EIA approaches and practices within existing government systems. It will also present how both successes and challenges resulted in rich collective learning related to the question of sustainability.

EIA's approach to sustainability

In its *Institutionalization & Sustainability Strategy* (EIA 2012d), the Programme agreed a number of terms and definitions to ensure clear communication with all stakeholders. The terms in Table 12.1 illustrate key aspects of the Programme's approach to sustainability.

EIA's four-phase model (see the Introduction) was designed with sustainability in mind, with activities determined by phase-specific sustainability strategies; sustainability was not something that could be left until the institutionalization phase. Working towards sustainability, while testing an innovation during piloting, is very different from finding ways to institutionalize proven solutions at scale, and each phase had different needs in terms of expertise and skills. The Programme therefore took a flexible approach to implementation, allowing continuous realignment with contextual changes and developments, for example, changes in the English language textbook. Government representatives were informed and involved right from the beginning.

Table 12.1 Definitions adapted from the EIA Institutionalization and Sustainability Strategy 2012

Sustainability:	'The capacity to endure.' In project terms this means ensuring that interventions started under the project can be continued without external support after the life of the project. Technical sustainability means that the actors involved in the interventions will have the ownership and capacity to continue services at appropriate levels of quality. Financial sustainability means the products or services provided are affordable for the intended beneficiaries and remain so after the termination of project funding.
Embedding:	'Inserted as an integral part of a surrounding whole.' In project terms: making sure that the interventions are a full part of existing processes, mechanisms, systems and institutions, rather than implemented as separate or parallel interventions.
Institutionalization:	'Officially placed in or committed to one or more specialized institutions.' Institutionalization is part of embedding, but with a special focus on embedding within existing institutions. It is about making sure that the interventions started by the project are fully owned and continued by the formal institutions of the Government of Bangladesh.
Capacity building:	The process of developing technical skills and institutional capability in a development context to enable the individuals working for these institutions to implement and sustain the services to be provided in a particular area of work independently beyond the lifetime of the project.
Partnership:	Established formal relationships with key institutions and personnel intended to achieve identified purposes with regard to specific objectives.

Source: EIA 2012d

Early in the Programme's life it was necessary to settle the 'what' question: what is it that will need to be sustained and embedded within existing systems? There was ready agreement that it was not the apparatus of EIA as a programme that would need to be sustained, but rather its approaches, methods and techniques that would need to be embedded in the mainstream classrooms and the government's teacher professional development (TPD) programmes. It followed, therefore, that interventions initiated by the Programme needed to be adopted and absorbed within the government and other (predominantly partner non-government organizations (NGOs)) institutions' structures and regular practices. Sustainability is about ensuring that the proven effective practices of an intervention can continue beyond its finite lifetime.

Successive sustainability strategies were linked to the major Programme elements, namely (i) TPD, (ii) materials development and (iii) research, monitoring and evaluation (RME). The Institutionalization and Sustainability (I&S) strategy identified core changes to be achieved within each of these domains.

Another question was where these project-initiated activities were likely to be located; what would be their new 'institutional home'? Answering this question needed to take into account that, within complex programmes, such transfer of ownership may happen at many levels, and the project identified three main ones at which to work: the classroom, where the teaching activities happen; the school, where teachers meet and support each other as well as those of surrounding support systems from cluster meetings and education officers; and the wider education system (Cambridge Education 2016).[2] Within the Government of Bangladesh (GoB) education system, EIA needed to respond to the specific needs of many levels of government (municipality, sub-district/upazila, district, division and central level), and with two education ministries and various managerial and technical departments and institutions, which have overlapping responsibilities. It was thus not an easy task for the project to determine strategies that would be equally applicable and well received by the various institutions.

As a discrete project under the Primary Education Development Programme (PEDP),[3] EIA found itself placed as both insider and outsider. It was a part of the education sector, but also had space to operate independently. For the pilot phase, DFID decided to test the new model of TPD at arm's length from the government, with the intention to subsequently 'sell a model that had proven to work' to the GoB. This both allowed EIA to develop and modify the model independently, and stressed the importance of gathering evidence in order to demonstrate to the government approaches and practices that brought visible, documented changes in the classroom. However, GoB maintained an essential role during piloting: its full approval was required for all the activities in government schools and EIA continuously engaged with GoB stakeholders at different levels to discuss progress. Because of the risk of bureaucratic delay during the pilot phase, work in government schools was supplemented by work in the schools of partner NGOs – Under-privileged Children's Educational Programmes (UCEP) and Friends In Village Development in Bangladesh (FIVDB). This meant that some very valuable early trialling could be undertaken before the Programme was able to launch in government schools (Shohel and Banks 2010; Shohel and Power 2010).

Shifting from a project mode of implementation carried the risk that the positive impact experienced at school level might be diluted or even negated in the move to an institutional mode, where institutions responsible for taking ownership may not have the supportive culture needed to sustain the innovations (Bold et al. 2013). This placed an onus on EIA staff to lobby and advocate for change effectively, as well as to develop a range of effective approaches to build the relevant capacity of the government institutions and staff. To deal with the risk that such an approach may not be fully successful, EIA's first I&S strategy included a 'two-route scenario', with a second route based on the creation of a 'bottom-up' demand for change in English language learning and practices by reaching – and enthusing – as many teachers and students about the EIA innovations as possible. Evidence of such grass-roots demand came from non-EIA localities where head teachers, Upazila Education Officers (UEOs) and other local education officials requested access to EIA materials and training.

As the above discussion shows, EIA's key approaches to sustainability were:

- in-built flexibility of the project design with scope for innovation at any point of implementation;
- ensuring key stakeholders at multiple levels felt ownership of the Programme activities;
- focusing on the approaches and principles of EIA rather than the project as a 'set design';
- combining top-down and bottom-up approaches within a multi-agency and multi-layered system;
- capacity-building of personnel in partnership with key stakeholders.

The remainder of the chapter will discuss and highlight how the sustainability approaches were operationalized in the EIA Programme during the period 2008–2017, as it moved from project to institutional mode. It will provide illustrations of the ways in which EIA, the government and NGO stakeholders engaged with the continuing processes of sustainability and institutionalization. It will also look at the degree of ownership felt by Bangladeshi institutions, the different roles taken by EIA project staff and the capacity development mechanisms established.

Sustainability in action

An analysis of selected EIA sustainability efforts that are part of the overall Programme experience is given in this section, within the context of the three fields of activity identified above: (i) TPD; (ii) materials development; and (iii) RME. Taking lessons from these experiences, in the last section of this chapter, a number of critical factors will be identified for the successful post-project sustainability of a complex and large-scale education programme.

Teachers' professional development

The TPD model, including the support structure and materials, were trialled and updated on the basis of experience gathered over successive phases. Interventions following a school-focused teacher development approach entailed a strong emphasis on capacity-development programmes for all personnel involved at the school level (head teacher and two teachers in each school) and those supporting the school (EOs, Upazila Resource Centre Instructors and others). These were run directly by the Programme. However, this intensive support and focus on capacity building in project mode developed into an institutional mode as direct project support diminished and government stakeholders' ownership increased. It was planned that, during the Institutionalization phase (Phase 4), a large number of teachers would be reached by EIA entirely through the government system. EIA TPD activities needed, therefore, to be embedded in the mainstream in-service programme and accordingly, capacities of the relevant personnel were developed.

EIA's independent stance during the pilot phase (Phase 2) had some unwanted consequences. Although a government project[4] with an effective model of TPD, EIA was not invited to contribute to the development of English Subject-based Training (SbT) (the existing in-service provision) until 2012, when the manual was fully developed and Programme staff could only take a reviewing role. At this later stage, significant advocacy and collaborative work was needed in order to ensure specific techniques, methods and activities and associated audio and video assets were embedded in the English SbT manual. This manual was used as the basis of capacity development of the government trainers and, at this advanced stage of development, EIA was not in a position to challenge the 'cascade' principle (discussed in Chapter 4) underlying it. Nonetheless it was important to work with the government system, even if it meant compromising on an important principle. More positively, at around the same time, it was encouraging to see that, in many upazilas, EIA teacher facilitators (TFs) were selected as government trainers, since this contributed to sustainability by increasing the number of competent trainers, experienced in effective school-based TPD, working in the system.

The gradual rapprochement between EIA and GoB institutions led ultimately to significant institutionalization of the former's TPD approach. By the final year of the project, the value of EIA's TPD work was recognized and Programme staff invited to contribute directly to the development of SbT materials for English teachers.

In contrast to the SbT case, those in government responsible for initial teacher education were quicker to recognize EIA's achievements and invited the Programme to work with the National Academy for Primary Education (NAPE) to develop a new initial teacher education programme, the Diploma in Primary Education (DPEd), which was intended for all beginner teachers in the country. During Phases 2 and 3, EIA made a major contribution to the development of the DPEd Framework and its materials for training in English proficiency and pedagogy. Having cohorts of teachers trained in learner-centred pedagogies entering the government system every year was expected to help to ensure the sustainability of EIA's impact. This multiple-donor-funded initiative relied on complex partnerships, and EIA worked successfully with NAPE, the Japan International Cooperation agency (JICA), UNICEF and other members of the donor consortium. However, agreement over approaches to generic (rather than English-only) pedagogy varied at the level of the individuals working directly on materials development at NAPE, or the programme delivery at the Primary Training Institute (PTI) level. While the Framework helped maintain consistency, the quality of training sessions at the PTIs were often found to be low and further investment for capacity building of the teacher educators/trainers during post-PEDP III (GoB 2017) has been called for. Nevertheless, effective pedagogical approaches tested through EIA interventions were embedded in the DPEd.

During the same period (Phases 2 and 3), in the absence of a sector-wide programme for the secondary education sector, EIA worked in project mode to reach secondary teachers. During Phase 4, at the invitation of the government and development partners, EIA worked on the development of the Secondary Education Sector Investment Programme (SESIP) framework. SESIP was the only GoB agency providing secondary TPD at the time. This created opportunities for continuing collaboration with Directorate for Secondary and Higher Education, where the SESIP team was based, and offered opportunities to embed principles of good practices in the programme's activities.

To establish joint ownership of the project activities, EIA personnel engaged simultaneously with the central and field-level government officials. This often involved a 'process facilitation' role for EIA bringing the two groups together in technical forums and other events, to raise awareness and ensure that effective classroom practices could inform policy-making (e.g. EIA 2014g). To build ownership on the part of the stakeholders at the central level, the EIA team also worked closely with the government Project Management Unit. To strengthen collaborative efforts with various government institutions and develop ownership in the process, EIA also worked through formal joint committees.

Fostering ownership of intervention activities in order to facilitate policy and systems change is a key tactic in the process of maintaining partnerships and, ultimately, sustainability through institutionalization, though the limits to what can be achieved do need to be recognized. For example, a Joint Implementation Group was formed with members of EIA and NAPE in order to work together to establish a Centre for Excellence (CfE). The aim of the CfE was to promote effective teaching and learning practices and English language skills development through focused capacity-building activities for the teacher educators and trainers. EIA's main role in this partnership was to provide assistance for designing, planning, facilitating and providing technical expertise in various capacity-development areas. Despite committed activity from both parties, it proved impossible for NAPE to secure sufficient funding under PEDP III for CfE activities.

A possibility that must be faced is that, unless NAPE is structurally reorganized and better supported by its governing ministry, the activities being taken under the CfE initiative in 2017 will not be sustainable. This is an example of how EIA's potential to contribute to the strengthening of educational capacity sometimes remained unrealized because of factors beyond its control. It also shows the need to be realistic about the potential for change and to take the absorption capacity of the system as the point of departure for sustainability-related initiatives.

Throughout the Programme's life, stakeholders at the local level (e.g. EOs and trainers) played an important role in implementing EIA activities. EIA always valued these partnerships, especially with those in positions of responsibility (e.g. head teachers, local EOs, training institution instructors), who took initiatives in their own upazilas and districts to support good practices of TPD in and beyond schools. This is an example where the 'bottom-up' strategy and a multi-level approach to ensuring sustainability were deliberately applied. To build capacity at the local levels, EIA engaged with the Upazila Resource Centre Instructors and used their venues for teacher development workshops. PTIs, too, were used as EIA workshop venues during the I&S phase. PTI Instructors and Superintendents were also introduced to the EIA Programme and to examples of best practice. Thus, relationships with these institutions were strengthened and in turn, these stakeholders became strong advocates for EIA approaches within the government system.

Materials development

As explained in Chapters 6 and 8, all EIA primary and secondary materials were closely linked with the contents of the national textbook *English for Today* (*EfT*). Local artists and musicians were engaged in developing the materials together with the English language teaching (ELT) experts from the OU team. Chapter 6 has already shown how the audio-visual (AV) materials were developed and revised with contributions from the teachers, TFs, EOs as well as technical experts, and also how filming took place in the authentic context of Bangladeshi classrooms. Crucially for sustainability, the EIA approach led to demand for the Programme's materials at school level, while basing the materials on the government curriculum made it easier to secure 'buy-in' at central level.

EIA developed two types of materials: materials for classroom use and materials supporting TPD. Embedding both types of materials within relevant government institutions and programme contents was essential to sustainability. For example, EIA provided technical support to the National Curriculum and Textbook Board (NCTB) to integrate audio contents for listening texts in the Teachers' Guides (TGs), which accompany the secondary English textbooks. In contrast, despite joint efforts made at the implementation level, embedding EIA TPD approaches and principles in the mainstream government training content was not a straightforward experience. Embedding EIA TPD approaches in NCTB's Teachers' Editions and TGs meant working closely with NCTB curriculum specialists, many of whom initially did not have a clear idea about EIA's status as a discrete project under PEDP. Hence advocacy was required to persuade NCTB personnel of the efficacy of EIA's methods and materials before they were willing to integrate them into their publications. The high level of staff turnover among key NCTB staff made this process extremely resource and time consuming for EIA. A further challenge in work with NCTB was its practice of not allowing in-house curriculum specialists to be closely involved with the development of materials, a job outsourced to external writers. Work with these consultants, contributed to individual capacity building but its power to strengthening long-term institutional capacity was attenuated.

However, a spirit of partnership, focused on the collective goal of improving English teaching and learning in schools, remained more or less strong throughout the collaboration and helped to facilitate the process. This has been observed in similar projects: 'This process of internal consultation slows down a project's progress but is, ultimately, time well spent' (Hunter and Alderson 2009: 79). During 2013, the Ministry approved the technical cooperation between EIA and NCTB on a number of curriculum reform activities. This formal partnership created further opportunities and enabled capacity building within the government system, which contributed to EIA's sustainability and ultimately its institutionalization.

EIA's partnerships were not, of course, solely with government bodies. The Programme worked, for example, with FIVDB to develop English readers. In partnership with this organization, EIA initiated a small-scale pilot initiative to develop an English Reading Scheme (ERS) through a series of capacity-development workshops. The ERS consisted of a set of eighteen graded reading texts and associated activities, closely linked with the *EfT* textbook and complementary to other EIA primary teaching and learning programme materials. During the last phase of EIA, Save the Children (SC) adopted the ERS package for its programme in the non-formal education sector for marginalized children, Shikhon. While this initiative is sustained within FIVDB and SC programmes, no way has been found to incorporate them within national provision, despite repeated discussion in many government forums.

EIA has been very successful in embedding and integrating its pedagogical approaches and materials within classrooms and TPD programmes; this required building the capacity of government institutions and personnel to develop materials and approaches according to the same principles. However, sustainability into the future depends on the presence within the system of the capacity to adjust and develop new materials in response to a changing environment (e.g. changes to the curriculum). After the conclusion of the Programme's activities, continuing major investment in capacity building remains essential to sustainability.

Research, monitoring and evaluation

As Chapter 11 explains, EIA's RME component informed the Programme's practices in each phase. The sustainability efforts in relation to RME focused on two specific areas of work: (i) research and evaluation and (ii) monitoring and quality assurance (QA). These will be briefly described below, in terms of partnerships and collaboration involved.

Research and evaluation

Data for many of EIA's evaluation studies were collected by a group of student-researchers appointed by the Institute of Education and Research (IER), Dhaka University (DU). They were recruited through a MPhil programme focused on English language teaching, learning and research, jointly developed by EIA and DU. One of the main purposes of this programme was to create an avenue to develop skilled researchers in ELT. A partnership was set up with IER, through which EIA-funded scholarships were provided to these student-researchers who simultaneously benefitted from relevant course components and related fieldwork. Three cohorts of them completed their studies and all graduates subsequently secured a post in the field. Thus, EIA contributed to developing a number of skilled ELT researchers. After the third cohort, IER, decided to absorb the MPhil programme into its list of mainstream programmes, creating a route for sustainability, although funding students through scholarships is not something DU was able to offer.

Monitoring and quality assurance (QA)

Monitoring and QA played an essential role in the development and success of EIA's model, and steps were taken to embed its QA processes in the government system. In particular, the skills of officials who visit classrooms were cultivated, so that they could observe more effectively and support improvement. As part of the scaling up, Upazila Education Officers (UEOs) were required to visit classrooms and use the 'classroom use' observation form, rather than the job being done by the Programme's own Teacher Development Coordinators. This required a large training programme that produced useful data (see Chapter 11). Although the use of UEOs and Assistant UEOs further embedded the QA process in the government system, it was not possible to ensure that all of these officers actually visited classrooms and submitted completed observation forms. During institutionalization, in the final stage of the EIA Programme, negotiation with the Monitoring and Evaluation (M&E) Division of the Directorate for Primary Education school inspectorate, to incorporate this kind of feedback into routine inspection procedures, was difficult. Eventually, EIA jointly conducted a pilot study in a number of upazilas. The findings of this pilot helped to strengthen the focus of the classroom observation activity on the quality of teaching and learning. The process also secured joint ownership and commitment from relevant government officials. Currently, the learning from this pilot is being fed into the design of the post-PEDP III processes. However, there remains a question around EIA's success in embedding its QA practices across the various levels of the system: while capacity of the decentralized levels has been built to some extent, this may not (yet) be fully supported by a wider systemic reform of M&E practices and associated strengthening of capacity at higher levels of the government.

Changing student assessment: limited success

The Programme was well aware of the 'backwash' effect of national assessments of English language learning, both from its classroom observation data and from the government's own policy papers, which identify serious shortcomings of the examinations, including their reliance on rote learning and their reinforcement of the use of traditional pedagogies (Das et al. 2014). The phenomenon of the examination 'tail' wagging the curriculum and pedagogic 'dog' is, of course, found throughout the world and Chapter 8 indicated some of the negative consequences for pedagogy noted by Programme members. The chapter also reported EIA's advocacy of forms of assessment that would reflect and encourage communicative ways of teaching, in particular by taking account of the essential communicative skills of speaking and listening. Aspects of the examination system were discussed at a number of the meetings held with the Ministry of Education on the integration and institutionalization of EIA approaches in the Secondary Education Sector Investment Programme (SESIP) activities (EIA 2015d). As a result of these meetings, the introduction of a speaking and listening component in the secondary education examinations was given full technical support by EIA, who worked with NCTB to make use of the Programme's audio materials to prepare students and teachers for oral/aural assessment activities. Through this work the Programme provided support for the development of a model for the evaluation of secondary students' speaking and listening (EIA 2015d).

EIA's advocacy role was enacted at a policy level, through the joint hosting of an assessment policy seminar, attended by prominent representatives of all relevant government educational bodies (EIA 2014g). During the life of the Programme, there were some changes to the examinations, notably in primary, where competency-based assessment was adopted, and EIA no doubt contributed to a change in climate which made such developments possible. However, there remained an anomalous situation where the classroom practices advocated by EIA and being endorsed by the government were at odds with the examinations. It may be that this element of the institutionalization was simply too large in its scope for EIA, with its finite resources, to instigate any substantial change.[5]

Lessons learnt: critical factors responsible for EIA's sustainability

The above account of EIA's experiences of embedding its practices within existing government and NGO systems suggests a number of key factors determining success (or otherwise) of attempts to achieve sustainability.

Demand and ownership

EIA addressed the importance of 'local roots of innovation' and of 'initial reforms addressing a well-understood local need and responding to significant local demand' (Samoff et al. 2011: 18). In Bangladesh, there was a strong demand from the government, and from a number of national NGOs, in relation to improving levels of English for Bangladeshi students and there was general acceptance of, and commitment to, the idea that such improvement could only be achieved through radical change in classroom practices. This had the potential to create ownership for such change by the government and NGO stakeholders.

Availability of time and resources

One of the key reasons why EIA achieved so many of its sustainability objectives was that, at the outset, DFID had taken a long-term view that the programme should be of nine years' duration. Educational reform is a process of 'moving mountains stone by stone' (Brock 2009: 454), requiring the time to build strong relationships and adjust models over time. Learning from implementation experiences, as well as institutional and contextual factors, gave EIA an advantage over many other international development projects. At the same time, we argue that even more time and resources are required to fully achieve sustainability of EIA practice, particularly in terms of building capacity within the government institutions. The task of transforming systems is often underestimated.

Adapting to the institutional context

As noted earlier, innovations that have worked in particular contexts regularly fail to deliver similar results in a new environment. EIA drew on some years of experience, and evaluation findings, to take contextual factors into account when determining its 'institutionalized model' (developed, but different, from the model tested during the pilot), as Chapter 5 shows. A balance was struck between making adaptations to fit with existing systems, and maintaining the critical elements of the original model that engendered the desired change (see Chapter 13). Thus, EIA benefitted from the fact that it was given the time to engage in an iterative process of continuous adaptation of the institutionalized model.

Evolving roles of EIA management and staff

Whilst there was a requirement to adapt the model in response to changing institutional context, EIA Programme staff also needed to adjust their roles and I&S activities in line with the evolving nature of the Programme. During the pilot phase, the activities were very strongly related to direct implementation, with a focus on the training of teachers and other education personnel. In the upscaling phase, EIA activities were increasingly mediated locally by government representatives, with EIA staff providing support for capacity building and technical assistance (TA) as well as working with central decision makers advocating the EIA model. In the institutionalization phase, a complete systems approach was adopted, with increased emphasis on TA at central levels of government, and a focus on institutional (rather than purely technical) capacity-building efforts. EIA had to be responsive enough to provide the specific expertise and skills required to change the way it supported various institutions throughout Phases 2–4. As already noted, sometimes capacity-building was focused on individuals and roles, rather than the institutions.

Using evidence for advocacy

The fact that EIA could demonstrate that the new model of TPD worked, with highly credible research showing classroom practice change and improved student learning outcomes, helped to convince stakeholders that EIA methods should be adopted. However, research evidence alone was not enough. EIA's ability to demonstrate visible change in the classroom through organizing field visits by education officials was a crucial element in convincing the government. This illustrates the importance of the *communication of evidence* in ways that are both accessible and of practical use in government decision-making.[6]

Affordability

The superior cost-effectiveness of an innovation compared to existing government programmes and competing solutions needed to be clearly established. This required obtaining comparable measures of cost-effectiveness, which can be hard to come by in low-resource situations (MSI 2012). For EIA, it also meant reducing the total cost of the model over time to result in expenditure that was more affordable for the government to absorb, so that the approach was not seen as an additional financial burden that would lead to a lack of sustainability. This is set out in detail in Chapter 13, with changes in the model explained to show how they met this affordability criterion.

Nature of local partnerships

The nature of the professional relationships between Programme staff and government and NGO staff was important. The demands and questions of the government and NGOs need to be taken as the point of departure, and EIA needed to avoid being too focused on wanting to institutionalize EIA as a whole Programme. Building long-term, respectful, relationships is key in being effective. Finally, relationship-development and capacity-building needed to happen at the different levels of the system, with a balance between the central and local government, and involving all institutions that needed to adopt elements of the new practice.

Deliberate sustainability goals and strategy from the beginning

To move from a project-based mode of implementation to an institutional one is a lengthy and complex process. Distinct and well-defined sustainability strategies that are integrated with the overall programme strategy, and which can be adjusted over time, are an absolute pre-requisite for success. Although the original bid envisaged a plan for institutionalization (ABMB 2007), the first I&S strategy was developed in 2011, six years before the end of the project. This allowed sufficient time to work meaningfully to achieve sustainability of EIA-initiated practices.

Institutionalizing a single subject within a general education system

An additional complexity was around operating within the single subject, English. While this in some ways made programme implementation simpler, and outcomes relatively easy to communicate, it became a challenge to institutionalize. The GoB system has no institution that implements only English teaching, and institutionalization efforts affected the whole system and required major changes in policy, TPD, curriculum and implementation across all subjects. This made the institutionalization efforts higher profile in political terms, and thus harder to negotiate.

'Holistic approach' to intervention design

EIA aimed to change classroom teaching and learning practices by working with teachers, EOs, teacher trainers, educators, curriculum specialists and policy-makers, and on the process for in-service teacher education within the sector programme. Evidence was gathered at each step to ensure planning for the next step was well informed. Advocacy and team work with local- and central-level stakeholders ensured ownership, contextual relevance, smooth communication and implementation of the activities. This 'holistic' approach would create a network of support around the teacher in the classroom. However, as experienced in relation to some of the other lessons, working effectively across all these fronts was difficult, and success was not achieved equally across the various dimensions.

Conclusion

EIA's journey towards sustainability has followed a route of success, but challenges and setbacks have been encountered along the way. Institutionalizing the project components within the mainstream government system and capacity-building were central to ensuring its sustainability. Every intervention of the EIA Programme was designed with a set of critical success factors that were closely linked to national programmes and implementation modalities. This increased the likelihood that the intervention would become embedded within the mainstream programmes and helped to link them to other donor-led major reform initiatives. At the same time, not everything that was achieved within the project mode of intervention was accomplished with the same level of quality when interventions were scaled up.

DFID's Bangladesh office has increasingly focused on providing support to government institutions through pooled funding within the sector programmes designed to develop capacity for planning and implementation. Towards the end of its life, EIA received further funding from the UK government for continued capacity-building activities and to support the design process of the next primary sector development programme. This opportunity, together with other representatives from the donor consortium (e. g. JICA, World Bank, Asian Development Bank, UNICEF, Australian Aid, Canadian International Development Agency etc.),[7] enabled direct contribution to the design of teacher education and ICT in education programmes post-PEDP III. This also meant that much of the learning from the experiences of implementing EIA TPD practices could be used to influence the design of the next sector programme.

Although EIA managed to embed examples of good practices in the teacher development contents and structures during the project's lifetime, unless the existing technical capacity amongst teacher trainers/educators in the system is improved at every level, the expected quality of the output is likely to be compromised in the long term. 'Notions of ownership and sustainability often belie local context where achievement of independence in technical competence is not easily compartmentalized into project cycles' (Hunter and Alderson 2009: 67). This is a major threat facing any intervention in a sector-wide programme that aims to raise the quality of education in schools in Bangladesh. Unless investment is secured in the sector budget for capacity-building among all education personnel involved in either providing management or subject and pedagogic support to the teachers in a planned manner, and with a longer term perspective, the potential effectiveness of a programme such as English in Action on a large scale may not be fully achieved.

Notes

1 www.unesco.org/new/fileadmin/MULTIMEDIA/HQ/ERI/pdf/Aichi-Nagoya_ Declaration_EN.pdf (accessed 19 October).
2 This is somewhat of simplification, as there is considerable interaction among these three sites of work.
3 The third PEDP details can be found at http://www.lged.gov.bd/ProjectHome. aspx?projectID=245.
4 EIA was a Technical Assistance (TA) project under the sector-wide PEDP III.
5 The business case for additional funding for institutionalisation in Phase 4, which was rejected by DFID, included a component on assessment: 'Contribute to framework for and design of new tests and related guidance to teachers in respect of revised national examination and assessment mechanisms' (EIA 2014f: 11).
6 Cambridge Education: From idea to impact – supporting innovation in Rwanda's education sector (https://www.camb-ed.com/intdev/article/391/from-idea-to-impact (accessed 30 October 2017).
7 The names of some of these agencies are now different.

13

Ensuring Value for Money

Claire Hedges, Kirsten Zindel and Bikash Chandra Sarkar

Introduction

The UK government, the funder of EIA via DFID, set out its Value for Money (VfM) agenda as:

> The purpose of the VfM drive is to develop a better understanding (and better articulation) of costs and results so that we can make more informed, evidence-based choices. This is a process of continuous improvement. VfM doesn't mean we only do the cheapest things, but we need to get better at understanding what is driving our costs and make sure that we are getting the desired quality at the lowest price.... We need to understand what works – a judgement based on the strength of evidence supporting an intervention and making our assumptions explicit.
>
> DFID 2011: 2

Yet VfM is often seen by projects as a process for reporting to a funder, a 'back office' function. In contrast, in EIA, VfM had a prominent role in programme design and implementation, being a cross-project, iterative process. The approach focuses on cost-effectiveness – maximizing results relative to the cost of inputs (Fleming 2013). Although projects routinely measure (unit) 'costs', 'results' are harder to gauge in education projects, particularly in quantitative terms, and therefore the relationship between costs and results is less well understood.

In line with DFID guidance, EIA's VfM framework therefore examined:

- economy – minimizing cost of inputs;
- efficiency – maximizing the conversion of inputs into outputs;
- effectiveness – maximizing the conversion of outputs into results (outcomes);
- equity – ensuring that benefits are distributed fairly;

- cost-effectiveness – maximizing results relative to cost of inputs;
- cost–benefit analysis – evaluating alternatives by identifying their costs and benefits in money terms.

This framework makes clear that VfM is not simply about cutting costs, but also about achieving results. It is not only about short-term results, but about long-term sustainable results. It is a way of thinking that applies across all project activities (Figure 13.1). EIA's VfM needs to be seen in the context of its theory of change (Figure 13.2), a necessary implication of the DFID agenda quoted above.

The VfM challenge posed to EIA is further set out in its logical framework, which sets out the inputs/activities with 'reach' targets, 'results' targets (based on the theory of change),[1] and 'funding allocations' over the project life (Table 13.1).

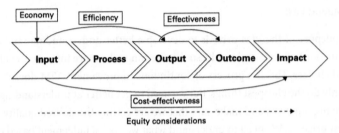

Figure 13.1 Value for Money as part of the overall process of inputs to impact

INPUT	Video, print and audio materials for teacher professional development (TPD) and classroom use, aligned with national curriculum and textbooks, and accessed by mobile technology. Ongoing follow up support through peer teachers, head teachers and education officials.
ASSUMPTION	Teachers' learning improves through direct access to TPD materials (with no intermediary mediation). Teachers and head teachers use this learning to try TPD activities in class.
OUTPUT	Primary and secondary teachers use EIA teaching approaches. Primary and secondary education officials orientated to support EIA-promoted TPD approaches.
ASSUMPTION	Improving classroom practice leads to improvements in student learning outcomes.
OUTCOME	Increased number of people able to communicate in English.

Figure 13.2 EIA theory of change (overview)

Table 13.1 EIA logical framework

Target	Phase 2	Phase 3	Phase 4
REACH (cumulative)			
Primary teachers	400	7,500	41,000
Primary students	35,000	540,000	3,000,000
Secondary teachers	200	5,000	10,000
Secondary students	83,000	2,080,000	4,200,000
RESULTS			
Classroom practice of primary and secondary teachers			
% of student talk in lessons	20%	20%	20%
% of that student talk that is in English	50%	60%	60%
Student learning outcomes			
% increase in primary students achieving GESE* level 1 or more (above baseline)	+5%	+5%	+5%
% increase in secondary students achieving GESE level 2 or more (above baseline)	+5%	+10%	+10%
FUNDING ALLOCATION			
Primary	£2.4M	£3.2M	£1.7M
Secondary	£3.1M	£2.3M	£1.0M

* GESE: Graded Examinations in Spoken English, Trinity College London (see Chapter 9)

This sets out a clear expectation that, across the life of the project, there will be a dramatic increase in 'reach' with 'results' maintained, all within a much reducing 'funding allocation'.

This chapter explores the EIA approach and arguments to achieving this. It elaborates on key procedures and tools used to successfully implement the VfM framework. It lays out what is behind the DFID Annual Review 2015 conclusion that:

> EIA does represent VfM and this is expected to increase over the life of the project, especially by factoring in the quality of products, the extent of reach and the sustainability of innovative delivery, behaviour change and language competence along with a pattern of declining unit costs.
>
> DFID 2015

The illustrative case studies and lessons learnt that appear in this chapter are drawn from various parts of the EIA journey.

Programme design principles enabling VfM

This section sets out how the school-based nature of the primary and secondary EIA components is integral to realizing economies of scale, how their cost profiles (i.e. what drives the costs) compare to more traditional face-to-face training methods, and how scalability is easier to achieve in the case of EIA than for traditional training methods.

As has been made clear earlier in the book (Chapters 4 and 5), a key design principle from the outset was the school-based nature of these components. The pilot phase was designed to explore different school-based teacher development (SBTD) resources, support models, and delivery mechanisms capable of working at large scale, to find out what worked and what did not. In this way, the project 'thought at scale' from its inception.

In conventional teacher education, teacher-training staff costs are generally the largest single budget item. These costs vary directly with the number of teachers, because traditional methods of teacher education are labour-intensive activities. However, in SBTD, training resources can be developed and recorded in advance, reproduced and distributed to large numbers of teachers, with positive results, as argued in Chapters 4 and 5. While significant fixed costs are incurred in developing the training resources, the variable costs of reproducing and distributing those resources and supporting their use for each additional teacher are modest (Oliveira and Orivel 2003; Banks et al. 2007; EIA 2016). For interventions like EIA, which aim to reach very large numbers, economies of scale can be achieved because the relatively high fixed costs remain the same, while the delivery of resources to very many teachers affects only the relatively low variable costs (i.e. costs which depend on the number of teachers). Scalability is key to the teacher development and support model for EIA (see Chapters 4 and 5). EIA resources place the site of learning in the teacher's classroom. As this method requires less face-to-face support from trainers than traditional methods (as other chapters have implied), the EIA model is economically more viable and also more feasible, as availability of expert trainers is no longer a constraint. Use of mobile communication media can enhance these economies of scale (see Chapter 6).

EIA's mobile technologies enable English to be brought directly into the classroom for both teachers and students. In contrast to common practices, like the use of ICT classrooms, as explained in Case Study 1 (below), EIA decided to search for low-cost, easy-to-use equipment; 'the trainer in your pocket', as characterized earlier, retains and supports unit costs for SBTD below those of more traditional alternatives.

Economy (minimizing cost of inputs)

This section outlines how economy (and minimizing unit costs) has revolved around three key principles within the school-based programme design.

1. Scale demands economical school-based implementation strategies

EIA's main variable cost drivers are:

1. teacher ongoing support (including face-to-face meetings);
2. reproduction and distribution of audio-video (AV) and print materials;
3. equipment (speakers, SD-cards and mobile phones).

The unit costs for each are shown in Table 13.2.

These unit costs fell from £600 per teacher in Phase 2 to £52 per teacher in Phase 4. This reduction came from streamlining materials, refining the teacher support model, increasing the use of local capacity, and moving to locally available teacher-owned mobile technology. This unit cost compares very favourably with other UK aid-funded projects, which focus more on taking teachers out of school for training, and with the Government of Bangladesh's (GoB) costs for in-service teacher training with similar objectives. However, as we will show, it does this with improved results even at scale.

Table 13.2 Unit costs over EIA phases (Primary)

Unit Cost	Phase 2	Phase 3	Phase 4
Teacher ongoing support	£270	£176	£35
Reproduction and distribution of materials	£105	£35	£15
Equipment	£225	£81	£2
Total	£600	£292	£52

2. The deployment in Phase 3 of a teacher-support model potentially affordable for the GoB to implement in Phase 4

As earlier chapters have discussed, the use of local cluster meetings (CMs) and teacher facilitators (TFs) was from the start designed to minimize the cost of implementation. Table 13.3 illustrates and sets out the kinds of changes made in Phase 3 in primary and secondary to prepare the ground for Phase 4.

Table 13.3 Changes in teacher support over EIA phases

	Phase 2	Phase 3	Phase 4
Workshops	Two Divisional residential workshops	None	None
Cluster Meetings	Twelve days of local cluster meetings	Eight days of local cluster meetings	Four days of local cluster meetings in government venues
Classroom Visits	Project-funded visits by project TFs	Project-funded visits by local education officials	Visits by local education officials within their government roles

3. A shift over time of the deployment of resources from international to national inputs as local capacity is developed

Chapter 5 has already indicated the need to depend upon local capacity, both from the point of view of localizing the Programme and responding to the local context. Table 13.4 illustrates the VfM incentive by explaining the changing role for the Open University (OU) over the project life – a key strategy in EIA's economy strategy and attempts to reduce unit costs.

Table 13.4 OU's changing role

Phase	OU Role	OU Key Activities
Phase 2 (2008–11)	Leading activities and capacity building core team in Bangladesh	Research and development of school-based training model and resources Facilitation of teacher development workshops
Phase 3 (2011–14)	Capacity-building local teacher support with core team in Bangladesh	Academic advice and support on upscaling of school-based training model and resources Capacity building of Teacher Development Coordinators (TDCs) and TFs
Phase 4 (2014–18)	Academic steering, advice and evaluation	Academic advice and guidance on supporting GoB's adoption of the teacher support model, resources and tools Academic leadership of research and evaluation

Case Study 1: VfM journey for materials and technology

From the outset, EIA has developed and produced high-quality audio-visual (AV) and print materials. VfM was one of the biggest drivers of this policy, and fixed production and variable reproduction costs have fallen each year through a number of different strategies.

In Phase 2, there was both strong leadership and 'hands-on' involvement from OU international experts who worked with national team members across a range of tasks, including academic writing, designing print materials, recording audio, filming in schools, AV editing etc. Subsequently, although receiving support from the OU staff, the local project team gradually took the lead on subsequent adaptions and additions, and the costs of developing materials fell across Phases 3 and 4.

In Phase 2, EIA piloted a wide range of materials. Primary teachers received materials for all five grades: audio recordings for each lesson within the *English for Today* textbook; posters; figurines (that is, modelling figures); flashcards; eighteen video clips illustrating student-centred classroom teaching practices and activities (for professional development); and an EIA-produced Teachers' Guide and a set of Activity Guides (to support teachers in the use of the above materials). Feedback was gathered on the teachers' response to, and use of, these materials.

In Phase 3, figurines were phased out, as they were used by only the most confident teachers; flashcards were also no longer provided, as these could be made by teachers and the humidity in the schools made it difficult to keep the cards in a good and usable condition. In Phase 4, the Activity Guides were dropped, as by this time EIA materials had been incorporated into the Government Teacher Editions accompanying the national textbooks. The amount of printed materials was therefore drastically reduced and, for Phase 4, all materials were made more standalone and flexible so that they might be used within different teacher professional development scenarios.

In contrast, audio materials have been constant across the phases. Once produced, copying them is fast, cheap and simple, and they can be used by thousands of people. New recordings were required only when the textbooks were changed by the government or for refinement purposes, and editing for such changes is also relatively speedy, cheap and easy.

Another constant has been the development of teacher professional development videos, although there has been a significant change in their content: actors and filmsets have been eschewed in favour of filming real teachers and classrooms (as explained in Chapter 6), which significantly reduced development costs.

In terms of technology, in Phase 2 EIA used the technology then available to pilot its AV materials with 750 teachers using Apple iPod Nano at £125 each (for primary teachers) and Apple iPod Touch (for secondary teachers) at £164 each, as well as rechargeable speakers (ION Block Rocker and Logitech Pure-Fi Anywhere) at £100 each. Although iPods were more expensive than other devices, they were chosen because they possessed the video functionalities needed to provide teachers with professional development through an ICT platform, and it was easy to navigate within the numerous audio- and video-files loaded on the SD card. Importantly, the AV resources could be uploaded and stored directly on the iPods without recourse to the internet, thus giving teachers zero cost of access. (Chapter 1 indicated that internet access was in any case low when EIA started.)

As EIA anticipated, available and appropriate technologies moved on during Phase 2. Therefore, in 2011, an equipment-testing study among a sample of the pilot teachers resulted in a new technology kit that was distributed to 12,000 teachers across Bangladesh by June 2014. The kit consisted of the Nokia C1–01 mobile phone (£35), a Lane SH–120 rechargeable amplifier/speaker (£42) and all of EIA's AV resources on 4 GB micro SD-cards (£4). This kit became known as the 'trainer in your pocket'.

In Phase 4, in order to reach 40,000 teachers, EIA provided only an SD card loaded with AV materials to teachers, who used these on their personal phones. Schools assumed the responsibility to find speakers to play the audio in the classroom, and 85 per cent of schools in the final primary teacher cohort were able to do so. Therefore, the only equipment cost left was the SD card, but even then it was found that interested teachers copied the AV materials onto other non-EIA teachers' SD cards. In addition, EIA materials are now available on Directorate of Primary Education and National Curriculum and Textbook Board websites and in teacher centres in every upazila across the country.

Efficiency (maximizing the conversion of inputs into outputs)

Efficiency is the key next step in the VfM process. This is an area where funders monitor projects to ensure strong financial control and this is often a central VfM indicator in funder reviews. Project teams need to consider if the same results can be obtained while saving costs, yet not jeopardizing sustainability and without incurring costs elsewhere.

Drawing on the logical framework (see Chapter 11) EIA's main efficiency indicators become:

- the number of teachers reached for the given financial input;
- percentage of student talk time in lessons for the given financial input;
- percentage of that student talk that is in English for the given financial input;
- the ability of the GoB to take forward EIA approaches after project end.

The achievements for the first three indicators for primary are shown in Table 13.5 (secondary follows a similar profile).

Table 13.5 Efficiency indicators achievements (Primary)

	Phase 2	Phase 3	Phase 4
Reach: number of participating teachers	508	7,015	35,185
Percentage of student talk in lessons	27%	27%	25%
Percentage of that student talk that is in English	81%	91%	91%

In addition to end-of-cohort evaluations of classroom practice, it is important to use monitoring data to provide an ongoing indication of progress (see Chapter 11). The project management information system and divisional monthly monitoring reports show the number of teachers starting the teacher development programme each month. Regular school visits, using a project-designed 'Classroom Use and Support Form' (see Chapters 11 and 12), monitor the use of pair and group work (which provides a key opportunity for more student talk and an interim proxy measure for student talk), and student use of English. These monitoring processes are essential to maintaining VfM. Budget and financial management is a matter of course for projects, but ongoing monitoring of expected changes is equally important, so that problems can be identified early and promptly acted upon. (There are also slower, but more reliable, data on classroom practice from the evaluation at the end of each cohort.)

Whilst one might expect to see trade-offs with regard to the extent of results as teacher numbers increase and unit costs fall, this was not the case for EIA; result levels were maintained across all the Phases (see Table 13.1 and Chapter 9). This is a strong argument in favour of the school-based, peer-supported teacher professional development adopted.

A further efficiency indicator is the position of the GoB to take forward EIA approaches after project end. This is explored in Case Study 2, which looks at how the teacher support model has changed over time, becoming ever closer to the GoB's systems and costs.

Case Study 2: Teacher support from international experts to government systems

This case study looks at the decision-making processes involved when considering changes to teacher-support strategies as EIA's scale dramatically increased over the project life. Three variables were articulated as questions:

1. What number of teachers is required to be reached by the project logical framework?
2. Can economies of scale be relied on or are more radical changes needed?
3. What level of intensity and which face-to-face support mechanisms are considered to have most impact on changing teachers' practice, in what ways and delivered by whom?

In Phase 2, EIA designed the teacher support to last sixteen months. Teachers were provided with an initial orientation workshop, twelve monthly CMs and a final evaluation workshop. All professional development meetings were held in rented private venues. Workshops were held at the divisional level and were residential. Project TDCs and international experts led the workshops and meetings. Local TFs very much played a supporting role. This was at a cost of £270 per teacher to EIA.

In Phase 3, the intensity and cost of support in Phase 2 could not be maintained. Critical decision-making, cross-project internal meetings were held, where different support models with associated financial models were hotly debated by the EIA partners. It was decided that all teacher meetings would take place closer to the teachers. There would be no residential workshops; instead, an initial extended CM was followed by seven one-day meetings. The focus of TDCs and international experts would be on building the capacity of the local TFs. The TFs would then lead the teacher CMs, drawing on their classroom experience of trying EIA professional development activities with their students and learning from the EIA support material provided. Key to making this possible were the AV materials, allowing the TFs' role to be that of a 'critical friend' in viewing and using the materials and activities. This was at a cost of £176 per teacher.

In Phase 4, further attenuation of the extent of face-to-face support was required to meet cost and government logistic constraints. With some trepidation, in the first Phase 4 cohort of 15,000 teachers, the number of teacher CMs was reduced to four (from eight) and held in government (not private) venues at almost no cost; yet, as Table 13.5 shows, classroom practice change (from the baseline situation) was maintained. Further, many EIA TFs became Government Teacher Trainers to be used in the institutionalized approach to EIA, bringing the project modality and the government systems closer together (see Chapter 12). The materials were adapted to be more stand-alone and flexible. The focus of EIA TDCs, and the now much-reduced academic expert inputs, was not only on the TFs, but also on the local education officer teams responsible for local teacher professional development. The cost per teacher reduced to £35, in line with government training. The focus now moved to local government providing the follow-on support to an initial orientation for teachers. Early signs (in late 2017) were encouraging; for example, upazilas were using EIA resources and activities in their local sub-cluster training for English; new dedicated meetings for EIA professional development were beginning to be locally funded; upazilas had formed English language clubs to improve teachers' English and their English language teaching.

Effectiveness (maximizing the conversion of outputs into results)

Effectiveness (the extent of results) is measured through the RME processes, and these show the proportion of students who achieve increases in English language competence (EIA 2014a; see Chapter 9).

The key effectiveness indicators for the EIA project were:

- the proportion of students who achieve competence increases for the given financial input;
- the increased likelihood of those looking for work, with better English, to find employment.

These indicators draw on the project's theory of change. First, it is assumed that changes in teachers' classroom practice (through the teacher development programme) lead to improvements in students' English language competence (ELC). Second, it is assumed that, if people have improved this competence, their economic and social opportunities improve, and assessing their ability to find employment is a proxy for this. The second indicator has been measured through a study of recruitment agencies (EIA 2014e).

The variation of these indicators over EIA's phases for primary are shown in Table 13.6. (secondary follows a similar profile).

Table 13.6 Effectiveness indicators (Primary)

	Phase 2	Phase 3	Phase 4
Proportion of students increasing their English language competence (ELC) grades	40%	30%	21%
Increased likelihood to find work	50%	50%	50%

It should be noted that the indicator for student ELC differs from the logical framework (log frame) target referred to earlier in this chapter. The log frame indicator looks at changes in specific grade criteria for ELC. For VfM calculations, it is important to capture all learning outcome improvements, and so here all students who improve one English language competence grade at any level (not just specific grade criteria) are included (EIA 2014f).

Here trade-offs in the extent of the results achieved, as numbers of teachers reached increases and unit costs fall, can arguably be seen. This contrasts with the classroom practice efficiency indicators, where results levels are maintained across the phases. However, it should be noted that in Phase 4, due to delays in Programme implementation as a result of nationwide protests, schools were only half way through the SBTD programme at the time of the ELC testing. The evidence suggests it is likely that previous results would have been achieved if the ELC assessments had been made at the end of the Programme.

Equity (ensuring that benefits are distributed fairly)

When judgements about the VfM of an intervention are made, issues of equity are vital considerations within this, in order to determine whether development results have reached the poorest, women and girls, and those most at risk of exclusion (e.g. those with special educational needs).

EIA has a strong inherent focus on social inclusion: the EIA English language approach is an important tool for improving inclusion (EIA 2014f), because the pedagogy and methods used strongly focus on the engagement and full participation of all learners. EIA focuses on: (i) addressing discrimination and negative perceptions towards marginalized/excluded groups, including raising awareness among those who are 'included', and helping them understand the potentially exclusive nature of their views, words and actions; and (ii) based on real needs, reaching out to marginalized groups and ensuring that they equally benefit from opportunities provided by EIA ('bringing them into the centre of the EIA interventions').

Since the start of Phase 3, the Programme selected schools located in disadvantaged areas, so that students from some of the poorest backgrounds would be reached. EIA also partnered with non-government organizations working with non-formal schools to reach out-of-school children and working children in urban areas, such as the Underprivileged Children's Education Programme. With the SBTD model, it can be seen in Table 13.5 that the classroom impact achieved in Phase 2 has been maintained (not compromised) in Phases 3 and 4, notwithstanding the greater and more socially inclusive reach. Similarly, when allowing for the timing issues of the Phase 4 ELC assessments, the impact on student learning outcomes tells a similar story (Table 13.6). This again is a strong endorsement of the school-based, peer-supported teacher professional development approach adopted.

The school-based design of the Programme, and its use of mobile technology, also reduces the barriers for female teachers to participate in professional development, minimizing periods away from their families and communities and allowing them 'anytime, anywhere' access to professional development activities and resources. 65 percent of primary teachers in the 2016 cohort were female, compared to the national average of 62 per cent. However, only 18 per cent of secondary teachers in the 2016 cohort were female, compared to the national average for English teachers of 23 per cent; here selection of teachers was less successfully influenced by the Project.

Improvements in ELC are found for both girls and boys throughout the project life. In the most recent assessments (EA 2017), the learning gains are similar for girls and boys in primary. However, in secondary, the extent of improvement is greater for boys than girls.

Cost-effectiveness (maximizing results relative to cost of inputs)

The economy and effectiveness indicators were combined to provide an indication of cost-effectiveness, which could then be used to make comparison across the different phases of the programme, and/or across alternative programmes that aim to reach the same goal (EIA 2017: vi). EIA's cost-effectiveness measure is the unit cost per student that increases one Trinity GESE English competence grade. Table 13.7 shows these figures for each EIA phase.

Table 13.7 Cost-effectiveness indicators (Primary)

	Phase 2	Phase 3	Phase 4
Unit cost per student that increases an English competence grade	£17	£13	£4

These indicators are calculated by taking the costs of the primary teacher development programme for a particular phase and dividing by the number of one-grade increases in English competence shown by students. It is only possible to do this because the EIA research and evaluation strategy measures student learning outcomes. As Chapter 4 indicates, it is rare for teacher education projects to do this; more frequently projects measure classroom practice change or teacher experience of the development programme. Calculating how many students improve their learning outcomes is complicated. First, a valid, credible and reliable method of assessment needs to be identified and implemented; in the case of EIA, the Trinity College London assessment is used. These assessments must then be analysed to find out how many one-grade increases are achieved by students. A statistical analysis routine had to be found that allowed for individual students who improved by more than one grade and ignored those students who improved, but by less than one grade.

The Project has found that the effort invested in this calculation has been worthwhile, not only in terms of proving its own VfM but also (and in particular) in advocacy to government and donors, as it makes the argument that large-scale SBTD programmes can be seen to produce evidence of results, with reducing cost, as scale increases to that of the GoB's own programmes.

Cost–benefit analysis (evaluating alternatives by identifying their costs and benefits in money terms)

Project teams and evaluators may also want to understand whether the benefits of an intervention outweigh its costs and also to use this knowledge to compare alternative programmes (EIA 2016).

EIA carried out a cost–benefit analysis of the primary programme, considering two options: (i) EIA would receive funding for the then last two years of its final phase (April 2015–March 2017); (ii) the 'counterfactual', i.e. that EIA would not receive any more funds, the project would stop and the Government English subject-based training (SbT) would be the only teacher training taking place. For this analysis the net present value of both the costs and benefits was calculated, using a discount rate of 10 per cent.[2]

The direct costs of EIA for these two years were identified from the project's nine-year financial perspective plan, and the Government costs of SbT were drawn from the Government's Annual Operation Plan. In addition, teacher opportunity costs were included to reflect the numbers of days teachers would spend out-of-school for training.

The numbers of students expected to increase one competence grade as a result of EIA were then taken, based on previous project evaluations, as were those expected to increase as a result of Government subject-based training, based on wider evidence of students' ELC (Education Watch 2011; Hamid and Baldauf 2008; Kraft et al. 2009; World Bank 2008).

The main quantifiable benefit for the project – the additional income earned (wage premium) for such an increase in English – was then factored in. EIA research found an average wage premium of 25–30 per cent across a wide range of employment types (EIA 2014e).

The balance of costs and benefits was then assessed, as summarized in Table 13.8.

Table 13.8 Summary of costs and benefits (GBP millions)

(All in £m)	EIA	SbT	Difference
Total economic benefit	57	24.5	32.5
Discounted economic benefit	16.5	7.1	9.4
Total economic cost	5.4	5.5	−0.1
Discounted economic cost	4.7	4.8	−0.1
Net Present Value	**11.8**	**2.3**	**9.5**

The net present value for EIA of £11.8M suggests the investment represented good VfM for DFID; and, compared to the alternative Government SbT, EIA had an additionality of £9.5M.[3]

Management support mechanisms (project ways of working)

As a partner of DFID, integrating a VfM agenda into an intervention is a requirement. DFID's guidelines around VfM are clear but broadly defined, because the diversity of portfolios does not allow a 'one-size-fits-all' strategy. Moreover, as this approach to VfM is still relatively new, EIA could not copy the strategy of similar and successful projects. EIA encountered several issues and difficulties, which, according to an international study executed by Mango and the Value for Money Learning Group (2016), are very common when designing and implementing a VfM agenda:

- how to define 'value';
- how to define the contribution of the project;
- how to find the appropriate internal and external benchmarks and comparisons;
- how to find the person-hours needed;
- how to convince staff and key stakeholders of the objectives behind the VfM strategy;
- how to maintain timely internal decision-making.

However, EIA experienced its benefits quickly after implementation, because the VfM strategy:

- enabled EIA to demonstrate value for its work to DFID and the GoB;
- helped the strategic decision-making processes;
- helped planning and budgeting processes;
- reduced costs;
- engaged staff in financial issues and decision-making.

Table 13.9 elaborates EIA's four key mechanisms to implement the VfM framework and the main challenges faced.

Lessons learnt

The above journey highlights the VfM drivers, processes and challenges faced by the project. It can be seen that some Programme elements have been strengthened over time, such as the increased use of mediated authentic video, the stronger reliance placed on TFs and the increased importance given to local teacher networks. Some elements remained core and have been maintained over time; for example, the school-based nature of the Programme has enabled learning inside the classroom, increased effectiveness and ensured low marginal costs to aid scalability and sustainability. Some elements have been streamlined or discarded over time; for example, the print guides have been streamlined,

Table 13.9 VfM mechanisms

Objective	Examples	Challenges
To implement VfM process, systems and tools for the required data.	Processes – procurement policy, decentralization of activities, handover to Government. Systems – monitoring and evaluation, financial planning, audits. Tools – monitoring instruments, quarterly progress checks against VfM plan.	1) Finding the optimal balance between cost, quality, monitoring and flexibility. 2) Measuring results and project benefits, finding appropriate comparisons, retrieving (confidential) information/data. 3) Data collection. 4) Setting up the most appropriate internal control systems and performance indicators.
To integrate VfM targets and actions into decision-making.	Inclusion of VfM agenda in management meetings, strategy workshops, all-staff meetings. Collaborative options appraisals on use of resources.	1) Creating a general understanding and acceptance about the importance of VfM and acknowledgement that VfM is a shared responsibility. 2) Embedding VfM cost and options analysis into EIA's main Programme activities and budgeting.
To build VfM skills and objectives amongst project staff.	Dedicated workshops on VfM framework, targets and objectives and allowing staff to think 'how' to achieve these targets. Set-up of a pool of staff members responsible for reporting on VfM practices and targets.	1) Bring Finance and Programme together to ensure joint planning and budgeting.
To learn and improve VfM.	Yearly assessment of VfM plan and redefining the VfM targets and objectives (Annual Review). Regular internal spot checks of EIA procedures and systems.	1) Creating a feedback loop to communicate lessons learned to staff and stakeholders in the field. 2) Adapting the strategy according to the lessons learned and progress made thus far.

teachers' own phones are now used rather than project-provided mobile phones, and Activity Guides were discarded when EIA-influenced Government Teacher Editions of the textbooks came into use.

Key lessons learned in relation to the Programme are:

- SBTD is a cost-effective alternative to more traditional cascade models, and there is critical importance, within this, of teachers receiving high-quality teacher professional support materials in their hands. This adds to the research evidence offered in Chapter 4, that it is an effective alternative.
- up-front investment in the teacher support design and materials reaps substantial benefits when scale-up is reached, but only if a project 'thinks at scale' from the outset.
- effectiveness and efficiency can complement each other (as well as at other times requiring trade-offs); for example, developing AV materials locally optimizes the use of local teachers and environments and maximizes teacher engagement, and is also lower in cost than that produced internationally.
- using AV materials can be very cost-effective, as reproduction costs are low and it is easy for teachers to copy and share the materials compared with printed texts.
- when reaching large scale, it is important, where possible, to use readily available technology that teachers already own and with which they are familiar.
- sustainable teacher networks inside and outside of school can be the driver for decisions relating to the investment of time and resources for teacher support.
- a well-articulated logical framework and RME strategy are vital to capture results.
- projects should demonstrate they can operate within government financial parameters and evidence results, if governments are to take on and sustain them.
- there is a danger that applying VfM could lead to a risk-averse culture, encouraging a focus on what is easier to measure rather than on what is most needed or effective.

Key lessons learned in relation to VfM management are:

- VfM targets and approaches need to be strategic, practical, realistic and cost-effective to use, taking into account the programme environment, with the benefits (additional benefits and savings) outweighing the costs (internal audits, time).

- monitoring tools should be practical and the systems should encourage staff to think about VfM and provide guidance, rather than restricting them in their daily activities.
- developing technical skills on financial management is important, as are soft skills such as open-communication, information sharing and transparency.
- time is an important success factor. With time the VfM strategy can be refined and streamlined with programme goals and objectives. It also allows the project team to learn and improve.
- a VfM task force with senior management champions and representation from all departments of the project, which is responsible for the VfM strategy implementation and monitoring, could be very effective.

Notes

1 These elements of the log frame were described in Chapter 11.
2 'Net present value' is a measurement of profit calculated by subtracting the present values (PV) of cash outflows (including initial cost) from the present values of cash inflows over a period of time; a positive net present value indicates that the projected earnings generated by a project or investment (in present pounds Sterling) exceeds the anticipated costs (also in present pounds Sterling).
3 The technicalities of this approach are demanding for a project, but an educational economist will be able to handle these calculations, provided the project has the kind of data illustrated above.

14

Strategic Issues

Critical Comments

Shamim Ahmed

Introduction

The final part of the book, on which this chapter offers some reflections, is about strategic issues. My expectation was that the focus of the 'strategic' chapters would be on a strategy for steering the Programme successfully through its planned lifetime. However, it soon became clear to me that central to EIA's strategy was the continuing life of the Programme's outcomes into the future and, though only one of the three chapters has 'sustainability' in its title, sustainability is the dominant theme in all three. I hope that my many years of working within the various agencies and ministries of Bangladesh's national education service will give some of my observations an insider perspective to complement the thoughts of the other authors in this part. Because my experience has mostly been in the primary sector, most of my reflections will refer to this phase of education.

Education in Bangladesh

In reflecting on the chapters in this part of the book, it is important to bear in mind some issues relating to the situation in Bangladesh, including some of the local 'culture' of the education system. One important contextual factor is the shortage of teachers with adequate English to teach the subject effectively. The decision to withdraw English from the school curriculum in 1971 (see Chapter 2) had the immediate consequence of seriously restricting the learning of English (and consequently having a limiting effect on education itself). Longer term, the action more or less ended the supply of future English teachers, because secondary-school teachers were (and still are) recruited from among arts, science or commerce graduates, and English teachers additionally require a strong background in the English language. Even now there is a serious shortage of English teachers at the primary and secondary level, leading to a situation where the proficiency of those who do teach English is often very low (see Chapter 9). This historical issue, it seems, has not only affected the teaching of English but, in the process, has also created a knowledge gap experienced by the whole educational community. Primary education did not figure significantly in the government's Five Year Plan until 1980, with a universal primary-education project (Lewis 2011), and according to a UNESCO review of progress, educational expansion 'only began to take place in the mid to late 1980s' (Latif 2004: 5). Ultimately, this prompted policy decisions to reposition English in the curriculum, with improved teaching methods. As Chapter 2 relates, EIA comes as the most recent in a succession of initiatives to improve English teaching. Past initiatives have failed to leave a significant legacy, and in the knowledge of this, EIA placed significant emphasis in its planning on sustainability. This entailed engagement with the system in all its diversity.

The primary education system in Bangladesh is very complicated and entirely managed by highly bureaucratic institutions. Nearly 85 per cent of the primary education system (schools and related agencies like the National Curriculum and Textbook Board (NCTB), National Academy for Primary Education (NAPE), Primary Teachers' Training Institutes (PTI) and (Secondary) Teacher Training Colleges) are totally under government management. This is unlike other countries in the region, such as India, Pakistan, Sri Lanka or Nepal, where the majority of primary schools are under private management. In Bangladesh, although there are local government management structures close to the schools, the community has little say in their management because school teachers, school-management procedures and curriculum are all dependent on a highly centralized system. For example, NCTB has sole responsibility for framing the curriculum, something that it does through the publication of textbooks for every subject and accompanying Teachers' Guides/Teachers' Editions, which assist educators in the required use of the textbooks. Review and revision are undertaken on a five- to ten-year cycle and work is therefore continuous. Despite many reports that teachers find the competency-based curriculum highly challenging, the model persists. NCTB's activities are fully supported by the Directorate of Primary Education (DPE), which, for example, recently sent a directive to schools requiring all the primary school teachers to follow the guidance given in the Teachers' Edition (TE) or Guide (TG) in all their lessons. Further, Assistant Upazila Education Officers were required to ensure this took place.[1]

The need for collaboration

Concentrating the power structure in this manner has created a feeling among all the stakeholders that they are not required to – and should not – listen to anyone outside the government's education structures. Thus, whatever teachers glean from any training is often left unimplemented if it is not specified within the guides and instructions from government. Similarly, DPE develops its in-service training manual and the training is also managed centrally by its Training Division. Under such a highly centralized system it is very difficult to accommodate or embed any innovative practice, whatever quality or practicality it demonstrates. Experience shows that only with the express consent of the directing ministry (in this case, the Ministry of Primary and Mass Education) can new practice be accommodated. In Bangladesh, the sustainability, institutionalization or embedding of any initiative can only succeed if these realities are taken into consideration.

EIA, therefore, had no option but to seek to embed its activities within the national system, as the only realistic hope that its materials and pedagogies would be entertained by schools and teachers and have a life after the end of the formal Programme. This is a decision that I commend.

Working with the grain

From the outset the EIA team was careful that the programme they would launch would be suitable for the Bangladeshi context, for example, by supporting the textbooks used in primary schools or NGO schools, and planning training or orientations totally acceptable to officials and teachers working at the primary level. This was one of the keys to sustainability through institutionalization. But institutionalization was an ultimate goal, and the path to that goal lay in the development of partnerships of the kind explained in Chapter 12. The chapter shows how different partnerships were appropriate to different phases, and how EIA made choices over which relationships should be prioritized, and in particular, how ownership of elements could pass from the Programme to the government agencies who would have the responsibility of maintaining their achievements thereafter. EIA's strategy of gradual transfer of control recognized that ownership of change is itself a particularly vital issue and something that must be engendered among both policy-makers and the practitioners.

During the pilot phase, EIA was in full control of the teacher professional development (TPD) approach. It gradually (though never completely) withdrew as the Programme progressed, giving ever greater responsibility to local government staff and teachers while it took on an oversight role and was mainly involved with central and local level government officials. EIA's key approaches to achieving sustainability lay in:

- 'in-built flexibility . . . ensuring key stakeholders' . . . ownership' (Chapter 12: p. 175) at the different levels;
- a willingness to accept changes through experience; adopting a mixed top-down and bottom-up approach;
- developing the technical capacities of local officials.

These approaches or strategies were planned on the basis of past experience and through discussions with the government's technical staff. Although, as Chapter 12 candidly admits, these potential partnerships did not always ultimately contribute to the Programme's goals, EIA is to be commended for its successes, and for its ability to achieve engagement with what is a complex and challenging education system.

Finding institutional homes

EIA has tried rightly to determine the elements that needed to be sustained and the location of an 'institutional home'. Getting such 'location' judgments right is always helpful but getting them wrong can be fatal for an initiative. And even if the correct home is identified, sometimes it has been difficult to make progress for other reasons. Chapter 12 indicates that there were difficulties with building capacity in such institutions as NAPE and NCTB, for example. Often a faculty or department would be represented by one or two individuals and only these individuals, rather than the institution as a whole, benefit from the interaction. As Chapter 12 recognizes, this represents a further obstacle to attempts to build capacity or institutionalize within the primary education system.

One example of a successful collaboration was the development of the Diploma of Primary Education (DPEd). It could be argued that although EIA was aware of the context of the education system and the history of the English language and English language teaching, it set out to deal only with the legacy of the situation by focusing on serving teachers. However, as Chapter 12 makes clear, it did try to assist new primary-school teachers with its collaboration with NAPE to develop a new initial teacher education programme, the DPEd. EIA contributed significantly to the development of the framework and to core materials and in particular, the English courses made great use of EIA materials. EIA consultants sometimes worked independently, but during editing and refinement, participation by NAPE practitioners was very important because it created a sense of ownership among NAPE Faculty, PTI Instructors and DPEd students. Thus, when some DPE representatives complained that the content of the English Resource Book was difficult, because they felt its vocabulary and contexts would be unfamiliar to teachers, NAPE faculty could successfully resist such objections. This collaboration with NAPE is a strong example of EIA acting imaginatively to take part in an undertaking which supported sustainability both by fostering ownership of its approaches on the part of influential figures in the educational establishment, and by embedding them in the training which would eventually be experienced by all new teachers. This is one way in which it was expected that the EIA model for improving the capacity of teacher educators, teacher trainers and teachers themselves would continue to enrich the system.

It is worth comparing the work of another partner in the development of the DPEd materials, Japan International Cooperation Agency (JICA), which collaborated with NAPE in the development of Mathematics and Science Resource Books. This project, 'Strengthening Primary Teacher Training on Science and Mathematics in Bangladesh',[2] has been running for many years and has worked closely with NCTB and the DPE Training Division as well as developing a close and long-standing relationship with NAPE. Their work with NCTB brought important changes to the Science and Mathematics textbooks and also helped develop Science and Mathematics Teacher's Edition and TG for Science for Grades 1 and 2. This collaboration has the elements of sustainability, embedding and ownership and to some extent, institutionalization. However, the project's impact on the wider education system has been limited. It was found, for example, that it was not clear whether the PTI instructors:

> ... were able to utilize and make the teaching packages a regular fixture in their lessons when they returned to each of their PTIs, or if they were able to improve the quality of Certification in Education (C-in-Ed) training.
>
> Aoki and Kogyo 2012: 4–5

And while a stated objective was the improvement of science and mathematics pedagogy, this was only in the fieldwork schools. JICA's input into the textbooks and ITE may have hoped to change practice in schools, but there has been no monitoring of any impact beyond the outcomes in the fieldwork schools[3] (Aoki and Kogyo 2012). JICA's partnership with NAPE has had clear benefits at central level, and the contribution to DPED materials has been invaluable. However, without large-scale monitoring and support, of the kind implemented by EIA, its effects have been limited and there is no evidence of the extensive reach and outcomes achieved by EIA.

The decision to establish a Centre of Excellence (CoE) in English teaching at NAPE, referred to in Chapter 12, in my opinion had the potential to be a key to sustainability and institutionalization for similar reasons. The Centre represented a significant collaboration between NAPE and EIA and there were hopes that it might play a major role in sustaining the Programme's outcomes in terms of practice into the future. Naturally materials produced in such collaborations would be included in TE/TG as well as DPE's training manual for subject-based training.

However, the decision to institute the CoE really needed to be taken three or four years earlier than it was. And timing is not the only issue: NAPE has no funds to support this initiative,[4] and at the time of writing (late 2017), has only one person with responsibility for this relationship, who, with the best will in the world, cannot have much effect in sustaining the learning from EIA. This supports the argument made in Chapter 12 that sustainability does not depend solely on the (funded) activities of the Programme itself; the educational environment also needs to be able to support it.

Given the byzantine complexity of the Bangladeshi education system and differing perspectives of government departments, it is perhaps not surprising that the DPE did not include all of EIA's principles and strategies in its subject-based training. However, in many upazilas, EIA teacher facilitators were selected as government trainers and this provided an alternative route to sustainability by increasing the number of competent trainers, experienced in effective TPD, working in the system. This then was more than a 'consolation', as it arguably kept EIA's successes visible to DPE, and later led to other opportunities. It is one of a number of examples where the two-track approach referred to in Chapter 12 ensured a degree of success despite frustrations. And it should be noted that later opportunities for engagement with the system were exploited more successfully. EIA was, for example, responsible for the authorship of three of the post-PEDP III design notes (see Chapter 12).

The role of research monitoring and evaluation

I have already argued that an effective research, monitoring and evaluation (RME) programme has a role to play in the sustainability of a programme, and Chapter 11 presents a complex account of the way monitoring and evaluation of EIA developed over the life of the project. The results produced were clearly part of its strategic purposes, as Chapter 12 notes in the critical factor 'Using evidence for advocacy'. But nevertheless, Chapter 11 makes clear that there was a persistent and increasing demand for more convincing evaluation evidence, which culminated in the design and execution of a quasi-experimental study. The earlier strategic decision to stay with repeats of studies at the end of each cohort was arguably unfortunate, though it may have been inevitable, given EIA's limited resources. Relying on a baseline to be valid for over five years carries its risks. Thus, it might have been prudent to at least try to repeat the pilot-year studies: a baseline before teachers and students started the Programme and one at the end of the full period (twelve months or more). After all, Chapter 11 makes it clear that the strength of the pilot studies was in their adoption of such an approach, which had commended itself to a seminar of stakeholders: 'EIA had "robust" evidence to show changes, which reflected pre- and post-treatment performance, seen as significant progress for evaluation in the "development education project" world' (Chapter 11:161). This endorsement may not have satisfied the UK's Department for International Development (DFID), which by 2015, was pressing for experimental studies.

It is also worth reflecting on the sources of some problems in the education system of Bangladesh, and to see what role research and evaluation could have had. A number of crucial historical events guided the destiny of the primary education system in Bangladesh. The most prominent of these is the nationalization of the primary education system in 1974, which centralized the entire structure under bureaucratic government management, as noted earlier. There is considerable evidence that an education system can thrive without a degree of teacher autonomy only in exceptional cases:

> Most countries whose students are among the highest performers in inter-national assessments of learning achievement have provided a high degree of autonomy to their local authorities and schools especially their teachers and parents, in deciding what courses to teach and how to use funds at the school.

> WB 2013b: 50

Teachers must have freedom to take decisions, to think independently and to develop their own beliefs, assumptions and knowledge based on their experience of what works. Often teachers are reluctant to change their beliefs, so innovative practices which are imposed without persuading them to change their beliefs are soon forgotten. (It has been said that teachers receive new ideas through training but leave them at the door of the training room.) David Pedder, in his critique of the TPD approach of EIA (Chapter 7), considers the consequences of such a practice–belief divide, which can include serious harm to a school's culture by creating an unbridgeable gulf between, among others, teachers and parents. The teachers believe that their accountability is only to the government and they have little responsibility to ensure children's learning. Pedder also makes the point that schools need to collect data to explore such practice–belief divides, but given the relatively poor record of the government system in its own RME efforts, this is a tall order for schools.

The complex situation prevailing in Bangladesh's primary education system calls for a thorough and accurate process of research, monitoring and evaluation that can provide valid and reliable findings based on robust evidence which enable appropriate follow-up initiatives. Such a rigorous strategy could go a long way to ensuring sustainability, not least by providing credible information to policy-makers about the effectiveness (or otherwise) of an initiative.

The evidence generated by the RME programme offers an abundant source for researchers, the government and other interested parties and represents a lasting effect, to the extent that it is possible to say that 'RME for sustainability' has been a success. In contrast, the sustainability of RME itself, the system's legacy, in terms of integrating its processes into the education system has been more modest. Attempts have been made to embed the monitoring system at the upazila level, through the academic supervision service. Although capacity-building should be a central feature of such embedding, EIA clearly did not have the resources to carry this out in any systemic way. EIA could rightly argue that it was a TDP and English language initiative, and not a monitoring and evaluation development project, and thus such capacity development could never be more than peripheral to its main activity. This again recalls the point made in Chapter 12, that sustainability also depends on investment outside the bounds of a single Programme. That EIA managed to train several cohorts of MPhil students at the University of Dhaka's Institute for Education and Research is to be commended, but this represents (as Chapter 12 also makes clear) capacity-development aimed at individuals rather than institutions.

Value for Money

The question in Chapter 11's subtitle, 'foundational cornerstone or luxury addition?' seems equally appropriate to Chapter 13's treatment of Value for Money (VfM). Certainly, in the early phases, many in the team were focused on developing crucial elements of the TPD model and probably gave the matter little thought. However, the chapter shows clearly how the search for the most cost-effective ways of using the Programme's budget enabled its activities to do more for less, through successive phases. It also shows how the quite bold assumption that technology costs, high in Phase 2, would come down to affordable levels was in the event correct.

At the Programme's inception in 2008, VfM did not have such a high profile as now and there was no easily identifiable external evidence base linking costs and results. DFID issued important guidance in 2011 (DFID 2011) that set a clear and high-profile agenda for this, which was strongly taken up by the project. Although not the fault of the EIA team, the lack of VfM-results-driven external debate in the early years limited the use of comparison and external benchmarking, and the opportunity to share and discuss data with other projects. The lack of an early VfM external perspective is to be regretted too as a lost opportunity to expedite the formation of partnerships with different constituencies within the education ministries. The vast majority of staff in DPE and Directorate of Secondary and Higher Education are from the administrative cadre, and earlier discussions could have taken place on this aspect of the Programme since it aligns well with their major concerns. It would have been an opportunity to 'speak the same language'.

As Chapter 13 makes clear, by the mid-point of the Programme, VfM was still central to EIA's thinking, but at a time when the resources for RME were both diminishing and highly stretched, opportunities to research in greater depth to understand which elements were particularly valuable in terms of promoting the Programme's outcomes could not be taken. For example, as Chapter 13 points out, the number of cluster meetings (CM) reduced at the same time as the unit costs were pared. However, although monitoring evidence showed the importance of CM (Chapter 6), this was not rigorous enough to be the basis of decisions. The act of bringing teachers together could not necessarily be seen as a crucial benefit; Bangladesh had fifteen years of sub-cluster meetings before EIA, and these had not produced dramatic advances in practice or learning outcomes. Stronger evidence of what aspects of the CM made the real difference would have strengthened the VfM model and made the Programme more effective and more valuable to other projects in similar fields, but that would have required a higher budget for RME.

But there is a lot of hindsight in the last few paragraphs. As I have already said, VfM as a theme in development projects has grown in prominence over recent years and its increasingly sophisticated application in EIA has no doubt made a considerable contribution to that growth.

Conclusion

The chapters in this final part of the book show how key strategies have worked together with the aim of ensuring not just the success of the Programme, but the sustainability of its improvements in classroom teaching and learning beyond its formal closure in 2018. The chapters effectively make the case that keeping a very close eye on developments through the RME programme, making sure every penny is spent to the greatest effect and building supportive relationships within the education system contributed to the Programme's sustainability. While my early observation of EIA events left me in no doubt of the uniqueness and high quality of the Programme presented by the EIA team facilitators working with the teachers and field officials, good practices were always at risk of attenuation with the Programme's expansion to reach nearly half of Bangladesh's school population. It is also true that over a decade of learning, some initiatives were not followed through and as a result the good practices advocated by EIA may not be fully accommodated in the system. It may be that the primary education system is not sufficiently prepared to adopt the practices suggested by EIA.

It would be premature at the time of writing (2017) to make predictions, positive or negative, about the Programme's effect. It appears, however, that through post-PEDP, the activities undertaken by EIA are likely to continue and additional schools will be brought under the Programme to complete implementation all over the country. Despite EIA being on the face of it an EL project, in the long run I believe it will be remembered for its endeavours to bring necessary changes to the education culture of Bangladesh.

Notes

1   In the past, as noted in Chapter 8, the publications themselves have often not been delivered to schools.

2   https://www.hiroshima-u.ac.jp/en/idec/research/jica.
3   Chapter 2 outlines how communicative features built into the English textbooks were routinely ignored by teachers, who did not understand what was intended.
4   At the time of writing, it is seeking funding from the Ministry of Primary and Mass Education (MoPME).

15

Final Reflections

Lessons Learnt

Marc van der Stouwe, Ian Eyres and Robert McCormick

Introduction

Our intention in this final chapter is both to draw out some of the over-arching lessons from the EIA experience, and to use this experience to reflect on what may be the future for educational interventions in developing countries such as Bangladesh.

Thus, first we will look back at the experience by drawing on some general themes that have emerged through the chapters of the book, but also distilling some of our experience gained from playing a leading part in the Programme for significant periods and in one case (Marc van der Stouwe's) throughout its life. We will, in particular, reflect on the Programme's focus on four key themes, identified below. In the last part of the chapter we will then consider implications for the future, some of which stem from new opportunities and some from new insights, while others arise from the changing priorities of governments and funding organizations working in the field of education in developing countries. We start, therefore, with hindsight.

Looking back

The four themes addressed in this reflection on the EIA experience, each of which features in several of the preceding chapters, will be: English language teaching (ELT); empowerment; flexibility, adaptability and the allocation of sufficient time; and partnerships.

ELT or not ELT: that is the question

Although the focus on a single subject may well have been a significant factor in the Programme's success, the strategy has risked some disadvantages, certainly in the context of upscaling and institutionalization. It is more difficult, for example, to effect change at whole-school level when only a relatively small proportion of the school's teachers are directly involved, or to persuade head teachers that a whole-school approach is needed. As Chapter 7 argued, this limits the depth of change that can be achieved. Students also have to adopt new habits and ways of responding and working in English lessons that are at variance with expectations in lessons in other subjects (which take up the other four-fifths of curriculum time). The relatively small number of English teachers in any school limits the scope for mutual support. Most Bangladeshi primary schools, for example, are unlikely to have more than two English teachers and there may be personal or practical reasons for some pairings to be unproductive, even in schools with five or six English teachers. At the level of local facilitation, not all education officers will feel confident to support and make judgments about English teaching, and the pool from which teacher facilitators can be drawn in each upazila is relatively small. While the Programme has no evidence that any of the foregoing were, in the event, significant negative factors, at the institutionalization level, as Chapter 12 points out, it has been difficult to integrate single-subject training into the government's cross-curricular continuing professional development programme. Moreover, as Fauzia Shamim argues in Chapter 3, any wider benefits of English language learning depend on the development of other essential skills, in particular, literacy and numeracy.

In addition, Chapter 2 raises the question (picked up again in Chapter 3) of whether English is the right subject to develop if the motivation is to promote economic development. Beth Erling and Masuda Khatoon present an array of evidence to support the proposition, but counsel caution in respect both of the partial nature of some sources and their scarcity, and are surely right to consider the case not proven. The research done by EIA on the link between English and economic development is adequate for a development project, though not what is needed for academic research. While further (and better) research is certainly needed, it must also be acknowledged that educational progress can never, on its own, engender economic development; put bluntly, jobs do not appear just because there are people with the skills to do them. In 1965 Foster coined the phrase the 'vocational education fallacy in development', when he questioned the use of schools to produce an economic effect when their students enter the workforce.[1] However, workforces with the appropriate skills must surely be better placed to compete for investment and employment when new opportunities do arise.

All that said, the single-subject focus on English language teaching has proven to offer distinct practical advantages, especially, but by no means exclusively, in the earliest days of the Programme. Whereas a programme attempting to improve general pedagogy would necessarily deal at a certain level of generality, EIA was able to demonstrate pedagogic principles through very precise examples of practice that all the participating teachers would be able to try out in their own classroom without the need for a high degree of interpretation or modification. It was also possible to design teacher professional development (TPD) activities and classroom materials which could closely scaffold the Programme's pedagogical approach. Moreover, this capacity – to give teachers clear messages in very concrete terms – facilitated discussion and shared reflection at cluster meetings and between paired teachers in their own school. Through reflecting on, and discussing, specific activities grounded in subject-based principles, participant teachers were able to arrive at shared understandings and a common professional perspective. Given that the Programme's capacity to engage teachers at the level of classroom realities is a major feature differentiating EIA from earlier, less successful projects, it is quite plausible to argue that without this ELT focus (or without the funding to support similarly highly focused TPD across the curriculum) there would have been no later successes to integrate into the government system.

Throughout the Programme's life there has been some – mostly anecdotal – evidence of teachers applying strategies learnt from EIA in the teaching of other subjects, and this is perhaps not surprising when one considers the similarities between communicative language teaching (CLT) and the dialogic pedagogies (Alexander 2017) promoted in many comparable projects focusing on other subjects (Westbrook et al. 2013). Moreover, given the lack of evidence of the kind of cultural resistance to such pedagogies reported by Westbrook, it seems that English (perhaps because it is unavoidably 'alien') provides a Trojan horse through which effective practices can gain acceptance in classrooms. As Chapter 12 relates, the Government of Bangladesh (GoB) was keen to draw on EIA's cross-curricular potential, which it wished to build into Primary Education Development Project III. EIA appears to have had at least some positive consequences for the wider curriculum, and lessons learnt from its implementation offer a firm foundation for further cross-curricular teacher development initiatives.

The empowering nature of EIA

Chapter 8 characterizes the Programme's approach to teacher development as 'Empowering teachers and learners' and sets out how EIA teachers have developed their practice through taking control of teaching and learning in their own classrooms. Indeed, Chapter 4 makes the idea of teacher agency a central theme in considering TPD. Chapter 14 argues that the highly centralized and directive nature of the national education system makes it very difficult for teachers to adopt innovative practices, and the experience of the Programme, certainly in its early days, was that the culture in and around schools was similarly conservative. This left teachers with no expectation that they should exercise any agency or choice in the way they taught (and, if anecdotal reports are to be believed, open to humiliating rebuke if they did choose to try something new). Looking in a different direction, Chapter 5 alerts us that, through their adoption of a transmission model, many past teacher development programmes (TDPs), have been similarly limiting. Both perspectives underestimate the value of teachers' commitment to their students and to achieving high quality in their own teaching.

Underpinning the CLT pedagogy espoused by the Programme is a welcoming of the place of active and purposeful participation to enable effective learning. Similarly, the Programme's TDP has, from the outset, sought to equip teachers not simply with a repertoire of techniques to 'deliver' to their classes, but an experiential understanding of effective pedagogies (Chapter 5). A key element to support this aim was the decision to make each teacher's classroom the primary location of their learning, so that participation in EIA meant the making of professional decisions and choices both in the planning and execution of lessons. This professional agency was amplified by teachers' own reflections and in discussions with both colleagues in school and in cluster meetings in which these reflections were shared. One noticeable outcome was the growth in confidence felt by teachers who could see their contribution as something needed by their school and encouraged by the Programme. This confidence enabled them to take risks with both imperfect English and new techniques and underpinned improvements in their pedagogy and their students' learning.

The case study of Shamima (Box 8.2, Chapter 8) shows how far her practice has advanced from the methods based on repetition and translation found in the baseline study (EIA 2009c), and the role of her self-evaluation in that progression.

Time and adaptiveness

From the outset, the Department for International Development (DFID) demonstrated a long-term perspective in planning for a nine-year programme (Chapter 12). DFID chose to allow the development of a purpose-designed model and to give it time to prove itself, rather than opting for a ready-made solution with the intention of immediately embedding it within government policy.

We believe that two core factors explain EIA's success in achieving its objectives: it was given *time for implementation*, ten years in total, and it was given *space to adjust* the interventions as necessary. In respect of *time*, the ten-year duration of the Programme meant that EIA had the opportunity to go through all stages of the innovation process, as outlined in Figure 15.1. Many educational initiatives focus on pilot testing innovative ideas and practices, collecting evidence on these interventions and producing convincing case studies. Rarely, however, do we find international development programmes that take an innovation through the next stages, i.e. replicating a pilot at scale and ensuring sustainability of an intervention through embedding and wider adoption.

EIA was exceptional in being designed as a programme that would move through all six stages of the innovation process. Thus, it moved from problem definition and the development of a concept that is translated into a practical solution in Phase 1, to pilot-testing with a strong focus on evidence collection in Phase 2, to scaling up a proven model in Phase 3. EIA went through these stages during its implementation period, while in the final stage (Phase 4) in particular, there was a shift to influencing the wider system and to advocating EIA

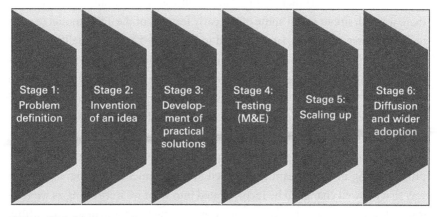

Figure 15.1 The innovation process

approaches, not just in the area of ELT, but in more general pedagogic and TPD contexts. This was combined with building the capacity of institutions and individuals within the government system to help them to sustain EIA-initiated methods and practices at decreasing levels of Programme support. This focus on the entire process in one single project, not often seen in development programmes, can be considered a major factor in EIA's success.

The issue of duration cannot be seen in isolation from the issue of programmatic *adaptiveness*. Such adaptations to the Programme were made in response to: (i) evidence from programme implementation; (ii) changes in the local context; and (iii) adaptation to the government system as EIA was embedded. In relation to *evidence*, EIA's RME activities generated information that fed into continuous programme adjustment (Chapter 11), thus enhancing the effectiveness of delivery and increasing the likelihood of achieving the desired outcomes. In other words, evidence was used to inform action. At the same time, and partly because of its long duration, the Programme experienced sometimes unpredictable *changes of the context* to which it needed to respond flexibly and rapidly. This did not mean that the Programme had not been planned carefully. Rather, it accepted that the complex of challenges and opportunities surrounding the Programme would change over time and require shifts in Programme design and implementation. An example is the move from the use of iPods (Phase 2) to mobile phones provided by the Programme (Phase 3), to the use of teachers' own mobile phones (Phase 4), enabled by beneficial changes in the technology landscape in Bangladesh. Another example of adaptation is provided by the changes made to the implementation model due to the increase in scale of implementation and EIA's improved understanding on how to work effectively with government and ensure 'political acceptability'. Thus, though there was a desire to retain some of the early features of the TPD model (e.g. six to eight cluster meetings), later this had to be reduced and eventually absorbed into the government sub-cluster meetings programme (as Chapter 13 explains from the value for money perspective). This change in the implementation model also resulted in lightening the Programme's central-level technical support function and a compensating increase in the technical support being provided through the digital TPD materials as well as through the decentralized support structures of the government rather than EIA as a Programme. Adaptive programming in EIA meant it 'designed and implemented a programme in a way that allowed change to be incorporated into what we were doing as we were doing it, within the framework of our overall impact and outcome goals within agreed timeframes'.[2]

Partnerships

Chapter 12 has already shown that building strong partnerships between Programme staff on the one hand and government and NGO staff on the other was important in allowing the EIA to develop its approach and materials, and in institutionalizing these at various levels within the education system. Building long-term, respectful relationships, based on the demands and needs of the system rather than the needs of the Programme, was key to being effective.

Behind this relationship building was EIA's own partnership, its implementing consortium of Cambridge Education, The Open University (OU) and the BBC Media Action. A particular example of this collaboration's contribution to the Programme's success relates to the beneficial combination of Cambridge Education's managerial strength and understanding of contextual development processes and the Open University's specialized technical knowledge and leadership. A salient dimension to the success of this partnership was the creative tension between the focus on change (and the need for change) brought by OU academics and the understanding on the part of Cambridge Education's Dhaka-based national staff of what was possible and what simply could not be changed in this particular context. The international Cambridge Education staff had an important facilitation role to play, often manifested as a bridging function between these two parties. EIA was, therefore, able to combine this focus and belief in change with realism and respect for the local perspective, based on a thorough understanding of local learning.

The commitment to change extended to changing minds within the EIA team. Early in the Programme, for example, some of the newly recruited Bangladeshi staff needed convincing that any change was possible, while later on members of the OU team needed to adjust their views on how to involve government institutions and officials in delivery, and accept the limitations set by the GoB's institutional set-up and absorption capacity. The processes of reflection and decision-making in this regard have been very thorough and constructive.

Looking forward

In this final section we wish to draw on EIA's lessons in order to look forward, sometimes considering initiatives that were only just emerging during the time of EIA and sometimes anticipating future developments in keeping with EIA's principles and practices. Our thoughts are themed as: empowerment into the future; school learning; investment in scale-up and embedding innovations; the role of technology; and out-of-school children and other marginalized groups.

Empowerment into the future

In the first half of this chapter we looked at how EIA had fostered a sense of professional agency among teachers, and we see this as an essential factor in the embedding of effective practice within the school system. Further evidence of a growing and collective sense of professional agency can be found in the work of the EIA-supported Teachers' Voices project,[3] which enabled teachers to undertake small classroom-based action-research studies. Over the course of a year, continuous support was provided by EIA staff both face-to-face and online.

The concluding two-day conference[4] gave the participants an opportunity to share their findings with other professionals, and the talk of 'action', 'reflection', 'observation', 'evidence', 'findings', 'unanswered questions' and so on signalled a marked change for teachers who had once thought only in terms of following and repeating the textbook.

Tempting as it is to hark back to a golden age of 'teacher-as-researcher', where curriculum development was a central concern and mainly located in the classroom (Stenhouse 1975), it seems optimistic to hope that this kind of 'teacher voice' activity can be maintained within existing education budgets. More significant, perhaps, is the evidence of the many teachers who, like Shamima (Chapter 8 and earlier in this chapter) are now much more self-critical and reflexive in changing their practice. Teachers across the Programme, like Shamima, feel empowered to experiment with different communicative approaches, and through reflection continue to adapt and improve. Teachers have been empowered by being shown practically (for example, through the use of MAV – Chapter 6) how such things could be done and through having the opportunity to work with colleagues to find the ways most suitable to their own classes. This allowed them to overcome the forces that led them to believe that innovative practice was impossible in the context of their schools (Kraft et al. 2009). It is this sense of agency and empowerment that will put teachers at the centre of a changed educational landscape.

School learning

Chapters 4 and 5 discussed how the Programme prepared head teachers (HTs) to support teachers in their learning, thus recognizing the school as an important arena for change. The evidence examined in Chapter 4, in particular, indicated a variety of functions for the HT from general support to teachers, to changing the culture of the school. Nevertheless, as Chapter 5 points out, while the role of the HTs within the Programme grew, it remained limited in its scope. This was in part for practical reasons, as only two teachers were involved in EIA from any one school (and in addition, with those head teachers who teach, in many primary schools, also fully participating as their teachers did). The discussion of ELT above (*ELT or not ELT: that is the question*), examined the limitations of the single-subject focus. It was a concern of EIA that its schools, as well as the individual teachers based in them, should be learning. This was the challenge articulated by David Pedder in his critical review of the EIA TPD model (Chapter 7): how to enable a school to learn in such a way that profound and lasting change is possible? Although EIA's head teacher development programme included training on leadership and providing support for EIA teachers, Pedder's 'Leadership and organizational learning capacity-building' goes further, in calling on schools to 'look critically at their organizational cultures and systems and prioritize in the life of the school the cultivation of supportive ecologies for innovation' (Chapter 7: p. 99). He goes on to argue for attention to be given to the 'influence of school-level beliefs and values on teachers' learning' (Chapter 7: p. 100), with the radical suggestion that schools should be self-evaluative, with staff examining the practice-value differences that exist within their collective experience and views.

This has important implications for future approaches that seek to address systemic change and particularly where there are several curriculum subjects involved (e.g. the Teacher Development Programme in Nigeria[5]) or where a whole-school approach is attempted (e.g. ZEST in Zambia[6]). The Nigerian project was aimed at primary and junior-secondary school teachers covering four subjects, using the same conception of TPD as EIA (indeed some staff on the project were drawn from EIA), with a number of teachers involved in a school and over a period of time. The plans up to 2015 envisaged a two-year engagement in a school with four teachers being involved in the following way:

Year 1 – Two new teachers for English and two new teachers for Mathematics from Primary 1–3 enrol into the Programme.

Y2 – Same pair of teachers for English language and pair of teachers for Mathematics receive materials on the next three grades (P4–6) in their respective subjects.

Y2 – Two of the four teachers are selected, on the basis of performance, interest and experience, to receive P4–6 Science and Technology materials and training.

Teacher Development Programme 2014: 13

The HTs are also involved for the two years and undertake training on leadership and on classroom observation (but not to establish a school-wide approach to this). At the time of writing it is too early to know how this will work in practice, but even this cross-curricular approach is limited, since not all of the school's teachers are involved.

If in such projects, a larger number of (or, better still, all) teachers could be involved there is potential for impact to be felt across the curriculum. Work on such whole-school approaches needs school-level strategies for implementation; for example, does the school start with a few 'champion' teachers or departments, or take all the teachers along at the same time?

The Zambian Education School-based Training (ZEST) has been required to undertake the latter approach, as the involvement of all teachers in a school in developing their practice of student-centred approaches, on the basis of their own assessment of needs, is mandated by the Zambian government. Such approaches have been tried in the developed world, for example with the Learning How to Learn project in the UK (James et al. 2007), which recognized the need to work at the classroom, school and network levels to improve the practice of assessment for learning in schools. But no particular model of how a school would take this forward was advocated, though schools were supported by project staff to develop suitable approaches for their individual circumstances. UK schools, and especially their head teachers, have the autonomy and hence agency to take individual approaches, something not always found in education systems in the developing world. As we have already stressed, EIA took teacher empowerment seriously and we have argued that this contributed to its success. It seems logical to extend this empowerment to whole schools, so that TPD is not just located in the school, but truly *school-based* as opposed to simply *based in a school*.

Investment in scale-up and embedding of innovations

Chapter 12 makes the case that if a project is serious about embedding change, sufficient time and resources are required. Before even being able to address the embedding of successful innovations, there is a need to address the identified problem that few successful pilots make the transition to working successfully at scale. The positive news is that this situation is changing: international development agencies are increasingly focusing funding and support onto the scale-up phase of interventions that have proven to work in their pilot stage (ESRC/DFID 2013). As mentioned above, we welcome this development as scale-up needs time as well as resources. It is important to stress that the current willingness to invest in scale-up also makes business sense for funders: continuing the investment in initiatives that have proven to work and are in demand by governments and other stakeholders, will have greater chances for impact at scale, while at the same time unit costs are likely to be lower as initial investment costs have been made already.

If such scale-up support is provided, it is important to take into account that first of all, pilot models need adjustment to work at scale: the model tested during the pilot will in most cases not be the same model used during scale-up, as Chapter 13 illustrated. This has affordability as well as delivery reasons, including the fact that a range of other institutions and stakeholders may get involved (and take ownership) during scale-up. Second, testing doesn't end at the pilot stage. There is a continued need to collect evidence about whether the intervention really does work at this larger scale too, while at the same time operating at scale comes with a different set of contextual factors, which also impact on the intervention. This could result in different outcomes. We make the case that investment in scale-up should include funding for continued research and evaluation as well, and that such evaluation should include a focus on the impact of contextual factors on an intervention (something pointed out in Chapter 11 in relation to randomized control trials), and not only on whether an intervention achieves its intended objectives (e.g. an improvement in learning outcomes).

However, it is imperative for the success of innovation in development to go a step further: in line with the discussion in Chapter 12, we stress that creating an intervention that proves itself to work at scale is a major achievement that deserves recognition. However, it is not the end of the story. Change will not be sustained by itself. It will need consistent and long-term support, especially in terms of technical assistance and system strengthening, with specific reference to Stage 6 of the innovation process outlined above (Figure 15.1). Our observation is that such long-term work on systems capacity-building is often not given the attention and resources it requires. There are general systems strengthening and education reform programmes in many countries, but what is insufficiently supported are the specific system-strengthening interventions that build systemic capacity to embed a *specific innovation* within government systems, i.e. as a logical next stage in the innovation process, rather than as a general system-wide reform approach. One of the reasons for this lacuna may be that innovation and system strengthening are seen as two rather different things, perhaps because the development of new ideas and the testing of innovations are often undertaken by different groups of people or even separate organizations. Another reason may be that capacity building and system strengthening are seen as the 'boring stuff', happening long after the initial excitement is over. Related to this is the above-mentioned donor tendency to fund short term and then move on to the next things, rather than to continue and deepen the investment of successful initiatives. This is a serious issue that donors must confront. A final explanation is that while, at earlier stages, an innovation could be given substantial freedom to 'run on its own', the process of embedding within systems, by definition, involves strong government involvement and buy-in, and dealing with the political and bureaucratic structures to which they are linked. Often external support to such processes may either not be welcomed by governments, or be blocked by politically circumspect donor agencies, or because of the latter's perceptions of a lack of immediate return on their investment.

In the case of EIA, the importance of embedding and institutionalization was recognized by DFID in their funding of EIA's long timescale. However, there was potential to do more. At later stages in the Programme, despite EIA's achievements in improving learning outcomes at scale, strong demand from the GoB for support to embed EIA's methods and practices within its systems, and the concerted efforts of DFID's Dhaka office, DFID did not take the opportunity to capitalize on the Programme's proven success; the decision was taken not to provide additional investment to support the technical assistance and capacity-building work necessary for fully embedding and sustaining the work of EIA. We believe that an additional and longer-term investment would have allowed the Programme to find better opportunities to address the issues and challenges of embedding a tangible and specific innovation in the area of English and TPD within a wider systems environment. Such embedding implies a multi-subject approach (not unproblematic as indicated earlier), and needs to include 'surrounding' areas such as assessment, curriculum, monitoring and evaluation and school support and supervision.

The role of technology

EIA had originally intended to use an increasingly sophisticated range of technologies to support more sophisticated professional development and pedagogic practices. The initial Programme design began with relatively simple devices for playing audio and video, but envisaged progressing onto using smartphones to build professional networks and laptops and digital cameras to support the creation of digital media by students undertaking photo-journalism, audio podcasting and participatory video projects, and teachers using video recording as part of their self-evaluation. However, these sophisticated and expensive technologies would have required correspondingly extensive training and support. After the initial workshops, the project accepted the need to 'keep it simple', in order to achieve affordable impact at scale, in keeping with the principles articulated in Chapter 13. Instead, EIA decided to focus upon targeted use of low-cost, widely available technology that by the final phase of the Programme most teachers would already own and use every day. This was effective, but relatively limited in its pedagogic affordances.

The Programmes' use of such available technology to improve classroom practice and learning outcomes rebuts two widely held views: (i) that technology must be expensive and therefore is not an appropriate investment in poor-country contexts; and (ii) that digital technologies requires major investment for people to learn how to understand and use them. The Programme demonstrates what is possible when technologies that people already own and are familiar with are used, rather than making large-scale investment in technologies that are complex and unfamiliar.

To reach an affordable solution that would bring technology within reach of teachers with an extremely modest salary, and of schools that had little budget of their own, EIA went through a number of iterations of the model and its technology, and benefitted from developments in the technology environment, not least reducing prices. There were also school developments that allowed them to use their school block grant for the purchase of hardware. Thus the technologies were within reach of the majority of schools and teachers, without further support from EIA, and so were sustainable.

With some of the common reservations about the use of technology addressed, there are three major points we wish to make in relation to the future of the use of technology in education interventions in an international development context. First, when designing future TPD interventions, technology should be seen as one element within a wider package of support, and not as a stand-alone solution capable of replacing all other forms of support. This book describes and advocates a technology-enhanced approach not technology as a panacea.

Second, using technology does more than simply provide content and support to teachers, it also has the potential to challenge and re-define 'cultures of learning'. In a context where people are used to learning (i) face-to-face, (ii) in groups and (iii) for defined time periods in selected training venues, it is a groundbreaking change to introduce technology-based learning, which is individualized, and designed in such a way (see Chapter 6) that it is accessible without the constant presence of a human trainer and can be done 'anytime, anywhere'. As we have just said, we do not believe that technology can 'deliver training' without other forms of support. However, successive generations are experiencing quite different digital cultures from those currently assumed, and imaginative ways to harness them need to be developed. The challenge for TPD and other education development programmes is to build on these developing learning cultures and styles, all the while challenging existing practices and introducing ways of learning. Digital technologies can provide excellent tools to enable such developments.

Third and finally, just as EIA tried within its adaptive programme design to second guess the future with regard to technology, so any future development in education should similarly *look forward*. Technology developments often move extremely fast: the way EIA was able to use technology at the end of the project was simply impossible to foresee at the pilot stage. New developments in relation to the next generations of smartphones, tablet technology, audio transmission and solar power all provide major opportunities in international development contexts, and the challenge for development interventions will be to look forward and be quick and flexible to grasp opportunities as they come along. For example, early research by colleagues working on the IGATE project (in Zimbabwe) suggests that all teachers already have smartphones and that they routinely access the internet on these devices (OU 2017). This provides technological opportunities well beyond our experience in Bangladesh (where, at the time of writing, many teachers still have no internet access) which the programme team will be wise to exploit.

Out-of-school children and other marginalized groups

The original programme design for the secondary sector included the deployment of boat schools to reach marginalized and out-of-school children, especially those in areas where schools were often not available owing to limited community access to land for building, or to schools being washed away by flooding. (At the time of project design, some 2,000–3,000 schools per year were being washed away in these areas.) It became clear, however, that such an ambitious initiative would be too demanding in terms of the Programme's human and financial resources.

EIA reached representatives of marginalized groups in Bangladesh in two different ways: (i) through the selection of locations in which EIA had its interventions; and (ii) by working with specific groups. On the first, EIA used the UNICEF composite deprivation index to select a high representation of remote and socio-economically disadvantaged areas.[7] Rather than having a separate intervention for marginalized groups, EIA thus reached a disproportionally high number of teachers and students from such groups through their high degree of inclusion in the EIA programme. Also at the request of UNICEF Bangladesh, EIA piloted materials and trained master trainers and teachers in the Ability Based Learning[8] non-formal education programme that reaches 200,000 working and street children, aged ten to fourteen years, in urban areas. Moreover, throughout the lifetime of EIA, the Programme reached many more working children through its partnership with the Underprivileged Children's Educational Programs[9] (UCEP) Bangladesh (see e.g. Shohel and Banks 2010).

However, although EIA schools component did include some marginalized groups during its implementation, out-of-school children and young people were not part of its core agenda. Addressing their needs would have been difficult to do within an approach to improving quality of learning which focused on working with teachers rather than directly with students. Yet there is a clear and urgent need to address the learning needs of these children: there are high numbers of out-of-school children in Bangladesh (Chapters 1 and 4), as is the case in many other parts of the world, and improving the learning opportunities of these children should be seen as a key priority, in line with both the SDGs and the 'Leave No One Behind' agenda.[10] Reaching out-of-school children and young people would obviously require distinct strategies and different delivery modalities from those used in the EIA's schools component.

The EIA experience may, however, provide some useful pointers in terms of how to open up learning opportunities for such new groups of learners. First of all, the way mobile phones provided an opportunity for individualized, 'anytime, anywhere' learning offers a model that could work for learning outside schools. These groups are expected to particularly benefit from a more flexible learning approach, as the reason they are out of school is often that they are working and unable to engage in scheduled activities.

Moreover, we see opportunities to use the EIA materials development experience to provide guidance for the development of new content. The technology may be suitable for use by community members who have no formal teaching role, but who could be supported to facilitate learning through educational materials. The materials could also be presented on a mobile device, but one that would need to require only minimal additional mediation by a community-based facilitator. The technology would have to be ubiquitous in the way that the mobile phone currently is, or cheap enough to supply to learners (or groups of learners). A new generation of technology (and associated learning materials) could provide ways of reaching these children.

Finally, the experience of using mass media, as well as community English-learning clubs in the adult learning component of EIA, may provide promising ways to support the learning of out-of-school children in more informal settings, with individual learning through technology integrated with new forms of community-based learning.

Lessons learnt

Constructing this chapter on the ideas of looking forward and looking back illustrates how learning lessons is a continuing process. The Programme's original team members brought together a great deal of past learning and experience in fields which included teacher development, international development, English language teaching, multilingual classrooms, general pedagogy, technology in education, project planning and management, RME, financial management and many more. It was perhaps this diversity of hinterland that resulted in a Programme that was imaginative and innovative in many ways, even though very little was wholly new. As EIA progressed and grew to reach and engage with many thousands of teachers, it continued to learn from other projects as well as from its own experience. It also began to contribute to learning, and so develop understanding of the elements which can make ELT and TPD programmes successful. This learning will inform new initiatives, some of them already emerging, which will in turn take the learning further. This book is an attempt to summarize some of the more important lessons learnt within English in Action. We trust that it is not the last word.

Notes

1   King and Martin (2000) reaffirmed the complexity of this link more recently.
2   EQUIP-Tanzania Adaptive Programming Reflections: Mid-Term Review January 2016 http://www.heart-resources.org/assignment/equip-tanzania-adaptive-programming-reflections-mid-term-review-january-2016/ (accessed 30 October 2017).

3 This is the project in which Shamima (Chapter 8) takes part.

4 http://eiabd.com/tvc.html (accessed 21 October 2017).

5 https://www.mottmac.com/article/9615/teacher-development-programme-nigeria (accessed 30 October 2017).

6 http://www.open.ac.uk/scotland/news/funding-ou-teacher-development-project-zambia (accessed 30 October 2017).

7 As noted in Chapter 11, this may have had unwanted consequences for the assessment of teacher and student progress when results were compared to a baseline established before this bias towards disadvantaged areas.

8 https://www.unicefusa.org/mission/protect/education/let-us-learn/bangladesh (accessed 30 October 2017).

9 http://www.ucepbd.org/ (accessed 30 October 2017).

10 https://www.theguardian.com/global-development/2015/aug/03/ban-ki-moon-hails-sdgs-agreed-by-193-nations-as-leaving-no-one-behind (accessed 21 October 2017).

Glossary

Classroom language the language spoken in English language lessons, particularly useful phrases that teachers are likely to use repeatedly, for example to present 'new' language items and patterns or to organize activities.

Cluster meeting a regular gathering of teachers from a local group of schools, for professional development purposes.

Code-switching the practice of switching between two or more languages in the context of a single conversation, e.g. alternating between English and Bangla.

Communicative language teaching (CLT) an approach to English language teaching based on the idea that language learning involves communication of real meanings.

Continuous professional development (CPD) developing professional skills, knowledge and experience whilst working. In teaching, this is also known as 'in-service', as distinct from 'pre-service' teacher education or development.

Cost–benefit analysis evaluating alternatives by identifying their costs and benefits in financial terms.

Cost-effectiveness maximizing results relative to cost of inputs (in DFID's value for money framework, results are considered in terms of poverty reduction).

Difference in differences a statistical technique used in quantitative experimental studies, comparing the average difference in outcome for the treatment group to the average difference in outcome for the control group.

Double-shift system where one 'shift' of students attends classes during the early part of the day and a separate second 'shift' attends later, thereby increasing the number of students a school can serve.

Economy minimizing the cost of inputs (within DFID's value for money framework).

Effectiveness maximizing the conversion of outputs/activities into outcomes/results (within DFID's value for money framework).

Efficiency maximizing the conversion of inputs into outputs (within DFID's value for money framework).

***English for Today* (*EfT*)** the national textbook series for English Language lessons in Bangladesh.

English Language for Teachers (EL4T) a self- or peer-study audio-course developed by EIA to improve teachers' own English Language, particularly developing speaking and listening skills using English language embodied in the curriculum.

English medium of instruction (EMI) when English is used as the primary medium of instruction, particularly when it is not the mother-tongue of most students.

Equity ensuring that benefits are distributed fairly.

Evaluation establishing whether a programme has been effective, usually over a period of one year or more.

First language the first language acquired by young people in their home, also known as 'mother tongue' or 'Language 1 (L1)'.

Logical framework (log frame) a tool for planning, implementing, monitoring and evaluating international development projects, highlighting a project's purpose, activities and anticipated results.

Mediated authentic video (MAV) a style of audio-visual resource developed by EIA: video clips showing teaching and learning within authentic classroom settings are mediated by a narrator to support teacher development.

Mobile learning/mLearning continuous access to learning activities/resources across a range of settings through mobile devices including phones, tablets or laptops.

Monitoring quick and relatively crude tracking of programme outputs/activities month-by-month, to ensure/improve the quality of programme delivery.

Net present value a measurement of profit calculated by subtracting the present values (PV) of cash outflows (including initial cost) from the present values of cash inflows over a period of time. A positive net present value indicates that the expected earnings generated by a project or investment (in present pounds sterling) exceeds the anticipated costs (also in present pounds sterling).

Pedagogy the theory, understanding and practice of teaching; the primary function of a teacher.

Qualitative studies research that gathers information that is not in a numerical form; for example, diary accounts, open-ended questionnaires, unstructured interviews and unstructured observations. Qualitative studies are typically descriptive or interpretative and as such are harder to analyse than quantitative studies.

Quantitative studies research that gathers information in numerical form, including structured questionnaires, interviews or observations and objective measurements. Quantitative studies usually gather large data-sets for analysis by statistical techniques.

Quasi-experimental study a quantitative study with an experimental design: comparing outcomes for treatment groups (who participate in some programme of treatment) and control groups (who do not participate in the programme). In all other aspects, the treatment and control groups are meant to be comparable, so differences in outcome are attributable to the treatment.

Randomized control trial (RCT) a quantitative study with an experimental design that requires matched control and treatment groups through randomized sampling of which groups receive the treatment and which do not (control).

School-based teacher development (SBTD) a form of workplace learning which is directed at becoming a teacher, or becoming a better teacher, through deliberate (thoughtful/purposeful) practice of teaching in schools.

Teacher facilitator (TF) a role within EIA for teachers who support their peers through the process of school-based teacher development within or between schools.

Technology-enhanced learning the use of digital technologies and materials to support teaching and learning: including how programmes are designed, teachers supported, communities developed and outcomes measured.

Translanguaging an approach to teaching and learning in the classroom that allows students and teachers to draw flexibly and fluidly on the range of languages available to them.

Upazila literally a 'sub-district' in Bangladesh, previously known as a 'thana'; upazilas are the second-smallest unit of regional administration in Bangladesh.

Value for Money (VfM) DFID views VfM as maximizing the impact of each pound invested in improving poor peoples' lives, through better understanding what drives costs and what influences results, so that more informed and evidence-based choices can be made.

References

ABMB (2007), *English in Action CNTR 200607629 Government of Bangladesh DFID*, Arnhem, Netherlands: ARCADIS BMB.

Alexander, D. (2008), *English Language Skills, Bangladesh. Written Ministerial Statements* (18 March) (online at: www.theyworkforyou.com/wms/?id=2008–03–18b.61WS.1 [accessed 2011, no longer available]).

Alexander, R. J. (2017), *Towards Dialogic Teaching: Rethinking Classroom Talk*, York, UK: Dialogos.

Altinyelken, H. K. (2010), 'Curriculum change in Uganda: Teacher perspectives on the new thematic curriculum', *International Journal of Educational Development*, 30 (2): 151–61.

Aminuzzaman, S., H. Baldersheim and I. Jamil (2003), 'Talking back! Empowerment and mobile phones in rural Bangladesh: a study of the village phone scheme of Grameen Bank', *Contemporary South Asia*, 12 (3): 327–48.

Amundsen, I. (2013), 'Dynasty or democracy? Party politics in Bangladesh', *CMI BRIEF*, 12 (6) (November) (online at: https://www.cmi.no/publications/file/4974-dynasty-or-democracy-party-politics-in-bangladesh.pdf [accessed 27 October 2017]).

Anamuah-Mensah, J., F. Banks, B. Moon, and F. Wolfenden (2013), 'New modes of teacher pre-service training and professional development', in B. Moon (ed.), *Teacher Education and the Challenge of Development*, 201–11, Oxon, UK: Routledge.

Aoki, Y. and K. Kogyo (2012) Ex-Post Evaluation of Japanese Technical Cooperation Project: 'Project for Strengthening Primary Teacher Training on Science and Mathematics (online at: https://www2.jica.go.jp/en/evaluation/pdf/2012_0602279_4.pdf).

Arcand, J.-L. and F. Grin (2013), 'Language in economic development: Is English special and is linguistic fragmentation bad?', in E. J. Erling and P. Seargeant (eds), *English and Development: Policy, Pedagogy and Globalization*, 243–66, Bristol: Multilingual Matters.

Argyris, C. (1993), *Knowledge for Action: A Guide to Overcoming Barriers to Organizational Change*, San Francisco, USA: Jossey Bass.

Argyris, C. and D. Schön (1978), *Organizational Learning: A Theory of Action Perspective*, Reading, MA: Addison-Wesley.

Argyris, C. and D. Schön (1996), *Organizational Learning II: Theory, Method and Practice*, New York, USA: Addison-Wesley.

Arkorful, K. (2012), *Complementary education programme and the opportunity to learn in the northern region of Ghana* (unpublished PhD thesis), Brighton, UK: University of Sussex.

Asian Development Bank (ADB) (2012), *The informal sector and informal employment in Bangladesh: Country report 2010*, Mandaluyong City, Philippines: ADB (online at: https://www.adb.org/sites/default/files/publication/30084/informal-sector-informal-employment-bangladesh.pdf [accessed 5 October 2017]).

Aslam, M., A. De, G. Kingdon and R. Kumar (2010), *Economic returns to schooling and skills: An analysis of India and Pakistan, RECOUP Working Paper No. 38* (online at: http://ceid.educ.cam.ac.uk/researchprogrammes/recoup/publications/workingpapers/WP38-returns_to_education.pdf [accessed 5 October 2017]).

Aslam, M., A. De, G. Kingdon and R. Kumar (2012), 'Economic returns to schooling and cognitive skills: A south Asian comparison', in C. Colclough (ed.), *Education Outcomes and Poverty: A Reassessment*, 94–118, London: Routledge.

Avaolos, B. (2011), 'Teacher professional development in Teaching and Teacher Education over ten years', *Teaching and Teacher Education*, 27(1): 10–20.

Azam, M., A. Chin and N. Prakash (2010), *The returns to English-language skills in India*. Discussion Paper No. 4802. Bonn: Institute for the Study of Labor (online at: http://ftp.iza.org/dp4802.pdf [accessed 5 October 2017]).

Baba, T. (2008), *A Study on the Program Approach Framework in International Cooperation and Japanese Style Education Model. Study Report*, Hiroshima, Japan: Hiroshima University. (In Japanese: Kokusaikyouryoku ni okeru Program Approach no Wakugumi to Nihongata Kyouiku Kyouryoku Model no Kousatu.)

Babaci-Wilhite, Z. (2015), *Language, Development and Human Rights in Education: Curriculum Policies in Asia and Africa*, London, UK: Palgrave Macmillan.

Bandura, A. (1997), *Self-efficacy: The Exercise of Control*, New York, USA: W. H. Freeman.

Banegas, D. L. (2009), 'Content knowledge in teacher education: Where professionalisation lies', *ELTED Journal*, 12: 44–51.

Banks, F., M. Bird, M. Deane, C. Hedges, J. Leach and B. Moon (2007), *Costing Open and Distance Teacher Education: Case Study Examples from Sub-Saharan Africa*, Milton Keynes, UK: The Open University.

Banu, R. (2005), 'Linguistic imperialism: The Bangladesh case', *Journal of the Institute of Modern Languages*, 17 and 18: 29–49.

Banu, R. and R. Sussex (2001), 'English in Bangladesh after independence: Dynamics of policy and practice', in B. Moore (ed.), *Who's Centric Now? The Present State of Post-colonial Englishes*, 122–47, Melbourne: Oxford University Press (Australia).

Barnes, A. (2006), 'Confidence levels and concerns of beginning teachers of modern foreign languages', *Language Learning Journal*, 34 (1): 37–46.

Barnett, M. (2006), 'Using a Web-Based Professional Development System to Support Preservice Teachers in Examining Authentic Classroom Practice', *Journal of Technology and Teacher Education*, 14: 701–29.

Barsoum, G. F. (2004), 'The employment crisis of female graduates in Egypt: An ethnographic account', *Cairo Papers*, 25 (3).

Baumgardner, R. J. (ed.) (1996), *South Asian English: Structure, Use, Users*, Urbana, IL: University of Illinois Press.

Belhiah, H. and M. Elhami (2015), 'English as a medium of instruction in the Gulf: When students and teachers speak', *Language Policy*, 14: 3–23.

Bell, M., P. Cordingley, C. Isham and R. Davis (2012), *Report of Professional Practitioner Use of Research Review: Practitioner Engagement in and/or with Research*. Technical report, Coventry, UK: CUREE, GTCE, LSIS and NTRP (online at: http://www. curee.co.uk/files/publication/1297423037/Practitioner%20Use%20of%20 Research%20Review.pdf [Accessed 4 June 2017]).

Berliner, D. C. (2002), 'Educational research: the hardest science of all', *Educational Researcher*, 31 (8): 18–20.

Bird, L., B. Moon and A. Storey (2013), 'The context for teacher education in developing countries', in B. Moon (ed.), *Teacher Education and the Challenge of Development*, 19–31, Oxon, UK: Routledge.

Birdsall, N., R. Levine and A. Ibrahim (2005), 'Towards universal primary education: investments, incentives, and institutions', *European Journal of Education*, 40 (3): 337–49.

Biswas, R., A. Joshi, R. Joshi, T. Kaufman, C. Peterson, J. P. Sturmberg, A. Maitra and C. M. Martin (2009), 'Revitalizing primary health care and family medicine/primary care in India – disruptive innovation?', *Journal of Evaluation in Clinical Practice*, 15 (5): 873–80.

Boissiere, M. (2004), *Determinants of Primary Education Outcomes in Developing Countries*, Washington, DC: World Bank, Independent Evaluation Group (IEG).

Bold, T., M. Kimenyi, G. Mwabu, A. Ng'ang'a and J. Sandefur (2013), *Scaling-up What Works: Experimental Evidence on External Validity in Kenyan Education*, Working Paper No. 321, Washington, D.C., USA: Centre for Global Development.

Bold, T., D. Filmer, G. Martin, E. Molina, B. Sacy, C. Rockmore, J. Svensson and W. Wane (2016), 'What do teachers know and do? A report card on primary teachers in Sub-Saharan Africa', in *RISE Annual Conference 2016*, Oxford: Research on Improving Systems Education, Blavatnik School of Government, University of Oxford.

Bondi, M. & F. Poppi (2007), 'Devising a language certificate for primary school teachers of English', *Profile Issues in Teachers Professional Development* (8): 145–64.

Bransford, J., A. Brown, and R. Cocking (2000), 'Teacher learning', in J. Bransford, A. Brown and R. Cocking (eds), *How People Learn. Brain, Mind, Experience and School*, 190–205, Washington: D.C., USA: National Academy Press.

British Council (n.d), *The English effect* (online at: https://www.britishcouncil.org/sites/ default/files/english-effect-report-v2.pdf [accessed 010817]).

Brock, A. (2009), 'Moving mountains stone by stone: Reforming rural education in China', *International Journal of Educational Development*, 29 (5): 454–62.

Brock-Utne, B. and H. Alidou (2011), 'Active students – learning through a language they master', in A. Ouane and C. Glanz (eds), *Optimising Learning, Education and Publishing in Africa: The Language Factor*, 187–216, Hamburg, Germany: UNESCO Institute for Lifelong Learning (UIL)/Association for the Development of Education

in Africa (ADEA)/African Development Bank (online at: http://unesdoc.unesco.
org/images/0021/002126/212602e.pdf [accessed 17 October 2017]).

Brock-Utne, B. and H. B. Holmarsdotti (2001), 'The choice of English as medium of
instruction and its effects on the African languages in Namibia', *International Review
of Education*, 47 (3–4): 293–322.

Buckler, A. (2011), 'Reconsidering the evidence base, considering the rural: Aiming for a
better understanding of the education and training needs of Sub-Saharan African
teachers', *International Journal of Educational Development*, 31 (3): 244–50.

Butler, Y. G. (2004), 'What level of English proficiency do elementary school teachers
need to attain to teach EFL? Case studies from Korea, Taiwan, and Japan', *Tesol
Quarterly*, 38 (2): 245–78.

Cable, C., P. Driscoll, R. Mitchell, S. Sing, T. Cremin, J. Earl, I. Eyres, B. Holmes, C. Martin
and B. Heins (2010), *Languages Learning at Key Stage 2: A Longitudinal Study*,
London: Department for Children, Schools and Families (online at: https://eprints.
soton.ac.uk/143157/1/DCSF-RR198.pdf [accessed 17 October 2017]).

Cambridge Education (2016), *Go Innovate! A Guide to Successful Innovation for
Education*, Cambridge, UK: Cambridge Education.

Canagarajah, S. (2009), 'The plurilingual tradition and the English language in South
Asia', AILA Review, 22 (1): 5–22.

Cavus, N. and D. Ibrahim (2009), 'M-Learning: an experiment in using SMS to support
learning new English language words', *British Journal of Educational Technology*, 40
(1): 78–91.

Chambless, K. S. (2012), 'Teachers' oral proficiency in the target language: Research on
its role in language teaching and learning', *Foreign Language Annals*, 45 (s1): s141–62.

Chester, M. and B. Q. Beaudin (1996), 'Efficacy beliefs of newly hired teachers in urban
schools', *American Educational Research Journal*, 33: 233–57.

Chowdhury, R. and P. Le Ha (2008), 'Reflecting on Western TESOL training and
communicative language teaching: Bangladeshi teachers' voices', *Asia Pacific Journal
of Education*, 28 (3): 305–16.

Chumbow, B. S. (2013), 'Mother tongue-based multilingual education: Empirical
foundations, implementation strategies and recommendations for new nations', in
H. McIlwraith (ed.), *Multilingual Education in Africa: Lessons from the Juba
Language-in Education Conference*, 37–56, London, UK: The British Council.

Cobb, P., J. Confrey, A. diSessa, R. Lehrer and L. Schauble (2003), 'Design experiments in
educational research', *Educational Researcher*, 32 (1): 9–13.

Coffey International Development (2012), *Activity-based Learning, Ghana* (Draft
synthesis report for DFID), Reading, UK: Coffey International Development.

Cohen, D.K. and J. D. Mehta (2017), 'Why reform sometimes succeeds: Understanding
the conditions that produce reforms that last', *American Educational Research
Journal*, 54 (4): 644–90.

Coleman, H. (1996), 'Darwin and the large class', in S. Gieve and I.K. Miller (eds),
Understanding the Language Classroom, 115–35, Basingstoke, UK: Palgrave Macmillan.

Coleman, H. (2010), *The English language in development*, London, UK: British Council (online at: https://www.teachingenglish.org.uk/sites/teacheng/files/UK011-English-Language-Development.pdf [accessed 12/07/17]).

Coleman, H. (2011), 'Introduction', *Dreams and Realities: English in Development*, 11–23, London, UK: The British Council (online at: https://www.teachingenglish.org.uk/article/dreams-realities-developing-countries-english-language [accessed 16 October 2017]).

Coleman, H. (2017a), 'Milestones in language planning and development aid', *Current Issues in Language Planning*, 18 (4): 442–68.

Coleman, H. (ed.) (2017b), Multilingualisms and development, Selected proceedings of the 11th Language & Development Conference, New Delhi, India. London, UK: British Council (online at: http://www.langdevconferences.org/publications/2015-NewDelhi/MultilingualismsandDevelopment-Coleman-ed-completepublications.pdf [accessed 16 October 2017]).

Coleman, H. (2018), 'An almost invisible "difficult circumstance": the large class', in H. Kuchah and F. Shamim (eds), *International Perspectives on Teaching English in Difficult Circumstances*, Basingstoke, UK: Palgrave Publishers.

Coleman, J. S. (1985), 'Schools and the communities they serve', *Phi Delta Kappan*, 66: 527–32.

Coleman, J. S. (1987), 'Norms as social capital', in G. Radnitzky and P. Bernholz (eds), *Economic Imperialism: The Economic Approach Applied Outside the Feld of Economics*, 133–55, New York, USA: Paragon House Publishers.

Coleman, J. S. (1990), *Foundations of Social Theory*, Cambridge, MA, USA: Harvard University Press.

Copland, F., S. Garton and A. Burns (2014), 'Challenges in teaching English to young learners: Global perspectives and local realities', *TESOL Quarterly*, 48 (4): 738–62.

Cordingley, P. (2013), *The contribution of research to teachers' professional learning and development. Research and teacher education: the BERA-RSA inquiry*, London, UK: British Education Research Association.

Damiani, E. and S. Gowland (2013), *English in Action Project Secondary Analysis of Evidence: The Impact of English on Economic Status in Bangladesh*, London: BBC Media Action.

Dang, T. H. (2013), 'Towards the Use of Mobile Phones for Learning English as a Foreign Language: Hesitation or Welcome?', *Language in India*, 13 (10): 474–85.

Das, S., R. Shaheen, P. Shrestha, A. Rahman and R. Khan (2014), 'Policy versus ground reality: secondary English language assessment system in Bangladesh', *The Curriculum Journal*, 25 (3): 326–43.

Day, C. and Q. Gu (2010), *The New Lives of Teachers*, London: Routledge.

de Segovia, P. and D. M. Hardison (2009), 'Implementing education reform: EFL teachers' perspectives', *ELT Journal*, 63 (2): 154–62.

Dearden, J. (2014), *English as a Medium of Instruction: A Growing Global phenomenon*, London, UK: Oxford University, Department of Education and British Council (online at: http://www.britishcouncil.org/education/ihe/knowledge-centre/english-language-higher-education/report-english-medium-instruction [accessed 16 October 2017]).

Department for International Development (DFID) (1999), *Strengthening primary education in Kenya: an evaluation of the strengthening primary education (SPRED) project, Kenya, 1991–1996,* Evaluation Summary 627, London, UK: DFID.

DFID (2010), *Learning For All: DFID's Education Strategy 2010–2015,* London, UK: DFID.

DFID (2011), *DFID's Approach to Value for Money (VfM),* London, UK: DFID (online at: https://www.gov.uk/government/uploads/system/uploads/attachment_data/file/67479/DFID-approach-value-money.pdf [accessed 16 October 2017]).

DFID (2013a), *Education position paper, Improving learning, expanding opportunities,* London, UK: DFID.

DFID (2013b), *Assessing the Strength of Evidence, How to Note, A DFID practice paper,* London, UK: DFID.

DFID (2013c), *International Development Evaluation Policy,* London, UK: DFID.

DFID (2014), *EIA 2014 Annual Review Report,* London, UK: DFID.

DFID (2015), *EIA 2015 Annual Review Report,* London, UK: DFID.

Department of Education (DoE) (2002), *Strategic Plan 2002–2007,* Washington D.C., USA: DoE (online at: http://www.ed.gov/about/reports/strat/plan2002–07/index.html [accessed 30 October 2017]).

Directorate for Primary Education (DPE) (forthcoming), *Post PEDP3 Draft Design Note. Sub-component: Pre-service Education,* Dhaka, Bangladesh: DPE.

Dladla, N. and B. Moon (2013), 'Teachers and the development agenda. An introduction', in B. Moon (ed.), *Teacher Education and the Challenge of Development,* 5–18, Oxon: Routledge.

Doiz, A., D. Lasagabaster and J. M Sierra (2011), 'Internationalisation, multilingualism and English-medium instruction', *World Englishes,* 30 (3): 345–59.

Donner, J. (2007), 'The use of mobile phones by microentrepreneurs in Kigali, Rwanda: changes to social and business networks', *Information Technologies and International Development,* 3 (2): 3–19.

Education Watch (2011), *Exploring low performance in Education: The Case Study of Sylhet division* (online at: http://www.campebd.org/Files/07042014023350pmEducation_Watch_Report_2009_10_Full_English.pdf [accessed 17 October 2017]).

EIA (2009a), *An Assessment of Spoken English Competence Among School Students, Teachers and Adults in Bangladesh, Baseline Study 1,* Dhaka, Bangladesh: EIA (online at: http://www.eiabd.com/eia/index.php/baseline-reports [accessed 5 October 2017]).

EIA (2009b), *Socio-linguistic Factors: The Motivations and Experiences of School Students, Teachers and Adults in the Community (Baseline study 2a),* Dhaka, Bangladesh: EIA.

EIA (2009c), *An Observation Study of English Lessons in Primary and Secondary Schools in Bangladesh, Baseline Study 3*, Dhaka, Bangladesh: EIA (online at: http://www. eiabd.com/eia/index.php/baseline-reports [accessed 5 October 2017]).

EIA (2009d), *The Demand for English Language in the Workplace and in Post-school Education (Baseline study 2b)*, Dhaka, Bangladesh: EIA.

EIA (2009e), *An Observation Study of English Lessons in Primary and Secondary Schools in Bangladesh (Baseline study 3)*, Dhaka, Bangladesh: EIA.

EIA (2009f), *An Audit of Current Materials for Teaching English in Bangladesh (Baseline study 4)*, Dhaka, Bangladesh: EIA.

EIA (2009g), *An Audit of a Range of English Language Teacher Training and Adult Provision (Baseline study 5)*, Dhaka, Bangladesh: EIA.

EIA (2009h), *The Technology Environment: Infrastructure and Supply in Bangladesh (Baseline study 6a)*. Dhaka, Bangladesh: EIA.

EIA (2009j), *The Technology Environment in Bangladesh: Access, Familiarity and Use (Baseline study 6b)*. Dhaka, Bangladesh: EIA.

EIA (2010a), *The Classroom Practices of Primary and Secondary School Teachers Participating in English in Action (Large-scale quantitative study 2a)*, Dhaka, Bangladesh: EIA.

EIA (2010b), *EIA Quality Assurance System. (Internal Paper to Annual Review 2010)*, Dhaka, Bangladesh: EIA.

EIA (2011a), *A Qualitative Observation Study of Primary and Secondary Lessons Conducted by Teachers Participating in EIA (Study 2b Practice), Cross-case Analysis*, Dhaka, Bangladesh: EIA.

EIA (2011b), *The Classroom Practices of Primary and Secondary School Teachers participating in English in Action (Study 2a1)*, Dhaka, Bangladesh: EIA.

EIA (2011c), *Perceptions of English Language Learning and Teaching Among Primary and Secondary School Teachers and Students Participating in English in Action (Study 2b3b)*. Dhaka, Bangladesh: EIA.

EIA (2011d), *EIA QA [Quality Assurance] analysis: Outputs 1 [Primary] & 3 [Secondary]* (unpublished internal document), Dhaka, Bangladesh: EIA.

EIA (2012a), *English Proficiency Assessments of Primary and Secondary Teachers and Students Participating in English in Action (Large-scale quantitative study 3a)*, Dhaka, Bangladesh: EIA.

EIA (2012b), *Students Lives Study: A Selection of Cases (Report 1: 2011)*, Dhaka, Bangladesh: EIA.

EIA (2012c), *The Classroom Practices of Primary and Secondary Teachers Participating in English in Action (Study 2a2)*, Dhaka: English in Action.

EIA (2012d), *EIA Institutionalisation & Sustainability Strategy* (unpublished internal document), Dhaka, Bangladesh: EIA.

EIA (2013), *Teacher lives: Case Study 1* (unpublished report), Dhaka, Bangladesh: EIA.

EIA (2014a), *English Proficiency Assessments of Primary and Secondary Teachers and Students Participating in English in Action: Second Cohort (2013)*, Dhaka: EIA.

EIA (2014b), *The Classroom Practices of Primary and Secondary School Teachers participating in English in Action: Second Cohort (2013)*, Dhaka, Bangladesh: EIA.

EIA (2014c), *Perceptions of English Language Learning and Teaching among Primary and Secondary Teachers and Students Participating in English in Action: Second Cohort (2013)*, Dhaka, Bangladesh: EIA.

EIA (2014d), *New Elements Research Studies*, Dhaka, Bangladesh: EIA.

EIA (2014e), *Synthesis Report: Evidence of the Relationship between English and Economic Gain in Bangladesh*, Dhaka, Bangladesh: EIA (online at: http://eiabd.com/publications/research-publications/research-reports/english-economic-gain.html [accessed 17 October 2017]).

EIA (2014f) *EIA Business Case for Additional Funding* (unpublished internal document), Dhaka, Bangladesh: EIA.

EIA (2014g), *Policy Seminar Proceedings: English Language Skills Assessment in the Primary and Secondary Education Sectors in Bangladesh* (Directorate of Primary Education, Mirpur, Dhaka, Bangladesh 16 March 2014), Dhaka, Bangladesh: EIA.

EIA (2015a), *English Proficiency Assessments of Primary and Secondary Teachers and Students Participating in English in Action: Third Cohort (2014)*, Dhaka, Bangladesh: EIA.

EIA (2015b), *Classroom Practices of Primary and Secondary School Teachers Participating in English in Action: Third Cohort (2014)*, Dhaka, Bangladesh: EIA.

EIA (2015c), *QA [Quality Assurance] Report 2013–2014* (unpublished internal document), Dhaka, Bangladesh: EIA.

EIA (2015d), *Working Paper: Integration and institutionalization of EIA approaches in the SESIP Activities* (unpublished working paper), Dhaka, Bangladesh: MoE

EIA (2016), *VfM submission to DFID Annual Review* (unpublished document), Dhaka, Bangladesh: EIA.

EIA (2017), *A Quasi-Experimental Study of the Classroom Practices of English Language Teachers and the English Language Proficiency of Students, in Primary and Secondary Schools in Bangladesh*, Dhaka, Bangladesh: EIA.

Ekanayake, S. Y. and J. Wishart (2014), 'Integrating mobile phones into teaching and learning: A case study of teacher training through professional development workshops', *British Journal of Educational Technology*, 46 (1): 173–89.

Elder, C. (2001), 'Assessing the language proficiency of teachers: are there any border controls?', *Language Testing*, 18 (2): 149–70.

Ellis, V. (2007), 'Taking subject knowledge seriously: from professional knowledge recipes to complex conceptualizations of teacher development', *The Curriculum Journal*, 18 (4): 447–62.

Erling, E. J. (2014), *The role of English in skills development in South Asia: Policies, interventions and existing evidence*, London: British Council (online at: http://www.britishcouncil.in/programmes/higher-education/internationalising-higher-education/policy-dialogues/report-role-english [accessed 5 October 2017]).

Erling, E. J. (2015), *The Role of English in Employability in the Middle East and North Africa (MENA): Policies, Interventions and Existing Evidence*, London: British Council.

Erling, E. J. (2017), 'Language planning, English language education and development aid in Bangladesh', *Current Issues in Language Planning*, 18 (4): 1–19.

Erling, E. J. and T. Power (2014), *Synthesis report: Evidence of the relationship between English and economic gain in Bangladesh*, Dhaka, Bangladesh: EIA (online at: https://www.gov.uk/dfid-research-outputs/synthesis-report-evidence-of-the-relationship-between-english-and-economic-gain-in-bangladesh [accessed 5 October 2017]).

Erling, E. J., P. Seargeant and M. Solly (2014), 'English in rural Bangladesh: How is language education perceived as a resource for development in rural communities?', *English Today*, 30 (4): 16–22.

ESRC/DFID (2013) *ESRC-DFID Education and Development: Raising Learning Outcomes in Education Systems Research Programme 2013–2014 Call Specification*, London: ESRC/DFID.

Euromonitor (2010), *The benefits of the English language for individuals and societies; Quantitative indicators from Cameroon, Nigeria, Rwanda, Bangladesh and Pakistan*, London: Euromonitor International (online at: http://www.teachingenglish. org.uk/article/benefits-english-language-individuals-societies [accessed 5 October 2017]).

Euromonitor (2013), *The economic benefit of learning English in Bangladesh* (unpublished internal report for English in Action), Dhaka, Bangladesh: EIA.

Fasih, T., G. Kingdon, H. A. Patrinos, C. Sakellariou and M. Soderbom (2012), *Heterogeneous returns to education in the labor market*, The World Bank. *Policy Research Working Paper 6170* (online at: https://openknowledge.worldbank.org/ handle/10986/12006 [accessed 30 September 2017]).

Fleming, F. (2013), *Evaluation Methods for Assessing VfM*, London, UK: Better Evaluation (online at: http://www.betterevaluation.org/sites/default/files/ Evaluating%20methods%20for%20assessing%20VfM%20-%20Farida%20Fleming. pdf [accessed 16 October 2017]).

FMRP (2005), *Secondary Education in Bangladesh: Assessing Service Delivery. Final Report Briefing note*, Dhaka, Bangladesh: FMRP.

Foster, P. (1965), 'The vocational school fallacy in development planning', in A. J. Anderson and M. J. Bowman (eds), *Education and Economic Development*, Chicago, USA: Aldine Publishing

García, O. and L. Wei (2014), *Translanguaging: Language, Bilingualism and Education*, London, UK: Palgrave Macmillan.

Geeves, R., E. Ly, S. Lorn, L. Borrmei and S. Saran (2006), *New Beginning: Children, Primary Schools and Social Change in Post-conflict Preah Vihear province – Cambodia*, Technical report, Norway: Save the Children.

General Economics Division (GED) (2015), *Millennium Development Goals: Bangladesh Progress Report 2015*, Dhaka, Bangladesh: Bangladesh Planning Commission Government of the People's Republic of Bangladesh.

Gladys, F. (2018), 'Towards a project based approach to teacher development in difficult circumstances: The Case of 2 English language teachers' professional development in Cameroon', in H. Kuchah and F. Shamim (eds), *International Perspectives on Teaching English in Difficult Circumstances*, Basingstoke, UK: Palgrave Publishers.

Glanz, C. (2013), 'Why and how to invest in African languages, multilingual and multicultural education in Africa', in H. McIlwraith' (ed.), *Multilingual Education in Africa: Lessons from the Juba Language-in Education Conference*, 57–68, London: British Council.

Glewwe, P. and M. Kremer (2006), 'Schools, teachers, and education outcomes in developing countries', *Handbook of the Economics of Education*, Volume 2, 945–1017, Amsterdam, Netherlands: Elsevier.

Government of Bangladesh (GoB) (2008), *Bangladesh Country Paper: Supply, Retention, Preparation and Career-long Development of Teachers in E-9 Countries*, Dhaka, Bangladesh: Ministry of Primary and Mass Education, Government of the People's Republic of Bangladesh.

GoB (2012), *Perspective Plan of Bangladesh 2010–2021: Making Vision 2021 a Reality*, Dhaka, Bangladesh: General Economics Division Planning Commission, GoB.

GoB (2017), *Post-PEDP III Programme* (unpublished document), Dhaka, Bangladesh: GoB.

Goddard, R. D. (2003), 'The impact of schools on teacher beliefs, influence, and student achievement: the role of collective efficacy beliefs', in J. Raths and A. C. McAninch (eds), *Teacher Beliefs and Classroom Performance: The Impact of Teacher Education*, 183–202, Volume 6, Advances in Teacher Education, Greenwich, CT: Information Age Publishing.

Hamid, M. O. (2009), *Sociology of language learning: Social biographies and school English achievement in rural Bangladesh* (unpublished PhD dissertation), Brisbane, Australia: University of Queensland.

Hamid, M. O. (2010), 'Globalisation, English for everyone and English teacher capacity: Language policy discourses and realities in Bangladesh', *Current Issues in Language Planning*, 11 (4): 289–310.

Hamid, M. O. (2011), 'Planning for failure: English and language policy and planning in Bangladesh', in J. A. Fishman and O. Garcia (eds), *Handbook of Language and Ethnic Identity: The Success-failure Continuum in Language and Ethnic Identity Efforts* (Vol. 2), 192–203, New York: Oxford University Press.

Hamid, M. O. and B. R. Baldauf (2008), 'Will CLT bail out the bogged down ELT in Bangladesh?', *English Today*, 24 (3): 16–24.

Hamid, M. O. and E. J. Erling (2016), 'English-in-Education policy and planning in Bangladesh: a critical examination', in R. Kirkpatrick (ed.), *English Language*

Education Policy in Asia, 25–48, Cham, Switzerland: Springer International Publishing.

Hamid, M. O., R. Sussex and A. Khan (2009), 'Private tutoring in English for secondary school students in Bangladesh', *Tesol Quarterly*, 43 (2): 281–308.

Hamid, M.O., I. Jahan and M.M. Islam (2013), 'Medium of instruction policies and language practices, ideologies and institutional divides: Voices of teachers and students in a private university in Bangladesh', *Current Issues in Language Planning*, 14 (1): 144–63.

Hamilton, D., D. Jenkins, C. King, B. MacDonald and M. Parlett (1977), *Beyond the Numbers Game: A Reader in Educational Evaluation*, Basingstoke, UK: Macmillan.

Hanushek, E. A. and S. G. Rivkin (2010), 'Generalizations about using value-added measures of teacher quality', *American Economic Review*, 100 (2): 267–71.

Hassan, M. K. (2013), *Teachers' and learners' perceived difficulties in implementing communicative language teaching in Bangladesh: A critical study* (unpublished PhD dissertation), Milton Keynes, UK: Open University.

Holland M., L. Long and L. Regan (2012), 'Implementing the thematic curriculum in Uganda: Implications for teacher education', in R. Griffin (ed.), *Teacher Education in Sub-Saharan Africa: Closer Perspectives*, Oxford, UK: Symposium Books.

Holliday, A. (1992), 'Tissue rejection and informal orders in ELT projects: Collecting the right information', *Applied Linguistics*, 13 (4): 402–24.

Holliday, A. (1994a), *Context-appropriate Methodology*, Cambridge, UK: Cambridge University Press.

Holliday, A. (1994b), 'The house of TESEP and the communicative approach: The special needs of state English language institutions', *ELT Journal*, 48 (1): 3–11.

Holliday, A. (2013), *The Struggle to Teach English As an International Language*, Oxford, UK: Oxford University Press.

Hopkyns, S. (2017), 'Emirati cultural identity in the age of "Englishisation": Voices from an Abu Dhabi university', in L. Buckingham (ed.), *Language, Identity and Education on the Arabian Peninsula*, 87–115, Bristol, UK: Multilingual Matters.

Hossain, A. (2000) 'Anatomy of Hartal Politics in Bangladesh', *Asian Survey*, 40 (3): 508–29.

Hossain, T., and J.W. Tollefson (2007), 'Language policy in education in Bangladesh', in A.B.M. Tsui and J.W. Tollefson (eds), *Language Policy, Culture, and Identity in Asian Contexts*, 241–57, London and Mahwah, NJ: Lawrence Erlbaum.

Howatt, A. (1984), *A History of English Language Teaching*, Oxford, UK: Oxford University Press.

Hu, G. (2005), 'English Language Education in China: Policies, Progress, and Problems', *Language Policy*, 4 (1): 5–24.

Hunter, T. and J. Alderson (2009), 'Micropolitical issues in ELT project implementation', in T. Hunter and J. Alderson, *The Politics of Language Education: Individuals and Institutions*, 64–84, Bristol, UK: Multilingual Matters.

Imam, S.R. (2005), 'English as a global language and the question of nation-building education in Bangladesh', *Comparative Education*, 41 (4): 471–86.

International Labour Organisation (ILO) (2012), Rethinking Economic Growth: towards productive and inclusive Arab societies, Beirut, Lebanon: ILO/UNRP (online at: http://www.ilo.org/wcmsp5/groups/public/---arabstates/---ro-beirut/documents/publication/wcms_208346.pdf [accessed 5 October 2017]).

James, M., R. McCormick, P. Black, P. Carmichael, M-J. Drummond, A. Fox, J. MacBeath, B. Marshall, D. Pedder, R. Procter, S. Swaffiedl, J. Swann and D. Wiliam (2007), *Improving Learning How to Learn: Classrooms, Schools and Networks*, London: Routledge.

Jull, S., S. Swaffield and J. MacBeath (2014), 'Changing perceptions is one thing...: barriers to transforming leadership and learning in Ghanaian basic schools', *School Leadership & Management*, 34 (1): 69–84.

Kachru, B (1983), *The Indianization of English: The Language in India*, New Delhi, India: Oxford University Press.

Kachru, B (1986), *The Alchemy of English: The Spread, Functions and Models of Non-native Englishes*, Champaign, USA: University of Illinois Press.

Kelly M. and M. Grenfell (2004), *European Profile for Language Teacher Education (EPLTE): A frame of reference*, Southampton, UK: University of Southampton.

King, K. (2007), 'Education, skills, sustainability and growth: Complex relations', Paper for the 9th UKFIET International Conference on Education and Development, *Going for Growth? School, Community, Economy, Nation*, Oxford 11–13 September.

King, K. and C. Martin (2000), *The vocational school fallacy revisited: education, aspiration and work in Ghana 1959–2000*, Edinburgh, UK: Centre for African Studies, University of Edinburgh (online at: http://www.cas.ed.ac.uk/__data/assets/pdf_file/0016/27322/No_085__The_Vocational_School_Fallacy_Revisited-_Education_as.pdf [accessed 27 October 2017]).

Kirkpatrick, R. and T.T.N. Bui (2016), 'Introduction: The challenges for English education policies in Asia', in R. Kirkpatrick (ed.), *English Language Education Policy in Asia*, 1–23, Cham, Switzerland: Springer International Publishing.

Kraft, R. J., A. Ehsan, and R. Khanam. (2009), *Comprehensive Primary Teacher Education and Continuing Professional Development: A Framework for Reform. Draft Final Report*, Dhaka, Bangladesh: UNICEF.

Ku, H. and A. Zussman (2010), 'Lingua franca: The role of English in international trade', *Journal of Economic Behavior and Organization*, 75 (2): 250–60.

Kuchah, H. & F. Shamim (eds) (2018), *Teaching English in Difficult Circumstances: International Perspectives on ELT*, Basingstoke, UK: Palgrave Publishers.

Kuchah, K. (2013) *Context-appropriate ELT pedagogy: an investigation in Cameroonian primary schools* (unpublished PhD thesis), Centre for Applied Linguistics, University of Warwick, UK.

Kuchah, K. and Smith, R. (2011), 'Pedagogy of Autonomy for Difficult Circumstances: Principles from Practice', *International Journal of Innovation in Language Learning and Teaching*, 5 (2): 119–39.

Lall, M. (2011), 'Pushing the child centred approach in Myanmar: The role of cross national policy networks and the effects in the classroom', *Critical Studies in Education*, 52 (3): 219–33.

Latif, S. (2004), *Improvements in the Quality of Primary Education in Bangladesh 1990–2002. Background paper for EFA Global Monitoring Report 2005*, UNESCO (online at: http://unesdoc.unesco.org/images/0014/001466/146657e.pdf [accessed 24 October 2017]).

Lawless, K. and J. Pellegrino (2007), 'Professional development in integrating technology into teaching and learning: Knowns, unknowns, and ways to pursue better questions and answers', *Review of Educational Research*, 77 (4): 575–614.

Leach, J. and B. Moon (2008), *The Power of Pedagogy*, London, UK: Sage.

Leach, J., A. Ahmed, S. Makalima and T. Power (2005), *DEEP IMPACT: an investigation of the use of information and communication technologies for teacher education in the global south*, Researching the issues, Technical Report 58, London, UK: DFID.

Lee, C. G. (2012), 'English language and economic growth: Cross-country empirical evidence', *Journal of Economic and Social Studies*, 2 (1): 5–20.

Leelen M. and R. Shaheen (2012), 'English in Action: useability and sustainability of audio-visual materials for English language teaching in Bangladeshi schools', *Proceedings from 11th World Conference on Mobile and Contextual Learning*, Helsinki, Finland, 15–18 October 2012.

Lei, J. and G. Hu (2014), 'Is English-medium instruction effective in improving Chinese undergraduate students' English competence?', *IRAL*, 52 (2): 99–126.

Lewin, K. (2011), *Making Rights Realities: Researching Educational Access, Transitions and Equity*, Technical report, Falmer, UK: University of Sussex.

Lewin, K. (2015), *Educational access, equity, and development; planning to make rights realities*, Fundamentals of Educational Planning 96, Paris, France: International Institute for Educational Planning, UNESCO.

Lewin, K. and J. Stuart (2003), *Researching teacher education: New perspectives on practice, performance and policy multi-site teacher education research project (MUSTER) researching teacher education: New perspectives on practice, performance and policy*, Educational Papers 49a, London, UK: DFID.

Lewis, D. (2011), *Bangladesh: Politics, Economy and Civil Society*, Cambridge: Cambridge University Press.

Li, D. (1998), '"It's Always More Difficult Than You Plan and Imagine": Teachers' Perceived Difficulties in Introducing the Communicative Approach in South Korea', *TESOL Quarterly*, 32 (4): 677–703.

Lo, Y. Y. and E. S. C. Lo (2014), 'A meta-analysis of the effectiveness of English medium education in Hong Kong', *Review of Educational Research*, 84 (1): 47–73.

Lockwood, J. (2012), 'Are we getting the right people for the job? A study of English language recruitment assessment practices in the business process outsourcing sector: India and the Philippines', *Journal of Business Communication*, 49 (2): 107–27.

Loewenberg Ball, D., M. H. Thames and G. Phelps (2008), 'Content knowledge for teaching: What makes it special?', *Journal of Teacher Education*, 59 (5): 389–407.

MacBeath, J. (1999), *Schools Must Speak for Themselves: The Case for School Self-evaluation*, London, UK: RoutledgeFalmer.

Malakolunthu, S., J. MacBeath, and S. Swaffield (2014), 'Improving the quality of teaching and learning through "Leadership for Learning": Changing scenarios in basic schools in Ghana', *Educational Management Administration and Leadership*, 42 (5): 701–17.

Management Systems International (MSI) (2012), *Scaling up? from vision to large-scale change: a management framework for practitioners*, Washington, DC, USA: Management Systems International.

Mango and the Value for Money Learning Group (2016), *Assessing and Managing VfM; Lessons for NGO's*, PPA Learning Partnership (online at: https://www.bond.org.uk/resources/assessing-and-managing-value-for-money-lessons-for-ngos-full-report [accessed 16 October 2017]).

Manik, J. A., G. Anand and E. Barry (2016), 'Bangladesh Attack Is New Evidence That ISIS Has Shifted Its Focus Beyond the Mideast', *The New York Times*, 2nd July 2016 (online at: https://www.nytimes.com/2016/07/03/world/asia/bangladesh-hostage-standoff.html?_r=0 [accessed 30 October 2017]).

Matin, K. A. (2014), *Income Inequality in Bangladesh*, Paper presented at the 19th Biennial Conference 'Rethinking Political Economy of Development' of the Bangladesh Economic Association (25–27 November) (online at: http://www.bea-bd.org/site/images/pdf/063.pdf [accessed 30 October 2017]).

McCormick, R. (2010), 'The state of the nation in CPD: a literature review', *The Curriculum Journal*, 21 (4): 395–412.

McCormick, R., A. Fox, P. Carmichael and R. Procter (2011), *Researching and Understanding Educational Networks*, London, UK: Routledge.

Miller, K. and X. Zhou (2007), 'Learning from Classroom Video: What Makes it Compelling and What Makes it Hard', in R. Goldman, R. Pea, B. Barron and S. Derry (eds), *Video Research in the Learning Sciences*, 321–34, Mahwah, NJ: Lawrence Erlbaum Associates.

Ministry of Education (2010) *National Education Policy 2010* (online at: http://www.moedu.gov.bd/index.php?option=com_docman&task=doc_download&gid=8493&Itemid [accessed 30 October 2017, in Bangla]).

Ministry of Education (2015), *Meeting minutes on the production and use of audio from English for Today listening text of Classes 6 to 9&10 (1st paper for English)* (unpublished paper), Dhaka, Bangladesh: MoE.

Mohanty, A. (2017), 'Multilingualism, education, English and development: Whose development?', in H. Coleman (ed.) (2017b): 261–80.

Moon, B. (2000), 'The Open Learning Environment: a new paradigm for international developments in teacher education', in M. Ben-Peretz, S. Brown and B. Moon (eds), *Routledge International Companion to Education*, London: Routledge: 756–70.

Moon, B. (2016), 'Building an agenda for the reform of teacher education and training', in B. Moon (ed.), *Do Universities have a Role in the Education and Training of Teachers? An International Analysis of Policy and Practice*, 251–62, Cambridge, UK: Cambridge University Press.

Moon, B. and C. Villet (2016), *Digital Learning: Reforming Teacher Education to Promote Access, Equity and Quality in Sub-Saharan Africa*, Technical report, British Columbia, Canada: Commonwealth of Learning.

Mott MacDonald (2013), *EIA Employer Survey 2013* (unpublished internal report for EIA), Dhaka, Bangladesh: EIA.

Mulgan, G. (2006), 'The process of social innovation', *Innovations: Technology, Governance, Globalization*, 1 (2): 145–62.

Nelson Mandela Foundation (2005), *Emerging Voices, A Report on Education in South African Rural Communities*, Cape Town, South Africa: HSRC Press.

Ness, D. and C.-L. Lin (eds) (2013). *International Education: An Encyclopaedia of Contemporary Issues and Systems*, London, UK: Routledge.

Nunan, D. (2003) 'The Impact of English as a Global Language on Educational Policies and Practices in the Asia-Pacific Region', *TESOL Quarterly*, 37 (4): 589–613.

O'Sullivan, M. C. (2006), 'Teaching large classes: The international evidence and a discussion of some good practice in Ugandan primary schools', *International Journal of Educational Development*, 26 (1): 24–37.

Oliveira, J. B. and F. Orivel (2003), 'The costs of distance education for training teachers', in B. Robinson and C. Latchem (eds), *Teacher Education Trough Open and Distance Learning*, London, UK: RoutledgeFalmer/The Commonwealth of Learning.

Onguko, B. (2014), 'JiFUNzeni: A blended learning approach for sustainable teachers' professional development', *Electronic Journal of E-Learning*, 12 (1): 77–88.

Ono, Y. and J. Ferreira (2010), 'A case study of continuing teacher professional development through lesson study in South Africa', *South African Journal of Education*, 30 (1): 59–74.

Open University (OU) (2017), *IGATE-T Rapid Analysis Initial summary report* (unpublished draft report), Milton Keynes, UK: The Open University.

Opfer, V. D., D. Pedder, and Z. Lavicza (2011), 'The role of teachers' orientation to learning in professional development and change: a national study of teachers in England', *Teaching and Teacher Education*, 27 (2): 443–53.

Orr, D., J. Westbrook, J. Pryor, N. Durrani, J. Sebba and C. Adu-Yeboah (2013), *What Are the Impacts and Cost-Effectiveness of Strategies to Improve Performance of Untrained and Under-Trained Teachers in the Classroom in Developing Countries?*, London, UK: EPPI- Centre, Social Science Research Centre, Institute of Education, University of London.

Osman, F. A. (2010), 'Bangladesh Politics: Confrontation, Monopoly and Crisis in Governance', *Asian Journal of Political Science*, 18 (3): 310–333.

Parlett, M. and D. Hamilton (1972), *Evaluation as illumination: a new approach to the study of innovatory programmes*, Occasional paper Edinburgh University (Centre for

Research in the Educational Sciences), Edinburgh, UK: Edinburgh University. (Reproduced in Hamilton *et al.*, 1977: 6–22.)

Pawson, R. (2013), *The Science of Evaluation: A Realist Manifesto.* London, UK: Sage.

Pawson, R. and N. Tilley (1997), *Realistic Evaluation*, London, UK: Sage Publishing.

Pedder, D. (2006), 'Organizational conditions that foster successful classroom promotion of learning how to learn', *Research Papers in Education*, 21 (2): 171–200.

Pedder, D. and J. MacBeath (2008), 'Organisational learning approaches to school leadership and management: teachers' values and perceptions of practice', *School Effectiveness and School Improvement*, 19 (2): 207–24.

Pedder, D. and V. D. Opfer (2013), 'Professional learning orientations: patterns of dissonance and alignment between teachers' values and practices', *Research Papers in Education*, 28 (5): 539–70.

Pedder, D., V. D. Opfer, R. McCormick and A. Storey (2010), 'Schools and continuing professional development in England – State of the Nation research study: policy context, aims and design', *The Curriculum Journal*, 21 (4): 365–94.

Phan, L.H. and O.Z. Barnawi (2015), 'Where English, neoliberalism, desire and internationalization are alive and kicking: Higher education in Saudi Arabia today', *Language and Education*, 29 (6): 545–65.

Popova, A., D. Evans and V. Arancibia (2016), 'Inside in-service teacher training: What works and how do we measure it?', *RISE annual conference 2016*, Oxford: Research on Improving Systems Education, Blavatnik School of Government, University of Oxford.

Powell-Davies, P. (2015), *The Social and Economic Case for Developing English Skills*, Thought pieces, Cairo Symposium 2015 (online at: https://www.britishcouncil.org.eg/en/symposium/thought-pieces/social-and-economic-case-developing-english-skills [accessed 16 October 2017]).

Power, T. (2012), 'Towards a new architecture for teacher professional development in South Sudan', *Transforming Government: People, Process and Policy*, 6 (4): 368–79.

Power, T. (2013), 'The "new" new technology: Exploiting the potential of mobile communications and open educational resources', in B. Moon (ed.), *Teacher Education and the Challenge of Development: A Global Analysis*, 212–26, London, UK: Routledge.

Power, T. (2015), *Aspects of School Based Teacher Development* (online at: *figshare*: https://doi.org/10.6084/m9.figshare.1294893.v1 [accessed 24, July, 2017]).

Power, T. and P. Shrestha (2009), 'Is there a role for mobile technologies in open and distance language learning? An exploration in the context of Bangladesh', Paper presented at *8th International Language and Development Conference*, 23–25 June 2009, Dhaka, Bangladesh (online at: http://oro.open.ac.uk/17795/ [accessed 12 October 2017]).

Power, T. and B. Thornton (2015), *Peer-supported, mobile enhanced School Based Teacher Development* (online at: *figshare*: https://doi.org/10.6084/m9.figshare.1294892.v1 [accessed 24, July, 2017]).

Power T., R. Shaheen, M. Solly, C. Woodward and S. Burton (2012), 'English in Action: School based teacher development in Bangladesh', *The Curriculum Journal*, 24 (4): 503–29.

Power, T., R. Gater, C. Grant and N. Winters (2014), *Educational Technology Topic Guide*, Technical report, London, UK: Health and Education Advice and Resource Team (HEART), DFID) (online at: http://www.heart-resources.org/topic/educational-technology/ [accessed 5 June 2017]).

Pryor, J., K. Akyeampong, J. Westbrook and K. Lussier (2012), 'Rethinking teacher preparation and professional development in Africa: an analysis of the curriculum of teacher education in the teaching of early reading and mathematics', *The Curriculum Journal*, 23 (4): 409–502.

Pyhak, P. (2018), 'Translanguaging as a pedagogical resource in English language teaching: A response to unplanned language education policies in Nepal', in H. Kuchah and F. Shamim (eds), *Teaching English in difficult circumstances. International Perspectives on ELT*, Basingstoke, UK: Palgrave Publishers.

Qi, S. (2009), 'Globalization of English and English Language Policies in East Asia: a Comparative Perspective' (Mondialisation de l'anglais et les politiques sur la langue anglaise dans les pays asiatiques: une perspective comparative), *Canadian Social Science*, 5 (3): 111–120.

Rahman, A. (2007), 'The history and policy of English education in Bangladesh', in Y.H. Choi and B. Spolsky (eds), *English education in Asia: History and policies*: 67–93, Seoul, South Korea: Asia TEFL.

Rahman, F. M. and A. Jahan (2011), 'Training English Teachers from Difficult and Rural Contexts in Bangladesh', in P. Gunashekar, A. Padwad and D. Pawalec (eds), *Starting, Stimulating and Sustaining English Language Teacher Education and Development. A selection of papers presented at the international Conference in Hyderabad in January 2011*, 86–92, London: British Council.

Richards, J. C., and T. S. Rodgers (2014), *Approaches and methods in language teaching*, Cambridge, UK: Cambridge University Press.

Rivkin, S., E. Hanushek, J. Kain (2005), 'Teachers, schools and academic achievement', *Econometrica*, 73 (2): 417–58.

Robinson, B. and C. Latchem (2003), 'Open and distance teacher education: uses and models', in B. Robinson and C. Latchem (eds) *Teacher education through open and distance learning*: 28–47, London: Routledge.

Robinson, V., M. Hohepa and C. Lloyd (2009), *School Leadership and Student Outcomes: Identifying What Works and Why: Best Evidence Synthesis Iteration (BES)*, Technical report, Wellington, New Zealand: Ministry of Education.

Rose, P. (2015), 'Lessons from 25 Years of Education for All', in S. McGrath and Q. Gu (eds), *Routledge Handbook of International Education and Development*, 390–400, London: Routledge.

Rosekrans, K. and M. Chatry-Komarek (2012), 'Education reform for the expansion of mother-tongue education in Ghana', *International Review of Education*, 58 (5): 593–618.

Saigal, A. (2012), 'Demonstrating a situated learning approach for in-service teacher education in rural India: The Quality Education Programme in Rajasthan', *Teaching and Teacher Education: An International Journal of Research and Studies*, 28 (7): 1009–1017.

Salameh, O. (2011), 'A multimedia offline cell phone system for English language learning', *International Arab journal of e-technology*, 2 (1): 44–8.

Samoff, J., M. Dembélé and E. M. Sebatane (2011), *"Going to scale"-nurturing the local roots of education innovation in Africa* (EdQual Working Paper No.28), Bristol, UK: EdQual RPC, University of Bristol.

Sampson, R. J., J. D. Morenoff and F. Earls (1999), 'Beyond social capital: spatial dynamics of collective efficacy for children', *American Sociology Review*, 64: 633–60.

Sandhu, A. K. and M. L. Rahman (2012), *Bangladesh Education Quality Background Study Education Sector Review Final Report — October 2012* (Background Report for the Bangladesh Education Sector Review [ESR]), Dhaka, Bangladesh: ESR.

Schuck, S., P. Aubusson, M. Kearney and K. Burden (2013), 'Mobilising teacher education: A study of a professional learning community', *Teacher Development*, 17 (1): 1–18.

Schweisfurth, M. (2011) 'Learner-centred education in developing country contexts: From solution to problem?', *International Journal of Educational Development*, 31(5): 425–32.

Seargeant, P. and E. J. Erling (2011), 'The discourse of 'English as a language for international development': Policy assumptions and practical challenges', in H. Coleman (ed.), *The English language in development*: 248–67, London: British Council (online at: http://www.teachingenglish.org.uk/transform/books/english-language-development [accessed 5 October 2017]).

Senge, P. M. (1990), *The Fifth Discipline: The Art and Practice of the Learning Organization*, New York, USA: Doubleday.

Sešek, U. (2007), 'English for teachers of EFL–Toward a holistic description', *English for Specific Purposes*, 26 (4): 411–25.

Shamim, F. (2009), 'Impact and sustainability of the Whole School Improvement Programme', in R. Qureshi and F. Shamim (eds), *Schools and Schooling Practices in Pakistan: Lessons for Policy and Practice*, 211–34, Karachi, Pakistan: Oxford University Press.

Shamim, F. (2011), 'English as the language for development in Pakistan: Issues, challenges and possible solutions', in H. Coleman (ed.), *Dreams and Realities: Developing Countries and the English Language*, 297–315, London, UK: British Council.

Shamim, F. and K. Kuchah (2016), 'Teaching large classes in difficult circumstances', in G. Hall (ed.), *Handbook of ELT*, 527–41, London, UK: Routledge.

Shamim, F., A. Abdelhalim, and N. Hamid (2016), 'English medium instruction in the transition year: Case from KSA', *Arab World English Journal*, 7 (1): 32–47.

Shohamy, E. (2013), 'A critical perspective on the use of English as medium of instruction at universities', in A. Doiz, D. Lasagabaster and J.M. Sierra (eds), *English* as *Medium of Instruction at Universities: Global Challenges*, 196–210, Bristol, UK: Multilingual Matters.

Shohel, M. M. C. and F. Banks (2010), 'Teachers' professional development through the English in Action secondary teaching and learning programme in Bangladesh: experience from the UCEP schools', *Procedia Social and Behavioral Sciences*, 2: 5483–94.

Shohel, M. M. C. and F. R. J. Banks (2012), 'School-based teachers' professional development through technology-enhanced learning in Bangladesh', *Teacher Development*, 16 (1): 25–42.

Shohel, M. M. C. and A. Kirkwood (2012), 'Using technology for enhancing teaching and learning in Bangladesh: Challenges and consequences', *Learning, Media and Technology*, 37 (4): 414–28.

Shohel M. M. C. and T. Power (2010), 'Introducing mobile technology for enhancing teaching and learning in Bangladesh: teacher perspectives', *Open Learning*, 25 (3): 201–15.

Shulman, L. (1986), 'Those who understand: knowledge growth in teaching', *Educational Researcher*, 15 (2): 4–14.

Shulman, L. (1987), 'Knowledge-base and teaching: foundations of the new reform', *Harvard Educational Review*, 57 (1): 1–22.

Slavin, R. E. (2002), 'Evidence-based education policies: transforming educational practice and research', *Educational Researcher*, 31 (7): 15–21.

Smith, R. and K. Kuchah (2016), 'Researching teacher associations', *ELT Journal*, 70 (2): 212–21.

Spear, P. (1938), 'Bentinck and Education: Macaulay's Minute', *Cambridge Historical Journal*, 6 (1): 78–101.

Stenhouse, L. (1975), *An Introduction to Curriculum Research and Development*, London, UK: Heinemann.

Street, B. (2003), 'What's "new" in New Literacy Studies? Critical approaches to literacy in theory and practice', *Current Issues in Comparative Education*, 5 (2): 77–91.

Sullivan, N. P. (2007), *Can You Hear Me Now? How Microloans and Cell Phones Are Connecting the World's Poor to the Global Economy*, San Francisco, CA, USA: Jossey-Bass.

Tatto, M. (2013), *The role of research in international policy and practice in teacher education. Research and teacher education: the BERA-RSA inquiry*, London, UK: BERA.

Teacher Development Programme (2014) *TDP In-Service Teacher Training (INSET) Strategy*, Abuja, Nigeria: Mott MacDonald.

The Daily Star (2016), 'Is Bangladesh all set to be a middle income country?', 6 March, 2016 (online at: http://www.thedailystar.net/op-ed/bangladesh-all-set-be-middle-income-country–786709 [accessed 30 October 2017]).

The International Research Foundation (TIRF) (2009), *The impact of English and Plurilingualism in global corporations* (online at: http://www.tirfonline.org/

wp-content/uploads/2010/09/TIRF_KeyQuestionsWorkforcePaper_
Final_25March2009.pdf [accessed 16 October 2017]).

Thijs, A. and E. van den Berg (2002), 'Peer coaching as part of a professional
development program for science teachers in Botswana', *International Journal of
Educational Development*, 22 (1): 55–68.

Thompson, H.R. (2007), 'Bangladesh', in A. Simpson (ed.), *Language and National
Identity in Asia*, 33–54, Oxford, UK: Oxford University Press.

Thornton, P. and C. Houser (2005), 'Using mobile phones in English education in Japan',
Journal of Computer Assisted Learning, 21: 217–28.

Thorton, H. (2006), 'Teachers talking: the role of collaboration in secondary schools in
Bangladesh', *Compare*, 36 (2): 181–96.

Tikly, L. (2015), 'What works, for whom, and in what circumstances? Towards a critical
realist understanding of learning in international and comparative education',
International Journal of Educational Development, 40: 237–49.

Timperley, H., A. Wilson, H. Barrar and I. Fung (2007), *Teacher professional learning and
development: Best Evidence Synthesis Iteration (BES)*, Wellington, New Zealand:
Ministry of Education (online at: http://www.oecd.org/edu/
preschoolandschool/48727127.pdf [accessed 3 June 2017]).

Trinity College London (2009), *Graded examinations in spoken English (GESE): Syllabus
from 1 February 2010*, London, UK: Trinity College.

UNESCO (2004), *EFA Global Monitoring Report 2005, Education for all*, Paris, France:
UNESCO (online at: http://www.right-to-education.org/resource/efa-global-
monitoring-report–2005-education-all-%E2%80%93-quality-imperative [accessed
29 October 2017]).

UNESCO (2006), *Teachers and educational quality: monitoring global needs for 2015*,
Montreal: Institute for Statistics, UNESCO.

UNESCO (2014), *Education for All: Global Monitoring Report 2014. Teaching and
Learning: Achieving Quality for All*, Paris, France: UNESCO.

UNESCO (2015a), *Education for All 2000–2015: achievements and challenges. EFA
Global Monitoring Report 2015*, Paris, France: UNESCO.

UNESCO (2015b), Sub-*Saharan Africa needs 6.2 million new primary teachers by 2030*,
Paris: UNESCO (online at: http://www.unesco.org/new/en/member-states/
single-view/news/sub_saharan_africa_needs_62_million_new_primary_teachers_
by/ [accessed 18 May 2017]).

UNESCO (2016), *Education for People and Planet: Global Education Monitoring Report
2016 – Education for People and Planet: Creating Sustainable Futures for All*, Global
education monitoring report series, Paris: UNESCO.

UNESCO (2017), *Education for Sustainable Development Goals: learning objectives*,
Paris, France: UNESCO.

UNICEF (2009) *Quality Primary Education in Bangladesh* (online at: http://
www.unicef.org/bangladesh/Quality_Primary_Education(1).pdf [accessed
30 October 2017]).

United Nations (UN) (2013), *Accelerating Progress to 2015: Bangladesh. A Report Series to the UN Special Envoy for Global Education*, New York: UN/Global Planet Foundation (online at: http://educationenvoy.org/wp-content/uploads/2013/07/BANGLADESH-UNSE-FINAL.pdf [accessed 27 October 2017])

Vaughan, B. (2007), *Islamist Extremism in Bangladesh*, CRS Report for Congress (Order Code RS22591), Washington, USA: Congressional Research Service, Library of Congress.

Verhelst, N., P. Van Avermaet, S. Takala, N. Figueras, and B. North (2009), *Common European Framework of Reference for Languages: learning, teaching, assessment*, Cambridge, UK: Cambridge University Press.

Verspoor, A. M. (2005), *The Challenge of Learning: Improving the Quality of Basic Education in Sub-Saharan Africa*, Paris, France: Association for Development of Education in Africa.

Vithanapathirana M. (2006), 'Adapting the primary mathematics curriculum to the multigrade classroom in rural Sri Lanka', in A. W. Little (ed.), *Education for All and Multigrade Teaching: Challenges and Opportunities*, Dordrecht, Germany: Springer: 127–54.

VSO (2002). *What Makes Teachers Tick? A Policy Research Report on Teachers' Motivation in Developing Countries*, London, UK: VSO (online at: http://www.bibalex.org/Search4Dev/files/288470/119513.pdf [accessed 19 May 2017]).

Walsh, C. and T. Power (2011), 'Rethinking Development and the Use of Mobile Technologies: Lessons from Bangladesh', *Global Learn Asia Pacific*, Global Conference on Learning and Technology, Melbourne, Australia, 28 April–01 May (online at: http://oro.open.ac.uk/28482/1/Rethinking_Development_and_the_Use_of_Mobile_Technologies-_Lessons_from_Bangladesh_walsh_power2011.pdf [accessed 11 October 2017]).

Walsh, C. S., T. Power, M. Khatoon, S. B. Kumar, A. K. Paul, B. C. Sarkar and M. Griffiths (2013), 'The "trainer in your pocket": Mobile Phones within a teacher continuing professional development (CDP) program in Bangladesh', *Professional Development in Education*, 39 (2): 186–200.

Walsh, C. S., C. Woodward, M. Solly and P. Shrestha (2015), 'The potential of mobile phones to transform teacher professional development to build sustainable educational futures in Bangladesh', *Association of Asian Open Universities Journal*, 10 (1): 37–52 (online at: http://oro.open.ac.uk/44416/8/WALSH_et_al_AAOU_Vol10_2015.pdf [accessed 11 October 2017]).

Walsh, S. (2006), 'Talking the talk of the TESOL classroom', *ELT Journal*, 60 (2): 133–41.

Wang, Q. and Lu, Z. (2012), 'A case study of using an online community of practice for teachers' professional development at a secondary school in China', *Learning, Media and Technology*, 37 (4): 429–46.

Waters, A and M. L. C. Vilches (2008), 'Factors Affecting ELT Reforms: the case of the Philippines Basic Education Curriculum', *RELC Journal*, 39 (1): 5–24.

World Bank (WB) (2008), *Education For all in Bangladesh: Where Does Bangladesh Stand in Achieving the EFA?*, Bangladesh Development Series Paper No. 24, Dhaka, Bangladesh: WB.

WB (2011), *Implementation, Completion and Results Report (IDA-38570) on a Credit in the Amount of SDR 104.2 Million (US$ 150 Million Equivalent) to the People's Republic of Bangladesh for a Primary Education Development Project II*, Dhaka, Bangladesh: WB.

WB (2013a), *Seeding Fertile Ground: Education that Works for Bangladesh: Volume IIa: A Policy Note on Access and Equity*, Washington, DC: World Bank.

WB (2013b), *Seeding Fertile Ground: Education that Works for Bangladesh: Volume IIb: A Policy Note on Education Quality*, Washington, DC, USA: World Bank

Wedell, M. (2008), 'Developing a capacity to make "English for Everyone" worthwhile: Reconsidering outcomes and how to start achieving them', *International Journal of Educational Development*, 28 (6): 628–39.

Wedell, M. (2011), 'More than just "technology": English language teaching initiatives as complex educational change', in H. Coleman (ed.) *Dreams and realities: Developing countries and the English language*, 269–90, London, UK: The British Council.

Wedell, M. and M. Lamb (2013), *Portraits of Inspiring English Teachers in China and Indonesia*, London, UK: British Council.

Westbrook, J., N. Durrani, R. Brown, D. Orr, J. Pryor, J. Boddy and F. Salvi (2013), *Pedagogy, Curriculum, Teaching Practices and Teacher Education in Developing Countries: Final Report. Education Rigorous Literature Review*, London, UK: EPPI-Centre, Social Science Research Unit, Institute of Education, University of London.

Whitehead, J., and B. Fitzgerald (2007), 'Experiencing and Evidencing Learning Through Self-Study: New Ways of Working with Mentors and Trainees in a Training School Partnership', *Teaching and Teacher Education*, 23: 1–12.

Williams, E. (2011), 'Language policy, politics and development in Africa', in H. Coleman (ed.), *Dreams and Realities: Developing Countries and the English Language*, 41–58, London: British Council.

Wilson, S. and J. Berne (1999), 'Teacher learning and the acquisition of professional knowledge: an examination of research on contemporary professional development', *Review of Research in Education*, Volume 24, 173–209, Washington, D.C., USA: American Educational Research Association.

Wolf, S. O. (2013), *The emerging Islamist plexus in Bangladesh?*, APSA Comment, Heidelberg: Applied Political Science of South Asia.

Woodward, C., M. Griffiths, and M. Solly (2014), 'English in Action: a new approach to continuing professional development through the use of mediated video, peer support and low-cost mobilephones in Bangladesh', in D. Hayes (ed.), *Innovations In The Continuing Professional Development Of English Language Teachers*, 227–48, London: British Council.

Woolcock, M. (2013), 'Using case studies to explore the external validity of 'complex' development interventions', *Evaluation*, 19 (3): 229–48.

Woolfolk Hoy, A., and R. Burke Spero (2005), 'Changes in teacher efficacy during the early years if teaching: a comparison of four measures', *Teaching and Teacher Education*, 21: 343–56.

Woolfolk Hoy, A., W. K. Hoy and H. A. Davis (2009), 'Teachers' self-efficacy beliefs', in K. Wentzel and A. Wigfield (eds), *Handbook of Motivation in School*, 627–55, Mahwah, NJ: Lawrence Erlbaum.

Young, J. W., D. Freeman, M. C. Hauck, P. G. Gomez and S. Papageorgiou (2014), *A Design Framework for the ELTeach Program Assessments. ETS Research Report Series*, 2014 (2): 1–29 (online at: http://onlinelibrary.wiley.com/doi/10.1002/ets2.12036/references [accessed 17 October 2017]).

Young, T. J. and S. Walsh (2010), 'Which English? Whose English? An investigation of "non-native" teachers' beliefs about target varieties', *Language, Culture and Curriculum*, 23 (2): 123–37.

Zhang, M., M. Lundenberg, M. Koehler and J. Eberhardt (2011), 'Understanding Affordances and Challenges of Three Types of Video for Professional Development', *Teacher and Teacher Education* 27 (2): 454–62.

Index

assessment: demands and processes, 95; for learning, 230; -oriented activities, 123; regimes and practices, 150

Bangla: 'decriminalizing' use of in classroom, 150; and national identity, 28; in development of nation, 33, 38; in the curriculum, 25; materials in, 27; role in society, 24; teachers' use of, 120; use in CLT, 141–2, 150

Bangladesh: administration, 12; bureaucratic institutions, 210; education in, 210–1; education system, 13–14; geography, 10–11, 21; local 'culture' of education system, 209; nationalization of primary education system, 215; population, 9, 10–11

capacity building: and formal partnership, 180; and relationship development, 185; definition, 173; EIA staff providing support for, 184; for individuals rather than institutions, 184; in project mode, 176; investment for/in, 177, 180; of individuals, 179; of personnel, 175; of systems, 231–2; sector budget for, 187

classroom: audio resources, 81; behaviour, 83; conditions, 15; management strategies, 115–6; primary and secondary resources, 72; talk, 104, 112; use of audio, 81; use of learning technology, 82–3; use of mobile technology, 86–7

classroom language, 19, 239; EIA audio files of, 93; EIA lists of, 119, 141; EIA materials emphasis, 142; EL for specific purposes (ESP), 149; rather than classroom English, 131; resources, 137; teacher use of, 139–40; to manage lesson, 114; university course, 131

classroom practice: and 'strong' form of CLT, 112; data as early warning, 197; EIA baseline studies, 157; EIA targets, 191; EIA teacher changes in, 83, 94, 113, 123, 139–40, 143, 184, 199; equity within, 50; evidence for HT support, 61; evidence for impact of educational technology, 63; evidence of change, 26; evidence of effective TDP, 202; evidence of effectiveness of teacher peer support, 59; evidence to inform policy, 178; for inclusion, 70; improving, 53, 70; nature pre-EIA, 17; pair and group work, 116; established pedagogic positions, 18; qualitative study of, 83; technology for, 68; training impact on, 53, 56; translate policy into, 37; use of technology to improve, 233; use of video, 89

cluster meetings: and change in ELT, 151–2; and teachers' confidence, 148; as a language-rich environment (translanguaging), 138; changes made over phases, 193, 198; encouraging appropriate use of Bangla, 120; evidence on, 217; guidance on use of visuals, 115; importance, 89; mediation of materials, 90; monitoring of, 111; reflection fostered at, 90, 118; teachers working in groups, 91; TFs filmed running, 90; transfer of ownership, 174; viewing of the MAV, 90

code-switching, 131–2, 138, 239

collaboration: and partnership, 179–80; EIA with NAPE on Centre of Excellence, 214; EIA with NAPE on development of the DPEd, 212–3; need for, 211; of JICA with NAPE, 213–4; with SESIP team, 177

communicative language teaching (CLT): and interaction, 131; and local context, 40; and teachers' proficiency (*see also*